English Language

For All SSC Exams

Latest Edition
Practice Kit

16 Tests

16 Topic-Wise Test

Topic Wise Chapters with Questions

✓ Thoroughly Revised and Updated

✓ Detailed Analysis of all MCQs

Title　　　　　　　　: English Language For All SSC Exams

Author Name　　　　: Mr. Rohit Manglik

Published By　　　　: EduGorilla Community Pvt. Ltd.

Publishers Address　: 12/651, First Floor Opp. Arvindo Park, Near Jama Masjid,
Indira Nagar, Lucknow, Uttar Pradesh-226016, India

Copyright EduGorilla

Disclaimer EduGorilla

ROHIT MANGLIK
CEO, EduGorilla

Dear Applicants,

People say *"Success comes to those who work hard."* But I've seen people working hard for their exams day in and day out for marginal success. While others succeed in their examinations by putting in just half the work. So are they God Gifted? No! I believe that it's because they work *smart* and not just *hard*. Similarly, for your exams, you should strategize your preparation so as to increase the likelihood of success. Well with EduGorilla get ready to increase your *chances of selection* in your exam by *16x*.

EduGorilla helps you in not only working *hard* but also working in a *smart and strategic* manner. With EduGorilla's preparation package, you get a chance to make your exam preparation easy, and a fun learning path towards selection. Finding the right path to your preparations can be difficult if you don't know in which direction to head. Don't worry, we have you covered! EduGorilla will be your guide to success in your journey. With our Preparation Package, you can prepare strategically and beat the exam in just one attempt.

EduGorilla's Preparation Package includes-

- **Test Series**
- **Books**

Our preparation package is handcrafted as per the latest changes, expert opinions, and students' discretion. Thus, enabling you to get through each stage of the selection process for your exam.

Our Books are designed by the teachers and experts of the respective exam with a combined 150+ years of experience; to provide you with easy, efficient, and effective learning. Our books are smart, in the sense that not only do they give you the answers to the questions but also provide similar questions for practice.

EduGorilla's competent Test Series gives you real-time experience and confidence through which you can clear your offline or online exam in just one attempt. We currently host 83,000+ mock tests for 1,440+ competitive and academic exams.

Thus, EduGorilla misses no chance to assist you in your preparation and covers all stages of the exam, so that you don't have to look anywhere else.

We provide complete preparation packages for defense, banking, teaching, and other National & State-Level exams. Hence, it doesn't matter which exam you aspire to because you will reach your success.

ALL THE BEST !
Let EduGorilla be your Guide to Success.

Rohit Manglik,
Founder and CEO, EduGorilla

INTRODUCTION

EduGorilla focuses on guiding students to succeed in their examinations. With that in mind, our book, titled "English Language : For All SSC Exams", has been drafted through the collective efforts of our distinguished experts with 150+ years of combined experience. This book consists of questions that are created following the latest changes in the syllabus and exam pattern. We compiled the book on the basis of questions that are most likely to appear in the SSC Exams. Through EduGorilla's "English Language : For All SSC Exams" your chances of success will increase 16x.

EduGorilla does this through our Complete Preparation Package. This package consists of well-conceptualized and structured content in the form of questions that are tailor-made according to your needs and will help you practice for exams in a smart way by pinpointing all the necessary information. It also provides hints and solutions, along with a smart answer sheet for your self-evaluation. You can assess your shortcomings and work accordingly on areas that may require more of your attention.

EduGorilla promises to help you succeed in your examination and accomplish your dream goals. We believe in our aspirants and see them at the top of the merit list. And the first step towards the top is to start preparing with us. EduGorilla's "English Language : For All SSC Exams" includes the following attributes.

➤ Well-Researched Content

➤ Top-Notch Quality

➤ Detailed Answers and Analysis

➤ Smart Answer Sheet

➤ Exam Relevant Questions

Therefore, EduGorilla fortifies your preparation and makes it durable enough to help you stand tall and beat the examination.

TABLE OF CONTENTS

English Language Test	1-163
Cloze test	1-11
Spotting Error	12-20
Fill in the blanks	21-28
Para jumble	29-40
Reading Comprehension	41-51
Sentence Rearrangement	52-66
Direct and Indirect	67-78
One word substitution	79-87
Phrase Replacement	88-96
Active and Passive voice	97-107
Sentence Improvement	108-115
Spelling	116-122
Idioms and Phrases	123-131
Sentence Connectors	132-143
Antonyms and Synonyms	144-154
Sentence correction	155-163

Ques (1-20):Direction: Read the given sentence and find out whether there are any grammatical errors in it or not and accordingly choose the correct option from the given alternatives.

The difficult thing about (1)________the science of habits is that most people when they hear about this field of research (2)______ to know the secret formula for quickly changing any habit. If scientists have discovered how (3)______ patterns work, then it stands to reason that they (4)________ have also found a recipe for rapid change, right? if only it (5)________ that easy. It's not (6)_______ formulas don't exist. The problem is that there isn't one formula for (7)________ habits. There are thousands. Individuals and habits are (8)________ different and so the specifics of diagnosing and changing the patterns in our lives differ from person to (9)_______ and behaviour to behaviour. Giving up cigarettes is different (10)_______ curbing overeating, which is different from changing how you communicate with your spouse, (11)______ is different from how you prioritize tasks at work. What's more, each person's habits are (12)______ by different cravings. As a result, this book does not (13)_______ one prescription, Rather, I hoped to deliver something else: a framework for understanding (14)________ habits work and a guide to experimenting with how they (15)_______ change. Some habits yield easily to analysis and influence. Others are (16)______ complex and obstinate and require prolonged study. And for others, change is a (17)______ that never fully concludes. But that does not (18)______ it can't occur. Each chapter in this book explains a different aspect of why habits exist and how they function. The framework (19)_________ in this section is an attempt to distill, in (20)________ very basic way, the tactics that researchers have found for diagnosing and shaping habits within our own lives.

Q.1 What would come in place of blank (1)?
[Indian Military Academy (IMA), 2020], [Officers Training Academy (OTA), 2020]

A. studying   **B.** study
C. studies   **D.** are studying

Q.2 What would come in place of blank (2)?
[Indian Military Academy (IMA), 2020], [Officers Training Academy (OTA), 2020]

A. wanting   **B.** wanted   **C.** wants   **D.** want

Q.3 What would come in place of blank (3)?
[Indian Military Academy (IMA), 2020], [Officers Training Academy (OTA), 2020]

A. those   **B.** this   **C.** these   **D.** that

Q.4 What would come in place of blank (4)?
[Indian Military Academy (IMA), 2020], [Officers Training Academy (OTA), 2020]

A. must   **B.** will   **C.** would   **D.** might

Q.5 What would come in place of blank (5)?
[Indian Military Academy (IMA), 2020], [Officers Training Academy (OTA), 2020]

A. are   **B.** were   **C.** was   **D.** will be

Q.6 What would come in place of blank (6)?
[Indian Military Academy (IMA), 2020], [Officers Training Academy (OTA), 2020]

A. these   **B.** this   **C.** that   **D.** which

Q.7 What would come in place of blank (7)?
[Indian Military Academy (IMA), 2020], [Officers Training Academy (OTA), 2020]

A. changing   **B.** changed
C. having changed   **D.** changes for

Q.8 What would come in place of blank (8)?
[Indian Military Academy (IMA), 2020], [Officers Training Academy (OTA), 2020]

A. full   **B.** all   **C.** complete   **D.** most

Q.9 What would come in place of blank (9)?
[Indian Military Academy (IMA), 2020], [Officers Training Academy (OTA), 2020]

A. people   **B.** persons
C. personnel   **D.** person

Q.10 What would come in place of blank (10)?
[Indian Military Academy (IMA), 2020], [Officers Training Academy (OTA), 2020]

A. from   **B.** since   **C.** to   **D.** into

Q.11 What would come in place of blank (11)?
[Indian Military Academy (IMA), 2020], [Officers Training Academy (OTA), 2020]

A. it   **B.** this   **C.** what   **D.** which

Q.12 What would come in place of blank (12)?
[Indian Military Academy (IMA), 2020], [Officers Training Academy (OTA), 2020]

A. broken   **B.** given
C. driven   **D.** prescribed

Q.13 What would come in place of blank (13)?
[Indian Military Academy (IMA), 2020], [Officers Training Academy (OTA), 2020]

A. contain   **B.** contains
C. contained   **D.** containing

Q.14 What would come in place of blank (14)?
[Indian Military Academy (IMA), 2020], [Officers Training Academy (OTA), 2020]

A. how   **B.** what   **C.** where   **D.** whose

Q.15 What would come in place of blank (15)?

[Indian Military Academy (IMA), 2020], [Officers Training Academy (OTA), 2020]

A. might   **B.** would   **C.** will   **D.** must

Q.16 What would come in place of blank (16)?
[Indian Military Academy (IMA), 2020], [Officers Training Academy (OTA), 2020]

A. quite   **B.** most   **C.** better   **D.** more

Q.17 What would come in place of blank (17)?
[Indian Military Academy (IMA), 2020], [Officers Training Academy (OTA), 2020]

A. process   **B.** processing
C. processed   **D.** processes

Q.18 What would come in place of blank (18)?
[Indian Military Academy (IMA), 2020], [Officers Training Academy (OTA), 2020]

A. means   **B.** meant   **C.** meaning   **D.** mean

Q.19 What would come in place of blank (19)?
[Indian Military Academy (IMA), 2020], [Officers Training Academy (OTA), 2020]

A. describing   **B.** described
C. will describe   **D.** description

Q.20 What would come in place of blank (20)?
[Indian Military Academy (IMA), 2020], [Officers Training Academy (OTA), 2020]

A. a   **B.** any   **C.** the   **D.** rather

Ques (21-30):Direction: In the following passage, there are blanks, each of which has been numbered. Choose the correct word from the given options which fits the blank appropriately.

Agriculture has often been conceptualized narrowly, _(1)_ specific combinations of activities and organisms: wet-rice _(2)_ in Asia, wheat farming in Europe, _(3)_ ranching in the Americas, and the like, but a more holistic perspective holds that _(4)_ are environmental engineers _(5)_ disrupt the _(6)_ habitats in specific ways. Anthropogenic disruptions such as clearing vegetation or tilling the _(7)_ cause a variety _(8)_ localized changes; common effects include an increase in the amount of light reaching ground level and a reduction in the competition among organisms. _(9)_ an area may _(10)_ more of the plants or animals that people desire for food, technology, medicine, and other uses.

Q.21 Which of the following words most appropriately fits the blank numbered _(1)_?
[SSC Sub Inspector (CPO), 2018]

A. in spite of   **B.** instead of
C. in terms of   **D.** in front of

Q.22 Which of the following words most appropriately fits the blank numbered _(2)_?
[SSC Sub Inspector (CPO), 2018]

A. making   **B.** production
C. inventing   **D.** preparing

Q.23 Which of the following words most appropriately fits the blank numbered _(3)_?
[SSC Sub Inspector (CPO), 2018]

A. dairy   **B.** agriculture
C. tree   **D.** cattle

Q.24 Which of the following words most appropriately fits the blank numbered _(4)_?
[SSC Sub Inspector (CPO), 2018]

A. humans   **B.** animals   **C.** cattle   **D.** crops

Q.25 Which of the following words most appropriately fits the blank numbered _(5)_?

A. whom   **B.** whose   **C.** who   **D.** which

Q.26 Which of the following words most appropriately fits the blank numbered _(6)_?
[SSC Sub Inspector (CPO), 2018]

A. heavenly   **B.** terrestrial
C. aquatic   **D.** celestial

Q.27 Which of the following words most appropriately fits the blank numbered _(7)_?
[SSC Sub Inspector (CPO), 2018]

A. chunk   **B.** tree   **C.** water   **D.** soil

Q.28 Which of the following words most appropriately fits the blank numbered_(8)_?
[SSC Sub Inspector (CPO), 2018]

A. of   **B.** off   **C.** till   **D.** by

Q.29 Which of the following words most appropriately fits the blank numbered _(9)_?
[SSC Sub Inspector (CPO), 2018]

A. due to   **B.** according to
C. as a result   **D.** in order to

Q.30 Which of the following words most appropriately fits the blank numbered _(10)_?
[SSC Sub Inspector (CPO), 2018]

A. present   **B.** produce   **C.** make   **D.** goods

Ques (31-40):Direction: In the following passage, some of the words have been left out. Read the passage carefully and select the correct answer for the given numbers out of the four alternatives.

Even though we're living in 2018, one can't (1) that there are (2) restrictions placed on women's behavior. One of which is the struggle of having a child and (3), having a successful career because our society believes that motherhood is a (4) when it comes to having a career; not for a man, but, (5) for a woman. But New Zealand's Prime Minister Jacinda Ardern has been (6) this (7) ever (8) she first ran for office and continues to do so as she's (9) new motherhood, a shortened maternity (10), and her political life. This firebrand PM of New Zealand has been breaking the glass ceiling and how.

Q.31 Find the appropriate word for (1).
A. Accept   **B.** Deny   **C.** See   **D.** Foresee

Q.32 Find the appropriate word for (2).
A. Some   **B.** Any   **C.** Certain   **D.** All

Q.33 Find the appropriate word for (3).
A. Yet   **B.** Though   **C.** But   **D.** Already

Q.34 Find the appropriate word for (4).
A. Gift   **B.** Boon   **C.** Difficult   **D.** Hurdle

Q.35 Find the appropriate word for (5).
A. Surely   **B.** Definitely
C. Must   **D.** Absolutely

Q.36 Find the appropriate word for (6).
A. Describing   **B.** Distributing
C. Dismantle   **D.** Debriefing

Q.37 Find the appropriate word for (7).
A. Stereotypes   **B.** Instances
C. Nuances   **D.** Mind-sets

Q.38 Find the appropriate word for (8).
A. By   **B.** From   **C.** At   **D.** Since

Q.39 Find the appropriate word for (9).
A. Avoiding   **B.** Juggle
C. Gestating   **D.** Harbouring

Q.40 Find the appropriate word for (10).
A. Off   **B.** Holiday
C. Leave   **D.** Departure

Ques (41-45):Direction: In the following passage, some of the words have been left out. Read the passage carefully and select the correct answer out of the four alternatives for the given numbers.

Can (1) work? Many individuals, having learned to exercise and avoid excessive caloric (2) are controlling their weight. The (3) of the (4) burden from the rich to the poor in many Western countries demonstrates that knowledge and the (5) to cure upon it are important.

Q.41 Find the appropriate word for (1).
A. Exercise   **B.** Prevention
C. Caution   **D.** Anything

Q.42 Find the appropriate word for (2).
A. Count   **B.** Index   **C.** Food   **D.** Intake

Q.43 Find the appropriate word for (3).
A. Mark   **B.** Distinction
C. Removal   **D.** Shift

Q.44 Find the appropriate word for (4).
A. Obesity   **B.** Corpulence
C. Physical   **D.** Fat

Q.45 Find the appropriate word for (5).
A. Vulnerability   **B.** Ability
C. Expertise   **D.** Insight

// Smart Answer Sheet //

Correct Indicates percentage of students who answered questions correctly.

Skipped Indicates percentage of students who skipped questions.

Q.	Ans.	Correct	Skipped
1	A	30.1 %	69.55 %
2	D	61.36 %	34.13 %
3	C	80.54 %	10.9 %
4	A	57.56 %	39.77 %
5	B	21.45 %	69.28 %
6	C	13.9 %	72.21 %
7	A	84.39 %	15.43 %
8	B	80.57 %	14.05 %
9	D	49.29 %	35.29 %

Q.	Ans.	Correct	Skipped
10	A	79.25 %	10.26 %
11	D	20.92 %	75.75 %
12	C	49.61 %	30.65 %
13	A	42.25 %	36.04 %
14	A	28.48 %	69.73 %
15	A	53.61 %	31.44 %
16	D	24.03 %	73.6 %
17	A	80.35 %	12.24 %
18	D	56.5 %	37.7 %

Q.	Ans.	Correct	Skipped
19	B	13.83 %	69.55 %
20	A	89.75 %	10.09 %
21	C	32.39 %	67.45 %
22	B	63.79 %	30.92 %
23	D	24.88 %	70.36 %
24	A	89.46 %	10.05 %
25	C	85.42 %	12.08 %
26	B	62.15 %	36.79 %
27	D	89.28 %	10.5 %

Q.	Ans.	Correct	Skipped
28	A	76.32 %	10.69 %
29	C	47.65 %	30.0 %
30	B	45.62 %	48.82 %
31	B	64.76 %	33.42 %
32	C	61.42 %	36.81 %
33	A	48.21 %	43.35 %
34	D	64.92 %	30.13 %
35	B	31.11 %	68.61 %
36	C	68.99 %	30.03 %

Q.	Ans.	Correct	Skipped
37	A	48.81 %	34.17 %
38	D	57.53 %	41.63 %
39	B	48.04 %	51.22 %
40	C	45.36 %	48.9 %
41	B	25.88 %	67.87 %
42	D	29.64 %	67.89 %
43	D	25.27 %	68.64 %
44	A	21.45 %	67.67 %
45	B	13.93 %	80.17 %

Performance Analysis	
Avg. Score (%)	35.56%
Toppers Score (%)	53.33%
Your Score	

//Hints and Solutions//

1. The correct answer is 'studying'.

A preposition is a word that shows direction (a letter to you), location (at the door), or time (by noon), or that introduces an object (a basket of apples).

Prepositions are typically followed by an object, which can be a noun (noon) or a gerund acting as a noun (falling), a noun phrase (the door), or a pronoun (you).

Let's look at the examples given below:

- I have been waiting for you since 2014. (preposition followed by a pronoun)
- He was excited about going to a hill station. (preposition followed by a gerund)

In the given sentence, the preposition 'about' must be followed by a noun, pronoun, or gerund.

Of the given options, we find that the gerund 'studying' is the most suited for the first blank.

The rest of the options are various verb forms.

Hence, the correct option is (A).

2. The correct answer is 'want'.

- The simple present tense is used when an action is happening right now, to state or ask about things in general, or when it happens regularly or unceasingly.
- The structure is given below:
  - Subject + V1 + object.
- The verb will take 's/es' if the given noun/pronoun (3rd person) is singular.
- Example: He plays badminton daily.
- Since the given sentence is in the present tense (as indicated by the earlier verbs), the plural verb 'want' will be used in the second blank as per the plural noun 'people'.

Hence, the correct option is (D).

3. The correct answer is 'these'.

The pronouns that connect a clause or phrase to a noun or a pronoun, is called a relative pronoun.

A demonstrative pronoun represents a thing or things. The most common demonstrative pronouns are:

this, that, these, those.

'This/that' are used with singular countable nouns and 'these/those' are used with plural countable nouns.

Example:

- This is my bag.
- Those were the days!

Since the patterns of habits (which is a plural countable noun) have already been discussed in the cloze test before, the

demonstrative pronoun 'these' will be the correct choice in the third blank.

Hence, the correct option is (C).

4. The correct answer is 'must'.

An auxiliary verb is a verb that adds functional or grammatical meaning to the clause in which it occurs, so as to express tense, aspect, modality, voice, emphasis, etc.

A modal or a modal auxiliary is a word such as 'can' or 'would' which is used with the main verb (the 1st form of the verb) to express ideas such as possibility, intention, or necessity.

Example:

- I have taken my breakfast. (have- auxiliary verb)
- One should obey one's elders. (should- modal)

The former part of the given sentence talks about the scientists discovering the mechanism of patterns and the latter part talks about them certainly finding a recipe for rapid change.

In the given condition, the modal verb 'must' will be used in the fourth blank of the cloze test as it provides the required conclusive tone.

Hence, the correct option is (A).

5. The correct answer is 'were'.

Conditional sentences are statements discussing known factors or hypothetical situations and their consequences.

One of the structures is mentioned below:

This particular type is followed when we talk about something in the past which is purely imaginary.

- If + Simple Past, Subject + Would + V1 + Object.

In the case of imaginary sentences, 'were' is used with all subjects irrespective of their number.

Example:

- If I had wings, I would fly like a bird.
- He shouted at me as if he were my coach.

Thus, in the fifth blank of the given cloze test, 'were' will be used as the given clause of the sentence is conditional/imaginary in nature.

Hence, the correct option is (B).

6. The correct answer is 'that'.

We use 'that' as a determiner, a demonstrative pronoun and a relative pronoun.

We also use it as a conjunction to introduce that-clauses.

Example:

- She picked up the hairbrush that she had left on the bed. (as a relative pronoun)
- I admit that I was wrong. (as conjunction)

In the sixth blank of the cloze test, we need a conjunction to connect the two clauses.

Thus the correct choice will be option (C) i.e., that.

Hence, the correct option is (C).

7. The correct answer is 'changing'.

A preposition is a word that shows direction (a letter to you), location (at the door), or time (by noon), or that introduces an object (a basket of apples).

Prepositions are typically followed by an object, which can be a noun (noon) or a gerund acting as a noun (falling), a noun phrase (the door), or a pronoun (you).

Let's look at the examples given below:

- I have been waiting for you since 2014. (preposition followed by a pronoun)
- He was excited about going to a hill station. (preposition followed by a gerund)

In the given sentence, the preposition 'for' must be followed by a noun, pronoun, or gerund.

Of the given options, we find that the gerund 'changing' is the most suited for the seventh blank.

The rest of the options are various verb forms.

Hence, the correct option is (A).

8. The correct answer is 'all'.

An adverb is a word or phrase that modifies or qualifies an adjective, verb, or other adverb or a word group, expressing a relation of place, time, circumstance, manner, etc.

Example:

- The haunted village was quite near to the railway station. (the adverb 'quite' qualifies the adjective 'near')

In the given sentence, we need an adverb to qualify the adjective 'different'.

Of the given options, only the 2nd option (all) and the 4th option (most) are adverbs. The other two are adjectives.

Hence in the eighth blank, 'all' will be used as there is no comparison made in the given sentence.

Hence, the correct option is (B).

9. The correct answer is 'person'.

Parallelism in grammar is defined as two or more phrases or clauses in a sentence that have the same grammatical structure.

It is used to balance nouns with nouns, prepositional phrases with prepositional phrases, participles with participles, infinitives with infinitives, clauses with clauses.

Example:

- My brother likes cooking and to read novels.
- My brother likes cooking and reading novels.

Since the preposition 'to' is preceded by the noun 'person', 'person' will be used in the ninth blank of the sentence as per the given rule.

Hence, the correct option is (D).

10. The correct answer is 'from'.

There are some verbs/nouns/adjectives which are followed by fixed preposition given below:

- Exonerate from, different from, liberalization of, interested in, inured to, accused of, a predilection for, a respite from, vexed at, etc.

Example:

- David was a different kid from others in his colony.

According to the rule and the example given above, 'from' will be used in the tenth blank of the sentence.

Hence, the correct option is (A).

11. The correct answer is 'which'.

Parallelism in grammar is defined as two or more phrases or clauses in a sentence that have the same grammatical structure.

It is used to balance nouns with nouns, prepositional phrases with prepositional phrases, participles with participles, infinitives with infinitives, clauses with clauses.

Example:

- My brother likes cooking and to read novels.
- My brother likes cooking and reading novels.

Since the previous clause in the sentence (which is different from...) starts with the pronoun 'which', 'which' will be used in the eleventh blank of the sentence as per the given rule.

Hence, the correct option is (D).

12. The correct answer is 'driven'.

Let's look at the meanings of the given options:-

- broken- to terminate
- given- to cause to have, in the abstract sense or physical sense
- driven- the act of applying force to propel something
- prescribed- to issue commands or orders for

As per the possible context of the sentence, a person's habits are propelled by various desires.

Therefore, from the given meanings, we find that the 3rd option i.e. driven is the correct choice in the twelfth blank.

Hence, the correct option is (C).

13. The correct answer is 'contain'.

The simple present tense is used when an action is happening right now, to state or ask about things in general, or when it happens regularly or unceasingly.

The structure is given below:

- Subject + V1 + object.
- Subject + do/does not + V1 + object. (negative sentence)

The verb will take 's/es' (except the negative sentences) if the given noun/pronoun (3rd person) is singular.

Example:

- He plays badminton daily.
- He does not play badminton daily.

Since the given sentence is in the present tense (negative sentence structure), the plural verb 'contain' will be used in the thirteenth blank.

Hence, the correct option is (A).

14. The correct answer is 'how'.

An adverb is a word or phrase that modifies or qualifies an adjective, verb, or other adverb or a word group, expressing a relation of place, time, circumstance, manner, etc.

The adverb 'how' most commonly means 'in what way' or 'to what extent'. We often use it with verbs such as tell, wonder and know in indirect questions:

Example:

- I just don't know how she manages to cook so well in such a small kitchen.

The former part of the given sentence talks about understanding the way habits work and the latter part talks about experimenting with a possible change in the habits.

In the given condition, the adverb 'how' will be used in the fourteenth blank.

Hence, the correct option is (A).

15. The correct answer is 'might'.

An auxiliary verb is a verb that adds functional or grammatical meaning to the clause in which it occurs, so as to express tense, aspect, modality, voice, emphasis, etc.

A modal or a modal auxiliary is a word such as 'can' or 'would' which is used with the main verb (the 1st form of the verb) to express ideas such as possibility, intention, or necessity.

Example:

- I have taken my breakfast. (have- auxiliary verb)
- One should obey one's elders. (should- modal)

The former part of the given sentence talks about understanding the way habits work and the latter part talks about experimenting with a possible change in the habits.

In the given condition, the modal verb 'might' will be used in the fifteenth blank of the cloze test as it provides the required tone of uncertainty.

Hence, the correct option is (A).

16. The correct answer is 'more'.

The three words—good, better, and best—are examples of the three forms of an adjective or adverb: positive, comparative, and superlative.

The positive form of an adjective or adverb is the basic form listed in a dictionary.

The comparative form is used when there is a comparison between two or more things.

The superlative form is used for a thing that is better than any other of the same category.

Example:

- She is a good Cricketer.
- Rohit is a better human being than his brother.
- He is the best singer in our class.

Since a comparison of habits (consider the noun 'habits' given in the previous sentence) is given in this sentence, 'more' will be used in the sixteenth blank.

Hence, the correct option is (D).

17. The correct answer is 'process'.

- Articles are words that define a noun as specific or unspecific.
- The definite article 'the' is used with the name of things that are unique or already mentioned before.
- The article 'a' is used with the name of things that are not specific.
- The article 'an' is used with the words starting with the sound of a vowel.
- A/An are used before indefinite singular countable nouns.
- Since the article 'a' is used before the seventeenth blank, the singular countable noun i.e., process will be the correct choice in the seventeenth blank.

Hence, the correct option is (A).

18. The correct answer is 'mean'.

The simple present tense is used when an action is happening right now, to state or ask about things in general, or when it happens regularly or unceasingly.

The structure is given below:

- Subject + V1 + object.
- Subject + do/does not + V1 + object. (negative sentence)

The verb will take 's/es' (except the negative sentences) if the given noun/pronoun (3rd person) is singular.

Example:

- He plays badminton daily.
- He does not play badminton daily.

Since the given sentence is in the present tense (negative sentence structure), the plural verb 'mean' will be used in the eighteenth blank.

Hence, the correct option is (D).

19. The correct answer is 'described'.

An adjective is any member of a class of words that modify nouns and pronouns.

Let's have a look at the meaning of the root verb:

- describe- to give a description of

The past participle of any verb i.e., the 3rd form is also used as an adjective.

Example:

- The story described by the narrator was applauded by the audience.

The words given in the 1st and 3rd option are various verb forms except for the 4th option i.e., description which is a noun.

Thus in the nineteenth blank, we need an adjective i.e. described (the 2nd option) to qualify the noun i.e., framework.

Hence, the correct option is (B).

20. The correct answer is 'a'.

Articles are words that define a noun as specific or unspecific.

The definite article 'the' is used with the name of things that are unique or already mentioned before.

The article 'a' is used with the name of things that are not specific.

The article 'an' is used with the words starting with the sound of a vowel.

A/An are used before indefinite singular countable nouns.

Since no particular way and a singular countable noun (way) are discussed in the sentence, the 1st option i.e., a will be the correct choice in the twentieth blank.

Hence, the correct option is (A).

21. The correct sentence is - Agriculture has often been conceptualized narrowly, in terms of specific combinations of activities and organisms.

In terms of means with regard to.

In spite of means regardless of; notwithstanding.

Instead of means in the replacement; in the place of.

In front of means in the presence of.

Hence, the correct option is (C).

22. The correct sentence is--Agriculture has often been conceptualized narrowly, in terms of specific combinations of activities and organisms like wet-rice production in Asia, wheat farming in Europe.

Production is the process of making or growing goods to be sold.

Inventing means creating or designing something.

Preparing means making something ready for use.

Hence, the correct option is (B).

23. The correct sentence is - Agriculture has often been conceptualized narrowly, in terms of specific combinations of activities and organisms like wet-rice production in Asia, wheat farming in Europe, cattle ranching in the Americas.

Cattle are large ruminant animals with horns and cloven hoofs, domesticated for meat or milk, or as beasts of burden; cows and oxen.

Dairy is a business enterprise established for the harvesting or processing of animal milk.

Agriculture is the science and art of cultivating plants and livestock.

A tree is a perennial plant with an elongated stem, or trunk, supporting branches and leaves.

Hence, the correct option is (D).

24. The correct sentence is - Agriculture has often been conceptualized narrowly, in terms of specific combinations of activities and organisms like wet-rice production in Asia, wheat farming in Europe, cattle ranching in the Americas and the like, but a more holistic perspective holds that humans are environmental engineers.

The passage is talking about agriculture, and also about a more holistic perspective that of the human-environmental engineers.

Animals, Cattle and Crops do not fit the context of the sentence.

Animals are all living beings except humans.

Cattle are ruminant animals with horns domesticated for meat or milk, or as beasts of burden; cows and oxen.

Crops are plants such as wheat and potatoes that are grown in large quantities for food.

Hence, the correct option is (A).

25. Thus the correct sentence is- A more holistic perspective holds that humans are environmental engineers who disrupt.

Who is the subject form and used for people.

Whom is the object form of the relative pronoun and mainly used for persons or animals with names and treated as people.

Whose is used for a person, animal and things and shows a sense of belonging.

Which is used for animals and things in general, it precedes a non-essential clause.

Hence, the correct option is (C).

26. The correct sentence is --A more holistic perspective holds that humans are environmental engineers who disrupt the terrestrial habitats in specific ways.

Terrestrial is related to the earth/ land.

Heavenly means divine.

Aquatic is related to water.

Celestial is related to heaven.

Since the sentence is about environmental engineers the obvious correct word is 'terrestrial'.

Hence, the correct option is (B).

27. The correct sentence is - Anthropogenic disruptions such as clearing vegetation or tilling the soil cause a variety of localized changes.

Soil is the top loose layer of the earth's surface in which plants grow.

Chunk is a roughly cut big piece of something.

Since the sentence is about 'clearing vegetation or tilling', the correct word is 'soil'.

Hence, the correct option is (D).

28. The correct sentence is - Anthropogenic disruptions such as clearing vegetation or tilling the soil cause a variety of localized changes.

Of is a preposition and shows belonging / origin-- a friend of mine.

Till is a preposition and means up to the time / until.

Off can be used as a preposition/adverb and shows separation-- 'flew off'.

By is a preposition and shows the agent used to carry out any action-- by car / by train.

The sentence is about the clearing vegetation or tilling causing changes, so the right word is 'of'.

Hence, the correct option is (A).

29. The correct sentence is - common effects include an increase in the amount of light reaching ground level and a reduction in the competition among organisms, as a result, an area may produce more of the plants or animals that people desire for food, technology, medicine, and other uses.

As a result means because of something that was done,

Due to means owing to.

According to means as stated by.

In order to express the purpose of something that needs to be done.

Hence, the correct option is (C).

30. The correct sentence is --common effects include an increase in the amount of light reaching ground level and a reduction in the competition among organisms, as a result, an area may produce more of the plants or animals that people desire for food, technology, medicine, and other uses.

Produce means to make/grow or manufacture.

Present means at this time / now.

Make means to build/ assemble/ produce something.

Goods mean things/merchandise.

Hence, the correct option is (B).

31. The correct answer is Deny.

Accept means consider or hold as true.

Deny means declare untrue; contradict.

See means perceive by sight or have the power to perceive by sight.

Foresee means realize beforehand.

From the above alternatives, we can conclude that deny is the word best suited for blank (1).

Hence, the correct answer is (B).

32. The correct answer is Certain. Certain is another word for confident.

It is something you know you are right about. Some is a word pertaining to quantity. Usually used when you do not know the exact quantity of things. "any" and "some" basically have the same meaning, but are used in different kinds of sentences. "Any" is used in "negative" statements, sentences that use the word "not". Restrictions are particular. So, all is a wrong choice.

Hence, the correct option is (C).

33. The correct answer is Yet.

Yet is used when something didn't take place at the time when it was expected.

But is used when two contradicting information is present, which is not in the given case.

Already is just the opposite of yet. It shows something happened sooner than it was expected. Tough when used at the end of the sentence, is an adverb that gives the sense of 'despite that'.

Hence, the correct option is (A).

34. The correct answer is Hurdle.

Gift means something acquired without compensation.

Boon means a desirable state.

Difficult means not easy; requiring great physical or mental effort to accomplish or comprehend or endure.

Hurdle means an obstacle that you are expected to overcome.

From the above alternatives, we can conclude that hurdle is the word best suited for blank 4.

Hence, the correct option is (D).

35. The correct answer is Definitely.

Definitely means without question and beyond doubt.

Surely means definitely or positively (`sure' is sometimes used informally for `surely').

Must means a necessary or essential thing.

Absolutely means completely and without qualification; used informally as intensifiers.

From the above alternatives, we can conclude that definitely is the word best suited for blank (5).

Hence, the correct option is (B).

36. The correct answer is Dismantle.

Dismantle means take off or remove.

Describe means give a description of.

Distribute means administer or bestow, as in small portions.

Debrief means to put someone through a debriefing and make his report.

From the above alternatives, we can conclude that dismantling is the word best suited for blank (6).

Hence, the correct option is (C).

37. The correct answer is Stereotypes.

Stereotypes mean a conventional or formulaic conception or image.

Instances mean an occurrence of something.

Nuances mean a subtle difference in meaning or opinion or attitude.

Mind-sets means a habitual or characteristic mental attitude that determines how you will interpret and respond to situations.

From the above alternatives, we can conclude that stereotypes is the word best suited for blank (7).

Hence, the correct option is (A).

38. The correct answer is Since.

Since from a specified time in the past.

By is used when medium is mentioned.

From with the source or provenance of or at.

At in or very near a particular place.

From the above alternatives, we can conclude that since is the word best suited for blank (8).

Hence, the correct option is (D).

39. The correct answer is Juggle.

Juggle means manipulate by or as if by moving around components.

Avoid means stay clear from; keep away from; keep out of the way of someone or something.

Gestate means have the idea for.

Harbor means a sheltered port where ships can take on or discharge cargo.

From the above alternatives, we can conclude that juggling is the word best suited for blank (9).

Hence, the correct option is (B).

40. The correct answer is Leave.

Leave means the period of time during which you are absent from work or duty.

Off means no longer on or in contact or attached.

Holiday means a day on which work is suspended by law or custom.

Departure means the act of departing.

From the above alternatives, we can conclude that leave is the word best suited for blank (10).

Hence, the correct option is (C).

41. The correct answer is Prevention.

Prevention means the action of stopping something from happening or arising.

Exercise means activity requiring physical effort, carried out to sustain or improve health and fitness.

Caution means care taken to avoid danger or mistakes.

Anything means used to refer to a thing, no matter what.

Hence, the correct option is (B).

42. The correct answer is Intake.

Intake means an amount of food, air, or another substance taken into the body.

Count means to determine the total number of (a collection of items).

Index means a set of items each of which specifies one of the records of a file and contains information about its address.

Food means any nutritious substance that people or animals eat or drink or that plants absorb in order to maintain life and growth.

'Calorie' is a unit of energy. 'caloric' is an adjective that would fit with any of the given options. But the only one that would affect 'weight control' is the calorie that we consume. Food with high calories wouldn't affect us until we consume it.

Hence, the correct option is (D).

43. The correct answer is Shift.

Shift means to change the emphasis, direction, or focus.

Mark means a line, figure, or symbol made as an indication or record of something.

Distinction means a difference or contrast between similar things or people.

Removal means the action of taking away or abolishing something unwanted.

Hence, the correct option is (D).

44. The correct answer is Obseity.

Obesity means the state of being grossly fat or overweight.

Corpulence means the state of being fat; obesity.

Physical means relating to the body as opposed to the mind.

Fat means (of a person or animal) having a large amount of excess flesh.

The blank requires a word that would provide additional information about what kind of burden we are talking about. Since the topic of the paragraph is obesity, both obesity and corpulence would ft. but, we have to select the most appropriate word which obesity is because corpulence is rarely used in day to day vernacular these days.

Hence, the correct option is (A).

45. The correct answer is Ability.

Ability means possession of the means or skill to do something.

Vulnerability means the quality or state of being exposed to the possibility of being attacked or harmed, either physically or emotionally.

Expertise means expert skill or knowledge in a particular field.

Insight means the capacity to gain an accurate and deep understanding of someone or something.

The 'to' following the blank is indicating towards something. The only option for which such directional or indication is necessary is ability. Whenever 'ability' is mentioned, we also have to mention, ability to do what.

Hence, the correct option is (B).

Ques (1-5):Direction: Identify the segment in the sentence, which contains the grammatical error.

Q.1 Prema is the girl in my class who write beautiful poems.

A. Prema is the girl

B. who write

C. beautiful poems

D. in my class

Q.2 Rahul was ready for accept any job, even a part-time one.

A. Rahul was ready

B. even a part-time one

C. any job

D. for accept

Q.3 The box of paper clips are kept in the drawer.

A. are kept

B. The box

C. of paper clips

D. in the drawer

Q.4 Each student will have to carry his own lunch on the picnic.

A. each student

B. his own lunch

C. on the picnic

D. will have to carry

Q.5 My father did never have an opportunity to go to a University.

A. an opportunity

B. a University

C. to go to

D. did never have

Q.6 Direction: In the following question, one part of the sentence may have an error. Find out which part of the sentence has an error. If the sentence is free from error, select the 'No error' option.

Rarely I have seen (A)/such a scene of (B)/ violence on the streets. (C)/ No error (D)

A. A   **B.** B   **C.** C   **D.** D

Ques (7-9):Direction: Identify the segment in the sentence, which contains the grammatical error.

Q.7 Sunita is senior to me in this office and know all the rules.

A. Sunita is senior to me

B. all the rules

C. and know

D. in this office

Q.8 One should be careful to re-read what they has written.

A. to re-read what

B. be careful

C. One should

D. they has written

Q.9 The files you were look for are placed on the table.

A. are placed

B. you were look for

C. The files

D. on the table

Q.10 Direction: In the following question, one part of the sentence may have an error. Find out which part of the sentence has an error. If the sentence is free from error, click the 'No error' option.

The border crisis is (A)/ present the biggest area in which voters (B)/ already view it as a failure. (C)/ No error (D)

A. A   **B.** B   **C.** C   **D.** D

Ques (11-17):Direction: Identify the segment in the sentence, which contains the grammatical error.

Q.11 The actor smiled to me when I entered the room as if she knew me.

A. the actor smiled to me

B. knew me

C. as if she

D. when I entered the room

Q.12 The list of candidates to be called for the interview were put up on the board.

A. for the interview

B. the list of candidates

C. were put up on the board

D. to be called

Q.13 We reserved tickets for a journey on train for the next morning for my sisters and me.

A. for a journey on train

B. for my sisters and me

C. for the next morning

D. we reserved tickets

Q.14 The Principal was extremely angry on the boys who threw the pieces of chalk at the teacher.

A. at the teacher

B. extremely angry on the boys

C. who threw the pieces of chalk

D. the Principal was

Q.15 No matter he tries hard he cannot play the guitar.

A. no matter   **B.** he tries hard

C. he cannot   **D.** play the guitar

Q.16 News of the calamity is reached the family members the next day.

A. the family members

B. news of the calamity

C. is reached

D. the next day

Q.17 The author's new novel, which is about social change, will launched soon.

A. the author's new novel

B. will launched soon

C. which is

D. about social change

Ques (18-29):Direction: Read the given sentence and find out whether there are any grammatical errors in it or not and accordingly choose the correct option from the given alternatives.

Q.18 Experience has shown that the change-over from a closed economy to a mercantile economy has presented in human society innumerable problems.

A. experience has shown that
B. the change-over from a closed economy
C. to a mercantile economy has presented
D. in human society innumerable problems

Q.19 A closed economy is identified as a human community that produces all it consumes and consumed all it produces.

A. a closed economy is identified
B. as a human community
C. that produces all it consumes
D. and consumed all it produces

Q.20 Iron is the most useful against all metals.

A. Iron is
B. the most useful
C. against all metals
D. No error

Q.21 Mumbai is largest cotton centre in the country.

A. Mumbai is
B. largest cotton centre
C. in the country
D. No error

Q.22 While every care have been taken in preparing the results, the company reserves the right to correct any inadvertent errors at a later stage.

A. While every care have been taken
B. in preparing the results,
C. the company reserves the right to correct
D. any inadvertent errors at a later stage

Q.23 My sister and me are planning a trip from Jaipur to Delhi.

A. My sister and me are
B. planning a trip
C. from Jaipur to Delhi
D. No error

Q.24 Despite the thrill of winning the lottery last week, my neighbour still seems happily.

A. Despite the thrill of winning
B. the lottery last week,
C. my neighbour
D. still seems happily

Q.25 Children are not allowed to use the swimming pool unless they are with an adult.

A. Children are not allowed
B. to use the swimming pool
C. unless they are with an adult
D. No error

Q.26 Her knowledge of Indian languages are far beyond the common.

A. Her knowledge
B. of Indian languages
C. are far beyond the common
D. No error

Q.27 The care, as well as the love of a father, were missing in her life.

A. The care, as well as the love
B. of a father,
C. were missing in her life
D. No error

Q.28 You look as if you have ran all the way home.

A. You look as if
B. you have ran
C. all the way home
D. No error

Q.29 The real voyage of discovery consist not in seeking new landscapes, but in having new eyes.

A. The real voyage of discovery
B. consists not in seeking new landscapes
C. but in having new eyes
D. No error

Ques (30-45):Direction: In the following question, the given sentence has four parts marked P, Q, R, and S. Choose the part of the sentence with the error and mark it as your answer. If there is no error, mark 'No error (S)' as your answer.

Q.30 Suresh have never (P) / encouraged nor (Q) /condoned violence. (R) / No error (S)
[SSC Sub Inspector (CPO), 2018], [SSC Sub Inspector (CPO), 2017]

A. P
B. Q
C. R
D. S

Q.31 Earth's deserts (P) / is a land of extremes,(Q) / constantly pushing life to the limit. (R) / No error (S)
[SSC Sub Inspector (CPO), 2018], [SSC Sub Inspector (CPO), 2017]

A. P
B. Q
C. R
D. S

Q.32 King penguins (P) / are active throughout (Q) / the long summer days. (R) / No error (S)
[SSC Sub Inspector (CPO), 2018], [SSC Sub Inspector (CPO), 2017]

A. P
B. Q
C. R
D. S

Q.33 The behaviour of resident spiders (P) / towards pirate spiders and their own prey (Q) / are quite different. (R) / No error (S)
[SSC Sub Inspector (CPO), 2018], [SSC Sub Inspector (CPO), 2017]

A. P
B. Q
C. R
D. S

Q.34 Scientists intended (P) / to reintroduce and conserve grey wolves (Q) / in their original habitats. (R) / No error (S)
[SSC Sub Inspector (CPO), 2017]

A. P
B. Q
C. R
D. S

Q.35 Tickle is (P) /one of the broadest and deepest (Q) / subject in science. (R) / No error (S)
[SSC Sub Inspector (CPO), 2017]

A. P
B. Q
C. R
D. S

Q.36 Throughout the history, (P) /humans have existed side-by-side (Q) / with bacteria and viruses. (R) / No error (S)
[SSC Sub Inspector (CPO), 2017]

A. P
B. Q
C. R
D. S

Q.37 Throughout the history, (P) /humans have existed side-by-side (Q) / with bacteria and viruses. (R) / No error (S)

[SSC Sub Inspector (CPO), 2017]

A. P   **B.** Q   **C.** R   **D.** S

Q.38 The scientists found that (P) / leopards tend to hoist prey (Q) / that are between half and one-and-a-half times it's own weight. (R) / No error (S)

[SSC Sub Inspector (CPO), 2017]

A. P   **B.** Q   **C.** R   **D.** S

Q.39 Bharatanatyam will also (P) / feature in the two-week (Q) / World Music Festival. (R) / No error (S)

[SSC Sub Inspector (CPO), 2018], [SSC Sub Inspector (CPO), 2017]

A. P   **B.** Q   **C.** R   **D.** S

Q.40 Ancient jewellery or decoration (P) / has a new meaning (Q) / with the discovery bone ornaments. (R) / No error (S)

[SSC Sub Inspector (CPO), 2018], [SSC Sub Inspector (CPO), 2017]

A. P   **B.** Q   **C.** R   **D.** S

Q.41 A prince were (P) / in search of a Sufi master (Q) / to help him in his mystical journey. (R) / No error (S)

[SSC Sub Inspector (CPO), 2018], [SSC Sub Inspector (CPO), 2017]

A. P   **B.** Q   **C.** R   **D.** S

Q.42 If you describe someone as a maverick, (P) / you mean that he is unconventional and independent (Q) / and does not think or behave in the same way as other people. (R) / No error (S)

[SSC Sub Inspector (CPO), 2017]

A. P   **B.** Q   **C.** R   **D.** S

Q.43 The consequence of (P) / his carelessness was (Q) / that the game was lost. (R) / No error (S)

[SSC Sub Inspector (CPO), 2018], [SSC Sub Inspector (CPO), 2017]

A. P   **B.** Q   **C.** R   **D.** S

Q.44 The place were (P) / Buddha was cremated (Q) / has recently been discovered. (R) / No error (S)

[SSC Sub Inspector (CPO), 2018], [SSC Sub Inspector (CPO), 2017]

A. P   **B.** Q   **C.** R   **D.** S

Q.45 Can you tell me (P) / the name of the person (Q) / whom wrote the book? (R) / No error (S)

[SSC Sub Inspector (CPO), 2018], [SSC Sub Inspector (CPO), 2017]

A. P   **B.** Q   **C.** R   **D.** S

// Smart Answer Sheet //

Correct   Indicates percentage of students who answered questions correctly.

Skipped   Indicates percentage of students who skipped questions.

Q.	Ans.	Correct / Skipped
1	B	19.94 % / 76.57 %
2	D	87.29 % / 11.82 %
3	A	78.68 % / 19.01 %
4	C	57.31 % / 38.17 %
5	D	22.46 % / 69.47 %
6	A	18.17 % / 69.78 %
7	C	47.14 % / 30.4 %
8	D	43.69 % / 44.84 %
9	B	85.84 % / 11.95 %

Q.	Ans.	Correct / Skipped
10	B	79.12 % / 20.21 %
11	A	55.82 % / 36.22 %
12	C	26.5 % / 71.51 %
13	A	40.36 % / 51.98 %
14	B	84.07 % / 15.56 %
15	B	83.01 % / 12.77 %
16	C	58.47 % / 36.9 %
17	B	52.95 % / 31.45 %
18	D	56.03 % / 32.01 %

Q.	Ans.	Correct / Skipped
19	D	63.39 % / 30.82 %
20	C	80.79 % / 12.38 %
21	B	88.74 % / 10.64 %
22	A	21.51 % / 67.2 %
23	A	65.51 % / 30.47 %
24	D	47.29 % / 48.11 %
25	D	67.39 % / 30.72 %
26	C	85.23 % / 12.24 %
27	C	68.97 % / 30.03 %

Q.	Ans.	Correct / Skipped
28	B	68.27 % / 31.22 %
29	B	69.14 % / 30.23 %
30	A	21.36 % / 74.5 %
31	B	54.27 % / 32.71 %
32	D	54.62 % / 37.11 %
33	C	89.13 % / 10.45 %
34	D	17.56 % / 71.96 %
35	C	55.79 % / 40.38 %
36	A	43.75 % / 41.57 %

Q.	Ans.	Correct / Skipped
37	D	60.93 % / 36.8 %
38	C	19.51 % / 74.69 %
39	D	41.28 % / 42.97 %
40	C	41.2 % / 42.11 %
41	A	42.24 % / 31.77 %
42	C	27.28 % / 69.19 %
43	D	69.58 % / 30.01 %
44	A	86.63 % / 12.13 %
45	C	60.25 % / 38.2 %

Performance Analysis

Avg. Score (%)	40.0%
Toppers Score (%)	53.33%
Your Score	

//Hints and Solutions//

1. The correct sentence will be: "Prema is the girl in my class who writes beautiful poems."

- Relative pronouns introduce relative clauses. The most common relative pronouns are who, whom, whose, which, that. The relative pronoun we use depends on what we are referring to and the type of relative clause.
- We use who in relative clauses to refer to people, and sometimes to pet animals. We use it to introduce defining and non-defining relative clauses.

Here, the speaker is referring to a third person i.e., Prerna, so we will use 'writes' instead of 'write'.

'Writes' is used with third person singular nouns.

Hence, the correct option is (B).

2. The correct sentence will be- "Rahul was ready "to" accept any job, even a part-time one."

Option (D) should use 'to' instead of 'for'.

In option (A) 'was' is correct as the sentence is in the past tense.

In option (B) the article 'a' is correct as it is used with indefinite things.

Option (C) is also grammatically meaningful.

'To' is used to indicate the relation between the person and the job.

'For' is used to indicate a purpose.

Hence, the correct option is (D).

3. The correct sentence is: "The box of paper clips "is" kept in the drawer."

Here, the box of clips is referred to as a single thing so we will use 'is' instead of 'are'.

We are referring to a specific box, so the use of 'the' before box is correct.

'Of' is used to define a relation.

'In' is used to define the location.

Hence, the correct option is (A).

4. The correct sentence will be: "Each student will have to carry his own lunch to the picnic."

In option (C), the preposition 'on' is incorrect and should be replaced with 'to' as 'to' is used to refer to a destination which is the picnic.

In option (A), 'each' is correct as it refers to each and every student.

In option (B), the pronoun 'his' is appropriately placed.

In option (D), 'will' is correct as it refers to an action in the future.

Hence, the correct option is (C).

5. The correct sentence would be: My father never did have an opportunity to go to a University.

In the above-given sentence, the error is related to adverb placement.

An adverb must come before the auxiliary verb in a sentence. For Example: I never was a fan of hers.

The structure of the sentence is incorrect.

Thus, 'did never' will be replaced by 'never did'.

Hence, the correct option is (D).

6. The error lies in part A of the given sentence.

Meaning of 'rarely': not often.

Inversion of sentences: sentences structure becomes: Verb+ subject.

Inversion of sentences takes place following negative adverbs and adverb phrases: hardly, never, rarely, seldom, scarcely, only later, on no account etc.

Therefore, we can see that the above-given sentence starts with 'rarely'.

So, inversion of sentence structure will take place and 'I have' will be replaced by 'have I'.

Thus, the part (A) is grammatically error.

Hence, the correct option is (A).

7. The correct sentence is:

'Sunita is senior to me in this office knows all the rules.'

The preposition 'to' correctly shows the relation between the two people.

Option (B) uses 'the' before 'rules' which is correct.

Option (D) uses the preposition 'in' which is correct.

Instead of 'know', 'knows' should be used as the subject is in the third person singular form.

Hence, the correct option is (C).

8. In option (D), the usage of 'they' is incorrect.

'One' will be used instead of 'they'.

Whenever the subject of the sentence is 'one' the pronoun should be used according to the subject of the sentence i.e., 'one'.

Let's see an example:

One should do one's duty sincerely.

The correct sentence will be:

One should be careful to re-read what one has written.

Hence, the correct option is (D).

9. The use of 'were' indicates that the sentence talks about an action that was being performed in the past.

So, we will use the past continuous tense.

Therefore, the correct form will be 'you were looking for'.

The correct sentence will be-

"The files you were looking for are placed on the table."

Hence, the correct option is (B).

10. The error lies in part B of the given sentence.

Presently: soon; not at the present time but in the future, after a short time.

'Present' is an adjective while 'presently' is an adverb

Therefore in the given sentence 'present' will be replaced by 'presently'.

Thus, the part (B) is grammatically error.

Hence, the correct option is (B).

11. The correct preposition, in this case, would be 'at', not 'to'.

We use the preposition 'at' with the verb 'smile'.

'At'- Here it means 'in the direction of somebody/something'.

Example:

He pointed a gun at the policeman.

He shouted at me.

Therefore, the correct sentence will be: The actor smiled at me when I entered the room as if she knew me.

Hence, the correct option is (A).

12. The error is under errors in subject-verb agreement.

Since the subject of the sentence is 'list' and not 'candidates', the verb which follows should be in the singular form.

We should write 'was' in place of 'were' in the present case.

The correct sentence is:

"The list of candidates to be called for the interview was put up on the board."

Hence, the correct option is (C).

13. We use the preposition 'by' when we talk about traveling with respect to any mode of transport.

So, the use of 'on' is incorrect.

The preposition 'on' will be replaced by 'by'.

The correct sentence will be:

'We reserved tickets for a journey by train for the next morning for my sisters and me.'

Hence, the correct option is (A).

14. We use the preposition 'at' or 'with' along with 'angry'.

So, 'on angry' is the wrong phrase to use in this case.

The correct preposition to be used here is 'with'.

The correct sentence would be:

The Principal was extremely angry with the boys who threw the pieces of chalk at the teacher.

Hence, the correct option is (B).

15. We always use how/where/what after 'no matter'.

The verb/adverb comes directly after 'how'.

The correct sentence would be:

"No matter how hard he tries, he cannot play the guitar."

Hence, the correct option is (B).

16. With the past tense form of a verb, we cannot use 'is'.

'Is' is used in the present forms of verbs.

Example:

She is reading.

He is driving.

So, the use of 'is' before 'reached' is incorrect. 'Is' + V_3 makes it passive which is incorrect.

We can use the continuous form of the verb with 'is'.

The sentence is in 'past tense' so 'simple past' will be used.

The correct sentence will be:

"News of the calamity reached the family members the next day."

Hence, the correct option is (C).

17. The given sentence is highlighting an event that will occur in the future as indicated by the word 'will'.

As the past participle of the verb used i.e., launched, we need to use an auxiliary verb i.e., be after 'will' to make the sentence grammatically correct.

All the other parts of the sentence are correct.

The correct sentence will be:

"The author's new novel, which is about social change, will be launched soon."

Hence, the correct option is (B).

18. The error is in the last part of the sentence 'in human society innumerable problems.' It should be replaced with innumerable problems in human society. The order of words has to be interchanged to make the sentence correct.

In the given sentence, it talks about something being caused (innumerable problems) and hence it should come first followed by to whom it has happened (human society).

The correct sentence is "Experience has shown that the change-over from a closed economy to a mercantile economy has presented **innumerable problems in human society**".

Hence, the correct option is (D).

19. The error is in the last part of the sentence 'and consumed all it produces'. The sentence is in the present tense and hence the second form of the verb (consumed) is incorrect. The verb should be used in the present tense (consume) in accordance with the entire statement.

The correct sentence is "A closed economy is identified as a human community that produces all it consumes **and consumes all it produces**".

Hence, the correct option is (D).

20. The error is in the last part of the sentence 'against all metals'.

The preposition 'of' is used when referring to or relating to something. Iron is metal itself and contextually the sentence means that iron is the most useful among all the metals. To make the sentence correct against must be replaced with 'of'.

The correct sentence is "Iron is the most useful **of** all metals".

Hence, the correct option is (C).

21. The error is in the second part of the sentence 'largest cotton centre' as a definite article 'the' is missing. The definite article 'the' is used with a superlative degree. For example: He is **the** tallest boy in the class.

The correct sentence is "Mumbai is **the** largest cotton centre in the country".

Hence, the correct option is (B).

22. The error lies in the first part of the sentence 'while every care have been taken.'

In the given sentence the subject 'care' is an abstract noun, so it will be followed by a singular verb (has). The plural verb (have) is incorrectly used in the given sentence. It must be replaced with 'has' to make the sentence correct.

The correct sentence is "While every care **has** been taken in preparing the results, the company reserves the right to correct any inadvertent errors at a later stage".

Hence, the correct option is (A).

23. The error is in the first part of the sentence 'My sister and me are.'

'Me' is an objective case of the pronoun 'I'. So that we can say that it is incorrect here because we need a subjective case. So it must be replaced with the subjective case 'I' to make the sentence correct.

The correct sentence is "My sister and **I** are planning a trip from Jaipur to Delhi".

Hence, the correct option is (A).

24. The error is in the fourth part of the sentence 'still seems happily'. The usage of 'happily' is incorrect in the given sentence. To make the sentence correct replace the adverb 'happily' with the adjective 'happy'.

According to the rule of grammar, seems is a linking verb and with a linking verb, we need to write an adjective (happy) and not an adverb (happily). For example: The eggs smell **rotten**. Here 'rotten' is an adjective.

The correct sentence is "Despite the thrill of winning the lottery last week, my neighbour still seems **happy**".

Hence, the correct option is (D).

25. The correct sentence is "Children are not allowed to use the swimming pool unless they are with an adult.

The sentence is error-free and grammatically correct. As both the plural subjects (children and they) are followed by the plural verb (are). The conjunction 'unless' is also correctly used in the sentence.

Hence, the correct option is (D).

26. The error lies in the last part of the sentence 'are far beyond the common.'

Knowledge is an uncountable noun and hence the usage of the plural verb 'are' is incorrect. It must be replaced with the singular verb 'is' to make the sentence correct.

The correct sentence is "Her knowledge of Indian languages **is** far beyond the common".

Hence, the correct option is (C).

27. The error lies in the last part of the sentence 'were missing in her life.'

As per the subject-verb agreement, the verb agrees with the subject in its number and person. Thus 'were' must be replaced with 'was'. When words joined to a subject by 'with, together with, in addition to, or, as well as, etc.,' the verb agrees with the main subject (care) only.

The correct sentence is "The care, as well as the love of a father, **was** missing in her life."

Hence, the correct option is (C).

28. The error is in the second part of the sentence 'you have ran.'

The given sentence is in the present perfect tense and expresses a finished action with a result in the present. In perfect tense, we shall use the 3rd form of the verb run. The three forms of the verb 'run' are: run - ran - run. Thus the usage of the verb 'ran' is incorrect and must be replaced with 'run'.

The correct sentence is "You look as if you have **run** all the way home".

Hence, the correct option is (B).

29. The error lies in the second part of the sentence 'consist not in seeking new landscapes.'

As per the subject-verb agreement, the verb agrees with the subject in number and person. The subject (voyage) is singular and hence the corresponding verb (consist) must also be singular. So 'consist' should be replaced with 'consists' to agree with the singular subject.

The correct sentence is "The real voyage of discovery **consists** not in seeking new landscapes, but in having new eyes".

Hence, the correct option is (B).

30. The given sentence is grammatically incorrect.

- Here, 'Suresh has neither' should be used instead of 'Suresh have never'.

- 'Neither' is used in the negative sense when we are presenting things that aren't true or valid. Neither...nor gives a negative meaning to verbs.

- And we also know that 'Neither' is always followed by 'nor'.

- Hence, 'never' should be replaced with 'neither' to form a grammatically correct sentence.

- We know that 'Suresh' is singular and it should be followed by a singular helping verb. Hence, 'has' should be used instead of 'have'.

Thus, the part (P) is grammatically error.

Hence, the correct option is (A).

31. The given sentence is grammatically incorrect.

- Here, 'are a land of extreme temperature' should be used instead of 'are a lamd of extremes'.

- Here, in the given sentence 'deserts' is plural. Therefore, it should be followed by a plural helping verb that is 'are'.

- Here, 'Extremes' is also incorrect.

- Rather it should be 'extreme temperature' to form a grammatically correct sentence.

Thus, the part (Q) is grammatically error.

Hence, the correct option is (B).

32. King penguins are active throughout the long summer days.

- The given sentence is grammatically correct.

- Here, 'King penguins' is plural.

- The king penguin (Aptenodytes patagonicus) is the second-largest species of penguin, smaller, but somewhat similar in appearance to the emperor penguin.

- Therefore, a plural helping verb that is 'are' is used.

Hence, the correct option is (D).

33. The given sentence is grammatically incorrect.

- Here, 'is quite different' should be used instead of 'are quite different'.

- 'Behaviour' is a singular noun, hence, the verb must also be singular to maintain the subject-verb agreement. Therefore, 'are' must be replaced with 'is' to form a grammatically correct sentence.

Thus, the part (R) is grammatically error.

Hence, the correct option is (C).

34. The given sentence is grammatically correct.

- The given sentence is talking about a past event. Hence, the use of second form of verb (intended) is grammatically correct.

- The word 'intended' means 'to have as a plan or purpose'.

- Example: The course is intended for intermediate-level students.

Thus, the part (S) is grammatically error.

Hence, the correct option is (D).

35. The given sentence is grammatically incorrect.

- Here, 'subjects in science' should be used instead of 'subject in science'.

- The noun following the phrase "one of the" is always a plural noun.

- Therefore, 'subject' must be replaced with 'subjects' to form a grammatically correct sentence.

Thus, the part (R) is grammatically error.

Hence, the correct option is (C).

36. Throughout history, humans have existed side-by-side with bacteria and viruses.

- The given sentence is grammatically incorrect.

- Here, 'Throughout history' should be used instead of 'Throughout the history'.

- In the given sentence usage of 'the' in Part P is grammatically incorrect.

- 'Throughout history' is correct. It means 'through the whole of some specified period or area'.

Thus, the part (P) is grammatically error.

Hence, the correct option is (A).

37. Wherever you live, there is surely some countryside or coastline not too far away that you are proud of.

- The given sentence is grammatically correct.

- In the first part, the usage of 'wherever' is completely correct.

- Here, it means 'to or in any or every place'.
    - Example: Wherever I go I always seem to bump into him.

- In the second part, the conjunction 'or' is used. It is 'used to connect different possibilities'.

Thus, the part (S) is grammatically error.

Hence, the correct option is (D).

38. The scientists found that leopards tend to hoist prey that are between half and one-and-a-half times their own weight.

- The given sentence is grammatically incorrect.

- Here, 'their own weight' should be used instead of 'it's own weight'.

- Here, 'their' should be used instead of 'its'.

- It's is a contraction of "it is" or "it has".

- We know that we don't use "it's" as a possessive pronoun usually for living things.

- In the given sentence possessive case should be used for the 'Leopards' so 'their' should be used because 'Leopards' are living things.
- 'Their' is a possessive determiner which means 'belonging to them'.
    - Example: Their house is very small, isn't it?
- In the given question 'Leopards' is the main subject. It is plural and refers to the whole class of Leopard.

Thus, the part (R) is grammatically error.

Hence, the correct option is (C).

39. Bharatanatyam will also feature in the two-week World Music Festival.

- Here, the given sentence is grammatically correct.
- We tend to go for 'Part Q' but it would be wrong because we 'use a hyphen with compound numbers'.
- Example: Radhika is sixty-three years old.

Thus, the part (S) is grammatically error.

Hence, the correct option is (D).

40. Ancient jewellery or decoration has a new meaning with the discovery of bone ornaments.

- 'Of' must be used between discovery and bone.
- We need a preposition to tell us about the relationship between one noun to another.
- Here, the preposition 'of' establishing the relationship between discovery and bone.

Thus, the part (R) is grammatically error.

Hence, the correct option is (C).

41. A prince was in search of a Sufi master to help him in his mystical journey.

- Replace were with was.
- We need a singular helping verb after a singular subject.
- Here, the subject is A prince(a singular noun) so we need a singular helping verb(was).

Thus, the part (P) is grammatically error.

Hence, the correct option is (A).

42. If you describe someone as a maverick, you mean that he is unconventional and independent and does not think or behave in the same way that other people.

- Replace as with that in part R.
- We often use that after the demonstrative pronoun the same.
- Ex: This is the same man that deceived me.

Thus, the part (R) is grammatically error.

Hence, the correct option is (C).

43. The word that acts as 'a subordinate conjunction' and the tense of the clause after that should be the same as the tense of the main clause.

Here, was is correct in both of the clauses.

Hence, the correct option is (D).

44. The place where Buddha was cremated has recently been discovered

- Replace 'were' with 'where' in part P.
- 'Were' is the past tense of 'be' when used as a verb. Where means in a specific place when used as an adverb, conjunction, or relative pronoun.
- Here, We need a relative pronoun to relate The place and Buddha, so Where is to be used here.

Thus, the part (P) is grammatically error.

Hence, the correct option is (A).

45. Can you tell me the name of the person who wrote the book?

- We need to replace 'whom' with 'who' to correct the sentence.
- We use Who as a relative pronoun to introduce a relative clause about people.
    - Ex: The police officer who came was a friend of my father's.
- Whom is the object form of 'who'. We use whom to refer to people in formal styles or in writing when the person is the object of the verb.
- Ex: Whom did he marry?

Thus, the part (R) is grammatically error.

Hence, the correct option is (C).

Q.1 Direction: Choose the appropriate word to fill in the blank.

A _______ of seagulls flew over the ship screeching raucously.

[Allahabad High Court Review Officer (RO), 2017]

A. drove **B.** fleet **C.** bunch **D.** flock

Q.2 Direction: Choose the appropriate word to fill in the blank.

She was the _____ of all eyes at the party.

[Allahabad High Court Review Officer (RO), 2017]

A. pride **B.** limelight **C.** star **D.** cynosure

Q.3 Direction: Choose the appropriate word to fill in the blank.

Ghaziabad is the _____ city in India.

[Allahabad High Court Review Officer (RO), 2017]

A. fast growing **B.** more fast growing
C. most fast growing **D.** fastest growing

Q.4 Direction: Choose the appropriate word to fill in the blank.

She _______ for a walk every morning to the park.

[Allahabad High Court Review Officer (RO), 2017]

A. is going **B.** goes **C.** has gone **D.** gone

Q.5 Direction: Choose the appropriate word to fill in the blank.

They did not want to leave ________ to chance while deciding on the trip.

[Allahabad High Court Review Officer (RO), 2017]

A. something **B.** nothing
C. anything **D.** someone

Q.6 Direction: Choose the appropriate word to fill in the blank.

Keep your friends close and your enemies _______.

[Allahabad High Court Review Officer (RO), 2017]

A. closer **B.** farther **C.** far away **D.** closest

Q.7 Direction: Choose the correct 'sound' word to describe.

The_____ of strange and unfamiliar dialects at the market held my interest.

[Allahabad High Court Review Officer (RO), 2017]

A. racket **B.** rumble **C.** clanging **D.** babble

Q.8 Direction: Choose the appropriate word to fill in the blank.

There are _____ takers for animal fur today, while ____ of the yesteryear stars were proud owners of mink coats.

[Allahabad High Court Review Officer (RO), 2017]

A. few, quite a few **B.** quite a few, a few
C. few, a few **D.** a few, few

Q.9 Direction: Choose the appropriate word to fill in the blank.

Complete the notice with the right word. Use of cell phones is _____ within the premises.

[Allahabad High Court Review Officer (RO), 2017]

A. avoided **B.** disallowed

C. prevented **D.** suspended

Q.10 Direction: Use the correct question tag to complete the sentence.

Suicide is not a solution to life's problems, ____?

[Allahabad High Court Review Officer (RO), 2017]

A. are they **B.** isn't it **C.** is it **D.** aren't it

Q.11 Direction: Choose the appropriate word to fill in the blank.

A mix of decayed wood, leaves and manure is known as ______.

[Allahabad High Court Review Officer (RO), 2017]

A. compose **B.** composed
C. composite **D.** compost

Q.12 Direction: Choose the appropriate word to fill in the blank.

He _____ goodbye to his friends before leaving.

[Allahabad High Court Review Officer (RO), 2017]

A. was bidding **B.** bidding
C. bid **D.** bode

Q.13 Direction: Choose the appropriate word to fill in the blank.

There are no sparrows chirping ____ the cities anymore. All ____ either died or flown far away as they had no space in ____ growing concrete jungle. The cunning pigeons have become _____ menace.

[Allahabad High Court Review Officer (RO), 2017]

A. at, are, a, the **B.** in, have, the, a
C. in, have, a, the **D.** by, are, a, the

Q.14 Direction: Choose the appropriate word to fill in the blank.

The hospital was too _____ from the scene of the accident to save the victim's life.

[Allahabad High Court Review Officer (RO), 2017]

A. farther away **B.** further ahead
C. far apart **D.** far

Q.15 Direction: Use the correct simile.

Her grandmother did not hear the noise. She was as deaf as _____.

[Allahabad High Court Review Officer (RO), 2017]

A. a stone **B.** a door **C.** a post **D.** a comb

Q.16 Direction: Choose the appropriate word to fill in the blank.

_____ a national holiday tomorrow.

[Allahabad High Court Review Officer (RO), 2017]

A. Its **B.** It's **C.** There's **D.** Will be

Q.17 Direction: Choose the appropriate word to fill in the blank.

Life has been hectic ______ I joined the army.

[Allahabad High Court Review Officer (RO), 2017]

A. ever after **B.** thereafter
C. when **D.** ever since

Q.18 Direction: Choose the appropriate word to fill in the blank.

A bunch of keys _____ found hanging from a nail on the wall.

[Allahabad High Court Review Officer (RO), 2017]

A. are **B.** were **C.** was **D.** have

Q.19 Direction: Choose the appropriate word to fill in the blank.

______ defendant was made to take ____ oath on ___ Bible that he would speak only ___ truth and nothing but _____ truth.

[Allahabad High Court Review Officer (RO), 2017]

A. a, the, a, the, a **B.** a, the, the, the, the
C. the, an, the, the, the **D.** the, the, the, the, the

Q.20 Direction: Choose the appropriate word to fill in the blank.

The parents of the girl did not ____ to her request.

[Allahabad High Court Review Officer (RO), 2017]

A. secede **B.** precede **C.** accede **D.** desist

Q.21 Direction: Complete the sentence by filling in the blank with the best option from those given below.

I have bought a new ____.

A. spectacle **B.** spectacles
C. pair of spectacle **D.** pair of spectacles

Q.22 Direction: Fill in the blank with a suitable Adverb.

He will ______ hate her.

A. always **B.** not
C. (A) and (B) both **D.** None of the above

Ques (23-45):Direction: Choose an appropriate word from the options to suitably fill the blank in the sentence below so that the sentence makes sense, both grammatically and contextually.

Q.23 During the freedom struggle in 1940s, he ________ a novel for 10 months.

A. has been writing **B.** wrote
C. had been writing **D.** was writing

Q.24 We ______ for the beach tomorrow evening.

A. will leaving **B.** will be leaving
C. are being left **D.** are leaving

Q.25 I can't quite ________ if it is a beauty or simply monstrous.

A. break **B.** decide **C.** take **D.** dither

Q.26 He currently resides in Raipur with his wife, daughter, and a mighty ______ of cats.

A. flock **B.** clowder **C.** sloth **D.** pack

Q.27 Do you have ____ books focusing on this war?
A. some **B.** any
C. the **D.** None of these

Q.28 The new laws are ________ and will not solve the real crime issue.
A. rational **B.** preposterous
C. inventive **D.** perceptive

Q.29 The _______ child kept on asking questions from his father to the point where he got irritated with the kid.
A. affluent **B.** erudite
C. candid **D.** inquisitive

Q.30 The government must now ________ its seriousness by moving away from the ________ policies of the past.
A. ensconce, conscientious
B. masquerade, equitable
C. shelter, scrupulous
D. demonstrate, flawed

Q.31 The ________ of the computer engineer really amazed us as it took him only a few minutes to recover the deleted files.
A. laconic **B.** gnome
C. ostentation **D.** dexterity

Q.32 The project believes that there may be a premium market for items that ________ using plastic reclaimed from the ocean.
A. made **B.** was made
C. have been made **D.** has been made

Q.33 The digital _______ of societies has resulted in sharply reduced demand for products such as paper and steel.
A. cohesion **B.** destruction
C. transformation **D.** divide

Q.34 The city was plunged ____ darkness due to sudden power failure.
A. through **B.** to **C.** into **D.** under

Q.35 She liked to be with him ________ than with the others, and when alone with him she sometimes laughed.
A. good **B.** better **C.** best **D.** over

Q.36 You haven't many teeth left, but ______ few you have are sharp enough to make me shudder.
A. a **B.** an **C.** very **D.** the

Q.37 "Don't you dare _____(shred) her ticket"?
A. think back **B.** think over
C. take out **D.** tear up

Q.38 Corruption is a standing hindrance ____ the nation's development.
A. of **B.** over **C.** to **D.** upon

Q.39 A cup of coffee and the sound of the falling rain was enough to ______ his troubled mind.
A. abhor **B.** hamper **C.** gambol **D.** soothe

Q.40 While the Chinese people may resent America for the current trade war, they have also for long looked at America with ________.

A. anxiety

B. admiration

C. inspiration

D. trepidation

Q.41 I have never ________ in the Raj Bhavan, but I hope to very soon.

A. set forth   **B.** set out   **C.** set foot   **D.** set up

Q.42 He actually lacked the ________ to go alone and talk to the Principal.

A. sense

B. wisdom

C. confidence

D. action

Q.43 Computing professionals ____________ of almost every aspect of the modern world.

A.   are trying to be conspicuous

B.   are evident

C.   are on the front lines

D.   are participating

Q.44 Bruce is an ______ who deceives others by claiming to be one of their relatives.

A. wager   **B.** priest   **C.** idol   **D.** imposter

Q.45 The thief ________ with the goods in broad daylight.

A. run away

B. ran off

C. run

D. run together

// Smart Answer Sheet //

Correct	Indicates percentage of students who answered questions correctly.
Skipped	Indicates percentage of students who skipped questions.

Q.	Ans.	Correct / Skipped	Q.	Ans.	Correct / Skipped	Q.	Ans.	Correct / Skipped	Q.	Ans.	Correct / Skipped	Q.	Ans.	Correct / Skipped
1	D	40.62 % / 31.22 %	10	C	67.91 % / 30.53 %	19	C	83.29 % / 15.32 %	28	B	68.97 % / 30.48 %	37	D	42.58 % / 45.97 %
2	D	58.52 % / 36.92 %	11	D	17.64 % / 75.0 %	20	C	48.35 % / 36.83 %	29	D	85.5 % / 10.88 %	38	C	65.65 % / 32.5 %
3	D	80.88 % / 15.28 %	12	C	42.12 % / 43.46 %	21	D	44.4 % / 33.3 %	30	D	54.41 % / 42.35 %	39	D	65.06 % / 30.93 %
4	B	66.45 % / 30.69 %	13	B	80.98 % / 11.66 %	22	A	87.19 % / 11.9 %	31	D	77.95 % / 13.6 %	40	B	64.36 % / 30.49 %
5	C	57.28 % / 35.65 %	14	D	56.11 % / 32.13 %	23	C	67.76 % / 30.33 %	32	C	76.95 % / 19.84 %	41	C	62.05 % / 31.96 %
6	A	14.84 % / 84.88 %	15	C	67.02 % / 31.41 %	24	D	56.12 % / 38.8 %	33	C	48.46 % / 36.45 %	42	C	55.42 % / 42.47 %
7	D	62.76 % / 35.09 %	16	B	64.34 % / 30.22 %	25	B	84.05 % / 14.62 %	34	C	52.92 % / 45.88 %	43	C	55.82 % / 38.09 %
8	A	88.47 % / 10.0 %	17	D	58.95 % / 35.84 %	26	B	65.64 % / 31.39 %	35	B	87.7 % / 11.58 %	44	D	82.53 % / 12.16 %
9	B	68.23 % / 31.72 %	18	C	59.94 % / 37.7 %	27	B	86.1 % / 12.52 %	36	D	82.47 % / 13.73 %	45	B	47.43 % / 52.28 %

Performance Analysis	
Avg. Score (%)	48.89%
Toppers Score (%)	57.78%
Your Score	

//Hints and Solutions//

1. The meaning of the given words:

- Flock: a number of birds of one kind feeding, resting, or travelling together.
- Drove: a herd or flock of animals being driven in a body.
- Fleet: a marshland creek, channel, or ditch.
- Bunch: a number of things, typically of the same kind, growing or fastened together.

Use of Collective Noun 'Flock' in the blank space of the sentence is appropriate.

Hence, the correct option is (D).

2. She was the **cynosure** of all eyes at the party.

The word 'cynosure' means- something that strongly attracts attention by its brilliance, interest, etc. The cynosure of all eyes, something serving for guidance or direction; a person or thing that is the center of attention or admiration.

Use of Noun 'cynosure' (attraction point) in the blank space of the sentence is appropriate.

Hence, the correct option is (D).

3. Ghaziabad is the **fastest growing** city in India.

The use of 'fastest growing' (Superlative degree) in the blank space of the sentence is appropriate.

Hence, the correct option is (D).

4. She **goes** for a walk every morning to the park.

As per the rule of subject-verb agreement, singular verb is used with singular subject.

The use of the singular verb 'goes' is appropriate in the space of the sentence.

Hence, the correct option is (B).

5. They did not want to leave **anything** to chance while deciding on the trip.

The meaning of the given words:

- Anything: used to refer to a thing, no matter what.
- Something: a thing that is unspecified or unknown.
- Nothing: not anything. no single thing.
- Someone: an unknown or unspecified person, some person.

The use of Pronoun 'anything' is appropriate in the blank space of the sentence.

Hence, the correct option is (C).

6. Keep your friends close and your enemies **closer**.

It is appropriate to use the Comparative Degree 'closer' of Noun 'close' in the blank space of the sentence.

Hence, the correct option is (A).

7. The **babble** of strange and unfamiliar dialects at the market held my interest.

The meaning of the given words:

- Babble: talk rapidly and continuously in a foolish, excited, or incomprehensible way.
- Racket: a loud unpleasant noise; a din.
- Rumble: make a continuous deep, resonant sound.
- Clanging: a pattern of speech observed in some types of mental illness.

The use of the word 'babble (sound word)' in the blank space of the sentence is appropriate.

Hence, the correct option is (D).

8. There are **few** takers for animal fur today, while **quite a few** of the yesteryear stars were proud owners of mink coats.

- Few: a small number of.
- Quite a few: being of a large but indefinite number.

It is appropriate to use 'few' and 'quite a few' respectively in the blanks of the sentence.

Hence, the correct option is (A).

9. Complete the notice with the right word. Use of cell phones is **disallowed** within the premises.

The use of Verb 'disallowed' (to prohibit, retaliate) is appropriate in the blank space of the sentence.

Hence, the correct option is (B).

10. The above question is based on Question Tag format. The first part of this type of English sentence is Assertive or Imperative and the second part is Interrogative. This second part is called Question Tag. It is a rule that the question tag of Affirmative (Affirmative) Sentences is Negative. That is, the question tag of Auxiliary Verb $+n't+$ subject $+?$ and Negative Sentences is Affirmative (Affirmative) i.e. Auxiliary Verb + Subject + ? Is used. Therefore, the use of 'is it' in the blank space is appropriate.

Ex. This novel is not interesting, is it?

Hence, the correct option is (C).

11. A mix of decayed wood, leaves and manure is known as **compost**.

The use of the word 'compost' (compound manure, vegetable manure, litter manure) in the blank space of the sentence is appropriate. The term 'compost' means- 'a mixture of various decaying organic substances, as dead leaves or manure, use for fertilizing soil, decayed organic material used as a fertilizer for growing plants.

Hence, the correct option is (D).

12. He **bid** goodbye to his friends before leaving.

Bid means to greet, command.

The given sentence is a simple indefinite sentense so use of bid is appropriate here.

In the simple present, most regular verbs use the root form, except in the third-person singular (which ends in -s).

Hence, the correct option is (C).

13. It is appropriate to use in, have, the, a respectively in the blank spaces of the sentence. So the meaningful sentence would be:

There are no sparrows chirping **in** the cities anymore. All **have** either died or flown far away as they had no space in **the** growing concrete jungle. The cunning pigeons have become **a** menace.

Hence, the correct option is (B).

14. The hospital was too **far** from the scene of the accident to save the victim's life.

The use of 'far' in the blank space of the sentence is appropriate. 'Too' implies a negative result.

Hence, the correct option is (D).

15. The use of 'a post' in the blank space of the sentence is appropriate. 'deaf as a post' means 'deaf as an adder'. Unable to hear or to listen, as in speak louder. Grandpa's deaf as a post.

The first simile has its origin in John Palsgrave's Acolastus (1540): "How deaf an ear I intended to give him...... he were as good as to tell his tale to a post". It has largely replaced deaf as an adder, alluding to an ancient belief that adders cannot hear; it is recorded in the Bible.

Hence, the correct option is (C).

16. It's a national holiday tomorrow.

It's is a contraction and should be used where a sentence would normally read "it is." the apostrophe indicates that part of a word has been removed. Its with no apostrophe, on the other hand, is the possessive word, like "his" and "her," for nouns without gender. For example, "The sun was so bright, its rays blinded me."

So, the use of It's is appropriate here.

Hence, the correct option is (B).

17. Life has been hectic **ever since** I joined the army.

The use of 'ever since' in the blank space of the sentence is appropriate. This is an Adverbial phrase.

Hence, the correct option is (D).

18. It is appropriate to use the singular verb 'was' in the space of the sentence. The structure of some sentences is as follows:

Singular collective Noun + of + Plural Noun

Example:

A team of students.

A set of books.

Hence, the correct option is (C).

19. The use of the, an, the, the, the respectively in the blank spaces of the sentence makes the sentence meaningful. Therefore, the correct and meaningful sentence would be:

The defendant was made to take **an** oath on **the** Bible that he would speak only **the** truth and nothing but **the** truth.

Hence, the correct option is (C).

20. The parents of the girl did not **accede** to her request.

Verb 'accede' means: 'to express approval or give consent, to agree to a request or demand,

Hence, the correct option is (C).

21. In grammar, when we refer to something that exists in numbers of 'two' for e.g. legs and trousers, ears and earrings, glasses or spectacles, we use the word 'Pair' to indicate that they are singular in number but two of them make one item a Pair of spectacles where the word 'spectacles' indicates that there are two i.e., one for each eye but together they make one item so they are referred to as 'a' Pair. Since the subject is 'Pair' which is singular, we use the phrase 'Pair'.

Hence, the correct option is (D).

22. Option (A): 'Always' is an adverb of frequency. It indicates that some action is taking place 'all the time'.

Option (B): 'Not' is not an adverb of frequency. It's a tool used to convert a positive sentence to a negative. It has no relation to time and hence, frequency.

Option (C) is incorrect because 'not' is not a frequency adverb.

Option(D) is incorrect because the answer lies in (A).

Hence, the correct option is (A).

23. During the freedom struggle in 1940s, he **had been writing** a novel for 10 months.

The mentioned action was taken in past and it continued for a certain period. Therefore Past perfect continuous tense should be chosen.

Hence, the correct option is (C).

24. We **are leaving** for the beach tomorrow evening.

The appropriate fit for the blank is 'are leaving' which is in present continuous tense. The present continuous tense is used for actions happening now or for an action that is unfinished. This tense is also used when the action is temporary. Another use of this tense is when we are talking about a planned event in the future.

Hence, the correct option is (D).

25. I can't quite **decide** if it is beauty or simply monstrous.

Decide - come or bring to a resolution in the mind as a result of consideration.

Hence, the correct option is (B).

26. He currently resides in Raipur with his wife, daughter, and a mighty **clowder** of cats.

A collective noun is a noun that represents a collection of animals and people.

Therefore, a group of cats is called 'clowder'.

Hence, the correct option is (B).

27. Do you have **any** books focusing on this war?

The correct determiner to be used is 'any'. 'Any' is the determiner used in negative sentences as well as in interrogative sentences.

Hence, the correct option is (B).

28. The new laws are **preposterous** and will not solve the real crime issue.

Preposterous means absurd, not logical, it is the only option that fits in the given blank.

Hence, the correct option is (B).

29. The **inquisitive** child kept on asking questions from his father to the point where he got irritated with the kid.

Inquisitive: having or showing an interest in learning things; curious.

The context talks about the curious child who kept on asking questions from his father to the point where he got irritated.

Hence, the correct option is (D).

30. The government must now **demonstrate** its seriousness by moving away from the **flawed** policies of the past.

Demonstrate - give a practical exhibition and explanation of (how a machine, skill, or craftworks or is performed).

Flawed - having or characterized by a fundamental weakness or imperfection.

Hence, the correct option is (D).

31. The **dexterity** of the computer engineer really amazed us as it took him only a few minutes to recover the deleted files.

Dexterity: skill; proficiency; adept at something.

The context talks about the skill of the computer engineer which amazed us as he took only a few minutes to recover the deleted files.

Hence, the correct option is (D).

32. The project believes that there may be a premium market for items that **have been made** using plastic reclaimed from the ocean.

Hence, the correct option is (C).

33. The digital **transformation** of societies has resulted in sharply reduced demand for products such as paper and steel.

Transformation means to change in composition or structure.

Hence, the correct option is (C).

34. The city was plunged **into** darkness due to sudden power failure.

In the above given sentence, 'into' will be used.

It is so because 'Plunged in/plunged into' is a phrasal verb meaning to suddenly start doing something actively or enthusiastically.

Hence, the correct option is (C).

35. She liked to be with him **better** than with the others, and when alone with him she sometimes laughed.

The word 'than' after the blank is a major hint that a comparative degree should be filled in the blank. Therefore, 'better' is the only appropriate choice here.

Hence, the correct option is (B).

36. You haven't many teeth left, but **the** few you have are sharp enough to make me shudder.

A few means some. It has a positive meaning. The few means not many, but all of those. Here we are talking about all the teeth that are left, so 'the' is the correct choice here.

Hence, the correct option is (D).

37. Don't you dare **tear up** her ticket.

The correct phrasal verb which should be used in the blank in the sentence is 'Tear up'.

The meaning of the phrasal verb 'Tear up' is rip into pieces.

Hence, the correct option is (D).

38. Corruption is a standing hindrance **to** the nation's development.

In the given sentence, the relation between the subject (corruption) and the object (nation's development) can be shown by either using 'to' or 'of'. However, hindrance (obstacle) will be followed by 'to' and not 'of'.

Hence, the correct option is (C).

39. A cup of coffee and the sound of the falling rain was enough to **soothe** his troubled mind.

Soothe: gently calm (a person or their feelings).

The context talks about the calming effect of coffee and the sound of rain on the troubled mind of a person.

Hence, the correct option is (D).

40. While the Chinese people may resent America for the current trade war, they have also for long looked at America with **admiration**.

Admiration means to feel respect and approval for.

Hence, the correct option is (B).

41. I have never **set foot** in the Raj Bhavan, but I hope to very soon.

To 'set foot' in a place means to be in a place, or go to that place.

'Raj Bhavan' is a place one visits and thus one cannot 'set forth' in Raj Bhavan, one cannot 'set out' in Raj Bhavan and one cannot 'set up' in the Raj Bhavan and thus 'set foot' is the most appropriate.

Hence, the correct option is (C).

42. He actually lacked the **confidence** to go alone and talk to the Principal.

The correct word here is 'confidence' which means 'the feeling or belief that one can have faith in or rely on someone or something.

Hence, the correct option is (C).

43. Computing professionals **are on the front lines** of almost every aspect of the modern world.

The given sentence describes the importance of computing professionals throughout the world. Option (C) fits correctly as 'on the front lines' means 'playing a very important part (in something); influential'. Someone who is in the front line has to play a very important part in defending or achieving something.

Hence, the correct option is (C).

44. Bruce is an **imposter** who deceives others by claiming to be one of their relatives.

Imposter means a person who pretends to be someone else in order to deceive others, especially for fraudulent gain.

Hence, the correct option is (D).

45. The thief **ran off** with the goods in broad daylight.

Ran off means to steal things and run.

Hence, the correct option is (B).

Ques (1-5):Direction: In the following question, sentences of a paragraph have been jumbled and labeled as A, B, C and D. You are required to rearrange the jumbled sentences of the paragraph and mark your response accordingly by selecting the correct option.

Q.1 A. But this drive expresses itself in many different ways.

B. Nietzsche sees the will to power as neither good nor bad.

C. According to him, it is a basic drive found in everyone.

D. The philosopher and the scientist direct their will to power into a will to truth.

A. DCAB   **B.** ADCB   **C.** CDAB   **D.** BCAD

Q.2 A. The element symbol for Plutonium is Pu, rather than Pl.

B. They later withdrew it as they realized it could also be used for an atomic bomb.

C. The researchers submitted the proposed name and symbol to the journal Physical Review.

D. This is because Pu was a more amusing symbol of the two.

A. DCAB   **B.** ADCB   **C.** CDAB   **D.** BCAD

Q.3 A: The opposite of demonetization is remonetization, in which a form of payment is restored as legal tender.

B: Sometimes, a country completely replaces the old currency with a new currency.

C: The current form or forms of money is pulled from circulation and retired, often to be replaced with new notes or coins.

D: Demonetization is the act of stripping a currency unit of its status as legal tender.

A. DCBA   **B.** DCAB   **C.** DBCA   **D.** ADCB

Q.4 A. It also describes how the elements and principles of artwork together in an art form.

B. Form is one of the seven elements of art.

C. It connotes a three-dimensional object in space.

D. Form is also used to describe the physical nature of the artwork.

A. DCAB   **B.** ADCB   **C.** CDAB   **D.** BCAD

Q.5 A. Transporting substances to and from our cells is a major function of blood.

B. Providing immunity and protection against bacteria and viruses is also another function of blood.

C. Blood is a component of the cardiovascular system.

D. It is composed of blood cells and an aqueous fluid known as plasma.

A. ADCB   **B.** DCAB   **C.** CDAB   **D.** BCAD

Ques (6-10):Direction: In the following question, sentences of a paragraph have been jumbled and labeled as A, B, C and D. You are required to rearrange the jumbled sentences of the paragraph and mark your response accordingly by selecting the correct option.

Q.6 A. The forest and trees filter the air and absorb harmful gases.

B. The environment gives us countless benefits that we can't repay our entire life.

C. Plants purify water, reduce the chances of a flood, maintain a natural balance, and many more.

D. As they are connected with the forest, trees, animals, water, and air.

A. CDAB   **B.** BDCA   **C.** ABCD   **D.** BDAC

Q.7 A: Hence, they are the most useful members of any society.

B: No one can deny that farmers form the backbone of any nation

C: They grow food for the whole country.

D: Yet they don't get the profit and recognition which they deserve.

A. ADCB   **B.** CADB   **C.** DCBA   **D.** BCAD

Q.8 A: For them it is the emotions.

B: For them happiness is not at all proportional to their income but their attitude towards life.

C: Which decide whether the person is happy or unhappy.

D: There are large number of people whose basic physical needs are easily satisfied.

A. DCBA   **B.** ABCD   **C.** DACB   **D.** ACBD

Q.9 A: After inspection the two would stand up.

B: Once a week Pratham led Heera, the elephant, down to river.

C: The elephant lay down on Pratham's side, then he looked at his feet and examined his whole body for sores.

D: The elephant knew it was time to return. So, both the elephant and trainer would return home.

A. BCAD   **B.** ADCB   **C.** DCBA   **D.** ACDB

Q.10 A: We feel deeply hurt when a friend says sharply, "I can't talk to you right now".

B: A friend's rudeness is much more damaging than a stranger's as it hurts us instead of making angry.

C: Or when a friend shows up late for a meeting with no valid reason, we get a little sad.

D: In these situations, we feel that we are being taken for granted.

A. CBDA   **B.** BACD   **C.** ADCB   **D.** DBCA

Ques (11-14):Direction: Rearrange the following given sentences to make a meaningful paragraph and then choose the correct order from the options given below.

Q.11 Pollution needs

P: otherwise our future generations

Q: to be tackled seriously

R: would suffer a lot

A. PRQ   **B.** QRP   **C.** RPQ   **D.** QPR

Q.12 (P) There is social conservation and revivalism

(Q) So advanced nations should help

(R) Above all there is stark poverty and hunger

(S) The threats to the newly independent nations are varied

(T) and we should try to become self-reliant

(U) And there are economic and social pressures

Which of the following is the correct order of the sentences:

A. SPURQT   **B.** RPQSTU

C. SRTQPU   **D.** TPQRSU

Q.13 1. As one might expect, people's happiness levels were positively correlated.

W. However, the two measures were not identical – suggesting that what makes us happy may not always bring more meaning, and vice versa

X. With whether they saw their lives as meaningful

Y. Feeling happy was strongly correlated with seeing life as easy, pleasant, being in good health and generally feeling well most of the time

Z. To probe for differences between the two, the researchers examined the survey

6. However, none of these things were correlated with a greater sense of meaning.

A. XWZY   **B.** WXZY   **C.** YZXW   **D.** ZXYW

Q.14 S1: There is an enemy beneath our feet-an enemy more deadly for his complete impartiality.

P: The enemy is the Earth itself.

Q: He recognizes no national boundaries, no political parties.

R: When an earthquake comes, the whole world trembles.

S: Everyone in the world is threatened by him.

S6: The power of an earthquake is greater than anything man himself can produce.

A. SRQP   **B.** QSPR   **C.** PRSQ   **D.** PRQS

Ques (15-18):Direction: Arrange these parts so as to form a complete meaningful sentence/paragraph and then choose the correct combination.

Q.15 A: by her indulgent parents

B: the child was so spoiled

C: when she did not receive all of their attention

D: that she pouted and became sullen

Which of the sequences present the most logical sentence?

A. C B A D   **B.** B C A D   **C.** B A D C   **D.** B D A C

Q.16 A : an image of a person in meditative pose

B : surrounded by animal, wild and tame

C : we have in the relics of Mohenjodaro

D : with eyes closed and indrawn

Which of the sequences present the most logical sentence?

A. C A D B   **B.** A B C D   **C.** C B A D   **D.** C A B D

Q.17 A : for the future

B : and poses the major challenge

C : commercial energy consumption

D : shows an increasing trend

Which of the sequences present the most logical sentence?

A. C B D A   **B.** C D B A   **C.** A D C B   **D.** A B C D

Q.18 A : disintegrates some part of the old truths, and

B : there by upsets the way of men's thinking and the ways of their lives

C : science does not merely add new truths to the old ones, but

D : sometimes the new truth it discovers

Which of the sequences present the most logical sentence?

A. A C B D   **B.** C D A B   **C.** A B C D   **D.** C B A D

Ques (19-28):Directions: Each question consists of six sentences of a passage. The first and the sixth sentences are given as S1 and S6. The middle four sentences in each have been jumbled up and labelled P, Q, R and S. You are required to find the proper sequences of the four sentences and mark your response accordingly.

Q.19 S1: The giant wall of the Dhauladhar range in Himachal Pradesh is one of the most stunning sights in the Himalayas.

P: As the life line of the region it acts as a watershed ridge between Chamba's Ravi river system and Kangra's Beas river system.

Q: Although of modest altitude compared to other Himalayan ranges - the highest Dhauladhar peak is less than 5,000 m.

R: Thus, the Dhauladhar could be stated as the life line of the region.

S: Despite of that, the range sweeps up an astounding 12,000 ft. from the valley floor, creating a barrier wall in that is striking to look at.

S6: Looming over the hill stations of Dharmsala and McLeodganj, the Dhauladhar is a popular trekking destination.

[Officers Training Academy (OTA), 2018], [Indian Military Academy (IMA), 2018]

A. QRPS   **B.** SPQR   **C.** QSRP   **D.** RQSP

Q.20 S1: Truth is far more important than the teacher.

P: Without self-knowledge, the air plane becomes the most destructive instrument in life; but with selfknowledge, it is a means of human help.

Q: Wisdom begins with self-knowledge; and without self-knowledge, mere information leads to destruction.

R: In other words, you have to be the perfect teacher to create a new society; and to bring the perfect teacher into being, you have to understand yourself.

S: Therefore you, who are the seeker of truth, have to be both the pupil and the teacher.

S6: So a teacher must obviously be one who is not within the clutches of society, who does not play power politics or seeks position or authority.

[Officers Training Academy (OTA), 2018], [Indian Military Academy (IMA), 2018]

A. QRSP   **B.** SRQP   **C.** QSRP   **D.** RQPS

Q.21 S1: Though most of us talk of discipline, what do we mean by that word?

P: The teacher would understand each child and help him in the way required.

Q: But if you have five or six in a class, and an intelligent understanding teacher with a warm heart, I am sure there would be no need for discipline.

R When you have a hundred boys in a class, you will have to have discipline; otherwise there will be complete chaos.

S: Discipline in schools becomes necessary when there is one teacher to a hundred boys and girls.

S6: And most of us are interested in mass movements, large schools with a great many boys and girls; we are not interested in creative intelligence, therefore we put up huge schools with enormous attendances.

[Officers Training Academy (OTA), 2018], [Indian Military Academy (IMA), 2018]

A. QRSP   **B.** SRQP   **C.** QSRP   **D.** RQPS

Q.22 S1: Tolstoy Farm was founded in 1910 by which time Gandhi had already conceptualized ideas that he would develop in India.

P: He was rich and used his money to buy the land and help set up the farm.

Q: A Jewish architect, Kallenbach was by his side through this period.

R: Tolstoy Farm became the subject of research for different kinds of cooperative communities across the world.

S: He first put in the social, moral, religious components of his doctrine.

S6 : Both he and Gandhi often referred to the time that they spent in Tolstoy Farm as among the happiest in their lives.

[Officers Training Academy (OTA), 2018], [Indian Military Academy (IMA), 2018]

A. QRSP   **B.** SQPR   **C.** SQRP   **D.** RQPS

Q.23 S1: Decentralized planning is a process of planning that begins from the grassroots level taking into confidence all the beneficiaries.

P: Under decentralized planning, the operation is from bottom to top.

Q: It can be said that it is more connected with the capitalistic economies.

R: It empowers the individuals and small groups to carry out their plans for their achievement of a common goal:

S: The decentralized planning is implemented through market mechanism.

S6: But it cannot be described as undemocratic for most national states adopt such a planning now.

[Officers Training Academy (OTA), 2018], [Indian Military Academy (IMA), 2018]

A. QRSP   **B.** SRQP   **C.** SQRP   **D.** SRPQ

Q.24 S1: It is doubtful if mankind, throughout his long history, has ever lived at all 'sustainably'.

P: But in general mankind has regarded the environment as an endless 'resource' to be exploited and plundered.

Q: Maybe a few isolated tribal groups finding the necessary balance with nature lived without the desire for endless 'more'.

R: Now we have reached a point where we are on the verge of destroying ourselves and most of the life on earth.

S: This process has accelerated greatly since the industrial revolution.

S6: The concept of 'sustainable' is so far from reality that it is almost laughable.

[Officers Training Academy (OTA), 2018], [Indian Military Academy (IMA), 2018]

A. PQRS   **B.** QPSR   **C.** PQSR   **D.** SRQP

Q.25 S1: Measurement is an important concept in performance management.

P: It also indicates where things are not going so well, so that corrective action can be taken.

Q: It identifies where things are going well to provide the foundations for building further success.

R: It is the basis for providing and generating feedback.

S: Measuring performance is relatively easy for those who are responsible for achieving quantified targets for example sales.

S6: It is more difficult in the case of knowledge workers for example scientists and teachers.

[Officers Training Academy (OTA), 2018], [Indian Military Academy (IMA), 2018]

A. RQPS   **B.** QPSR   **C.** PSQR   **D.** SPQR

Q.26 S1: Equity theory is concerned with the perception people have about how they are being treated compared with others.

P: To be dealt with equitably is to be treated fairly in comparison with another group of people or a relevant other person.

Q: Equity involves feelings and perceptions and is always a comparative process.

R: Equity theory states, in effect, that people will be better motivated if they are treated equitably and demotivated if they are treated inequitably.

S: It is not synonymous with equality, which means treating everyone the same, since this would be inequitable if they deserve to be treated differently.

S6: This explains only one aspect of the process of motivation and job satisfaction, although it may be significant in terms of morale

[Officers Training Academy (OTA), 2018], [Indian Military Academy (IMA), 2018]

A. PQRS   **B.** PQSR   **C.** RSQP   **D.** QPRS

Q.27 S1: We cannot understand the power of rumours and prophecies in history by checking whether they are factually correct or not.

P: The rumours in 1857 began to make sense when seen in the context of the policies the British pursued from the late 1820s.

Q: Rumours circulate only when they resonate with the deeper fears and suspicions of people.

R: Under the leadership of Governor General Lord William Bentinck, the British adopted policies aimed at "reforming" Indian society by introducing Western education, Western ideas and Western Institutions.

S: We need to see what they reflect about the minds of people who believed them - their fears and apprehensions, their faiths and convictions.

S6: With the cooperation of sections of Indian society they set up English-medium schools, colleges and universities which taught Western sciences and liberal arts.

[Officers Training Academy (OTA), 2018], [Indian Military Academy (IMA), 2018]

A. SQPR   **B.** QSPR   **C.** PRSQ   **D.** RSPQ

Q.28 S1: The Constitution of India thus emerged through a process of intense debate and discussion.

P: This was an unprecedented act of faith, for in other democracies the vote had been granted slowly, and in stages.

Q: However, on one central feature of the Constitution there was substantial agreement.

R: Many of the provisions were arrived at through a process of give-and take, by forging a middle ground A between two opposed positions.

S: This was on the granting of the vote to every adult Indian.

S6: In countries such as the United States and the United Kingdom, only men with education were allowed into the charmed circle.

[Officers Training Academy (OTA), 2018], [Indian Military Academy (IMA), 2018]

A. PRSQ   **B.** RQSP   **C.** SPRQ   **D.** QSRP

Ques (29-33):Direction: In the following question, sentences of a paragraph have been jumbled and labeled as A, B, C and D. You are required to rearrange the jumbled sentences of the paragraph and mark your response accordingly by selecting the correct option.

Q.29 A. One of the best-known examples of North Indian sculpture.

B. And hints at the richness and grandeur of the ancient Mauryan Empire.

C. Is the Lion Capital of Ashoka, Sarnath.

D. It is the source for the national emblem of India.

A. ABDC   **B.** ACDB   **C.** ADCB   **D.** ABCD

Q.30 A. Before the 12th century, It is to be identified as Carnatic classical music.

B. And has been evolving since the 12th century.

C. It is a tradition that originated in Vedic ritual chants.

D. Shastriya Sangeet is the classical music of North India.

A. DCBA   **B.** DCAB   **C.** ABCD   **D.** ABDC

Q.31 A. "It is mine. I saw it first," claimed one cat.

B. Suddenly they spotted a loaf of bread lying beneath a tree.

C. Once upon a time, two cats were passing through a street.

D. Both pounced upon it and caught the loaf at the same time.

A. ADBC   **B.** BADC   **C.** DBCA   **D.** CBDA

Q.32 A. It is one of the most popular pastimes.

B. Finding fault with others is the most common human folly.

C. But while railing at others, we hardly realize that we have the same faults in ourselves.

D. We like to sit in idle groups and rail about the shortcomings of others.

A. DBCA   **B.** CBDA   **C.** BADC   **D.** ADBC

Q.33 A. She understood my signs, and I could make her do as I wished.

B. My constant companion was Martha, our cook's daughter.

C. We even helped in feeding the hens which crowded around the kitchen steps.

D. This pleased me greatly and we spent a lot of time together.

A. BADC   **B.** CBDA   **C.** DCAB   **D.** ADCB

Ques (34-37):Direction: The question below consists of a set of labelled sentences in which first and the last sentence is given. Out of the four options given, select the most logical order of the sentences to form a coherent paragraph.

Q.34 S1- Climatic changes have become more prominent now because of global warming which is a global concern.

P- Such gases never let sun rays go back to the atmosphere, however, trap heat from them.

Q- The release of various greenhouse gases in the atmosphere by many natural means and human activities causes an increase in atmospheric temperature because such gases have a capability to absorb all the heat of environment from the sun, burning coal, etc.

R- Both are hot issues of the current time and it is the time to analyse causes and prevention methods to prevent global warming.

S- Fossil fuels burning release more carbon dioxide which is increasing day by day because of deforestation.

S6- Plants are the main source to utilize carbon dioxide as a food, however, we are disturbing the natural cycle by cutting more plants.

A. SRPQ   **B.** QPRS

C. RQPS   **D.** None of these

Q.35 S1- Reading books has a lot of psychological benefits.

P- It is helpful for gaining lots of knowledge and information but reading a good book is healthier for our brain and a completely different experience.

Q- When it comes to reading, most of us these days are addicted to reading online blogs, articles, stories and tweets.

R- Those who have a habit of reading are aware of the pleasure and value of reading books then.

S- They know its magic and power that renders knowledge and makes one wiser.

S6- It does wonder for our brains as it is the activity that helps us focus. Reading is the best exercise for your brains.

A. QRSP   **B.** SQRP

C. RSQP   **D.** None of these

Q.36 S1- In such a competitive world, it is must for all to have a good education.

P- The importance of higher education has become increasingly in getting good job and position.

Q- It makes us strong mentally, socially and intellectually by increasing our knowledge level, technical skills and a good position in the job.

R- Each and every kid has their own dream of doing something different in life.

S- Proper education creates lots of ways to go ahead in the future.

S6- There is only one way to all dreams which is a good education.

A. PSQR   **B.** RQPS

C. SPRQ   **D.** None of these

Q.37 S1- Better standard of living for the family is one of the advantages of women/female education.

P- An educated mother will earn as good as the father of the family and will look after the financial needs of her family in a much better way.

Q- It doesn't take a mathematician to conclude that a family relying on double wages is more content and happy than a family which relies on the income of a single parent.

R- Women are more concerned about the health of their family than men and have a great sense of hygiene too.

S- Two incomes under the same roof will improve the quality of living and also ensure better education and facilities to the children, not to mention that a happy family will ultimately lead to a happy society.

S6- Even working women are constantly concerned about their family's health and don't compromise with it at any cost.

A. SPRQ   **B.** QPSR

C. RSPQ   **D.** None of these

Ques (38-41):Direction: In this question, each item consists of six sentences of passage. The first and sixth sentences are given in the beginning as SI and S6. The middle four-sentence in each have been jumbled up and labelled as P, Q, R and S. You are required to find the proper sequence of the four sentences.

Q.38 S1: The British rule in India has brought about the moral, material, cultural and spiritual ruination of this great country.

S6: We are not to kill anybody but it is our dharma to see that the curse of this Government is blotted out.

P: I regard this rule as a curse.

Q: Sedition has become my religion

R: Ours is a non-violent battle

S: I am out to destroy this system of Government.

[UPSC NDA, 2019]

A. S P R Q   **B.** P S Q R   **C.** Q R P S   **D.** S R P Q

Q.39 S1: Mr. Sherlock Holmes and Doctor Watson were spending a weekend in a University town.

S6: It was clear that something very unusual happened.

P: One evening they received a visit from an acquaintance, Mr. Hilton Soames.

Q: On that occasion, he was in a state of great agitation.

R: They were staying in furnished rooms, close to the library.

S: Mr. Soames was a tall, thin man of a nervous and excitable nature.

The proper sequence should be

A. P R S Q   **B.** R P S Q   **C.** P Q R S   **D.** R P Q S

Q.40 S1: The machines that drive modern civilisation derive their power from coal and oil.

S6: Nuclear energy may also be effectively used in this respect.

P: But they are not inexhaustible.

Q: These sources may not be exhausted very soon.

R: A time may come when some other sources have to be tapped and utilised.

S: Power may, of course, be obtained in future from forests, water, wind and withered vegetables.

The proper sequence should be

A. P Q R S   **B.** Q P R S   **C.** S R Q P   **D.** S P Q R

Q.41 S1: The body can never stop.

S6: It comes from food.

P: To support this endless activity, the body needs all the fuel for action.

Q: Sometimes it is more active than at other times, but it is always moving.

R: Even in the deepest sleep we must breathe.

S: The fuel must come from somewhere.

The proper sequence should be

A. P Q R S   **B.** P R Q S   **C.** Q R P S   **D.** S R Q P

Q.42 Direction: In this question, each item consists of six sentences of passage. The first and sixth sentences are given in the beginning as S1 and S6. The middle four-sentence in each have been jumbled up and labelled as P, Q, R and S. You are required to find the proper sequence of the five sentences.

S1: The machines that drive modern civilisation derive their power from coal and oil.

S6: Nuclear energy may also be effectively used in this respect.

P: But they are not inexhaustible.

Q: These sources may not be exhausted very soon.

R: A time may come when some other sources have to be tapped and utilised.

S: Power may, of course, be obtained in future from forests, water, wind and withered vegetables.

The proper sequence should be:

A. PQRS   **B.** QPRS   **C.** SRQP   **D.** SPQR

Q.43 Direction: In this question, each item consists of six sentences of passage. The first and sixth sentences are given in the beginning as S1 and S6. The middle four-sentence in each have been jumbled up and labelled as P, Q, R and S. You are required to find the proper sequence of the five sentences.

S1: The body can never stop.

S6: It comes from food.

P: To support this endless activity, the body needs all the fuel for action.

Q: Sometimes it is more active than at other times, but it is always moving.

R: Even in the deepest sleep we must breathe.

S: The fuel must come from somewhere.

The proper sequence should be:

A. PQRS   **B.** PRQS   **C.** QRPS   **D.** SRQP

Q.44 Direction: Read the following group of sentences. The 1st and the last sentences are numbered 1 and 6, the rest are numbered P,Q,R,S. Arrange these four sentences in proper order to form a meaningful paragraph/sentence.

1. Optimism is not a deep complicated philosophy

P. In some persons it is an inborn trait.

Q. In fact, it is always taking a positive and bright view of life.

R. It is more of a general attitude of life.

S. They are tuned that way by nature and temperament.

6. However, in most cases it is an acquired and nurtured habit.

A. RQPS   **B.** QRPS   **C.** PSRQ   **D.** PSQR

Q.45 Direction: Given below are sentences which have been presented in a random order. Arrange the following sentences in a proper sequence to form a meaningful paragraph and identify the correct sequence.

A. This is because your witness will be called upon to testify in court if the will is ever challenged.

B. Lawyers advise people to use witnesses who are younger than they and are likely to outlive them.

C. You can make a will as simple as you want. You will need to sign the document in the presence of two witnesses, who will then have to put the signature on it.

D. It helps if a doctor is a witness or the document is signed in his presence.

E. This is because he could be called upon to testify to the stability of your mental condition when you drew up the will.

A. ABCDE   **B.** CBADE   **C.** DCBAE   **D.** CDBAE

// Smart Answer Sheet //

Correct — Indicates percentage of students who answered questions correctly.

Skipped — Indicates percentage of students who skipped questions.

Q.	Ans.	Correct / Skipped
1	D	68.58 % / 30.56 %
2	B	63.37 % / 30.64 %
3	A	41.68 % / 51.79 %
4	D	56.92 % / 36.97 %
5	C	56.72 % / 34.28 %
6	D	59.26 % / 39.29 %
7	D	56.27 % / 36.79 %
8	C	60.59 % / 38.21 %
9	A	52.81 % / 43.12 %

Q.	Ans.	Correct / Skipped
10	B	41.77 % / 53.94 %
11	D	20.3 % / 67.25 %
12	A	55.9 % / 39.92 %
13	A	65.38 % / 33.45 %
14	B	51.67 % / 42.43 %
15	C	54.02 % / 38.95 %
16	A	67.63 % / 30.4 %
17	B	69.26 % / 30.34 %
18	B	62.17 % / 34.99 %

Q.	Ans.	Correct / Skipped
19	C	66.23 % / 30.45 %
20	D	44.51 % / 33.57 %
21	B	26.29 % / 69.39 %
22	D	81.84 % / 14.85 %
23	D	10.31 % / 72.32 %
24	B	48.87 % / 31.57 %
25	A	67.45 % / 30.44 %
26	C	29.25 % / 68.83 %
27	B	43.87 % / 51.32 %

Q.	Ans.	Correct / Skipped
28	B	89.37 % / 10.19 %
29	B	57.39 % / 40.44 %
30	A	55.47 % / 37.35 %
31	D	66.62 % / 32.79 %
32	C	48.73 % / 36.11 %
33	A	69.29 % / 30.6 %
34	C	55.09 % / 42.42 %
35	C	47.31 % / 46.28 %
36	A	44.81 % / 53.8 %

Q.	Ans.	Correct / Skipped
37	B	19.18 % / 74.43 %
38	B	66.17 % / 31.44 %
39	B	22.61 % / 69.61 %
40	B	69.99 % / 30.0 %
41	C	48.92 % / 37.3 %
42	B	66.47 % / 30.11 %
43	C	47.12 % / 32.69 %
44	A	25.29 % / 71.44 %
45	B	46.71 % / 32.91 %

Performance Analysis	
Avg. Score (%)	53.33%
Toppers Score (%)	60.0%
Your Score	

//Hints and Solutions//

1. When ordering the sentences, it is easier to find the first few and then eliminate the options. The first sentence is always independent and introduces a topic. Here, only sentence B is independent and introduces the topic of 'Nietsche and will to power'. So, B must be the first sentence. This order is only shown by option (D).

Thus, the correct sequence is: BCAD.

Hence, the correct option is (D).

2. When ordering the sentences, it is easier to find the first few and then eliminate the options. The first sentence is always independent and introduces a topic. Here, only sentence A is independent and introduces the topic of 'Plutonium'. Out of the given options, only option (B) begins with A.

Thus, the correct sequence is: ADCB.

Hence, the correct option is (B).

3. D is the first sentence because it introduces the subject of demonetization. C further explains how it is carried out. So, C is the continuation of the explanation of the subject introduced in D. C talks of the replacement of the current form of money with new notes using the word 'often'. And B talks of the replacement using the word 'sometimes'. Both the two sentences refer to the replacement of currencies, so, both should be written subsequently, and placing C before B is contextually more meaningful. A is a different point, so, it must come after DCB.

Thus, the correct sequence is: DCBA

Hence, the correct option is (A).

4. When ordering the sentences, it is easier to find the first few and then eliminate the options. The first sentence is always independent and introduces a topic. Here, only sentence B is independent in meaning, which introduces the topic of 'form in as an element of art'. So, B must be the first sentence in the correct order. Out of the given options, only option (D) begins with B.

Thus, the correct sequence is: BCAD.

Hence, the correct option is (D).

5. When ordering the sentences, it is easier to find the first few and then eliminate the options. The first sentence is always independent and introduces a topic. Here, only sentence C is independent and introduces the topic of 'blood'. So, C must be the first sentence. This order is only given by option (C).

Thus, the correct sequence is: CDAB.

Hence, the correct option is (C).

6. The given paragraph is related to the importance of the environment. So, sentence 'B' will be the first sentence after rearrangement as it establishes the subject matter. The word 'they' in the sentence 'D' is used for 'countless benefits' mentioned in sentence 'B' so it will be followed by sentence 'D'. Sentence 'A' follows 'D' as it talks about the 'benefits of trees and forests' and is in the continuation of 'D'. Sentence 'C' is the logical successor of 'A' as it further explains the 'benefits of plants'.

Thus, the correct arrangement is BDAC.

Hence, the correct option is (D).

7. B is the sentence that introduces the topic- farmers. So, it will be the first sentence after rearrangement.

C follows B as it gives the reason for what is mentioned in B.

A follows C as it starts with 'hence' showing that it is indeed right to say that farmers are the most useful members of society.

D follows A as it connects with it by yet. 'Yet' signifies 'still'. Farmers are the most useful members of society, still, they don't get much profit or recognition.

Thus, the correct arrangement is: BCAD.

Hence, the correct option is (D).

8. D is the sentence that establishes the subject matter. Hence, it'll be the first sentence after rearrangement.

A will come after D because it further explains the characteristic of those people.

C is connected to A by 'which'. Which is used to refer to something already mentioned.

B contextually follows C. As it summarizes by stating that happiness is not at all proportional to income.

Thus, the correct arrangement would be: DACB

Hence, the correct option is (C).

9. B is the sentence that introduces the characters 'Pratham' and his elephant 'Heera'. Hence, it will be the first sentence after rearrangement.

C contextually follows B because it states the activities of elephant what it does next.

Third sentence will be A because it mentions what they did after the inspection was over,

D is the concluding sentence of arrangement as here they are returning home after everything is done.

Thus, the correct arrangement would be: BCAD

Hence, the correct option is (A).

10. B is the sentence that establishes the subject matter. Hence, it will be the first sentence after the rearrangement.

A is the logical successor of B as it describes what a friend does that can hurt us.

C connects with A through 'or' and presents another situation where our friends hurt us.

D is the closing sentence because it gives a conclusion- 'we feel taken for granted'.

Thus, the correct arrangement would be: BACD

Hence, the correct option is (B).

11. The correct logical order is QPR.

'Pollution needs' must follow Q as all other options are unviable. P and R forms a logical pair because 'otherwise' in sentence P should be followed by a reason which is mentioned in R 'suffer a lot'.

Hence, the correct option is (D).

12. The correct logical order is SPURQT.

The passage is about threats faced by a newly independent nation so the opening sentence should be S which tells that the threats are varied. PU is a logical pair joint by the conjunction 'and'; they tell about the kinds of threats. U is followed by R which adds on with the most dangerous threats. QT is a logical pair joint by the conjunction 'and'. So advanced nations should help.

Hence, the correct option is (A).

13. X. The sentence X is the continuation of the first sentence because correlation needs another object to be correlated with, which here is 'a meaningful life'.

W. Contradicting the general belief, i.e. the two terms happy life and meaningful life are correlated as discussed in the previous sentence, sentence W follows X

Z. The sentence Z further talks about attempts to probe for differences between the two factors.

Y. Sentence Y attempts to explain the differences and precedes statement 6.

Hence, the correct option is (A).

14. After the rearrangement the correct order will be QSPR.

'There is an enemy beneath our feet - an enemy more deadly for his complete impartiality. He recognizes no national boundaries no political parties. Everyone in the world is threatened by him. The enemy is the Earth itself. When an earthquake comes, the whole world trembles. The power of an earthquakes is greater then, anything man himself can produce'.

Hence, the correct option is (B).

15. B contains the subject 'the child' and is thus the first part. A will follow B because it is a passive sentence and the verb will be followed by the doer. D makes complete sense after A.

Complete sentence is: " The child was so spoiled by her indulgent parents that she pouted and became sullen when she did not receive all of their attention".

Hence, the correct option is (C).

16. C will be the first part since it contains the subject, B cannot preceed A as in (C) because B describes what is in A, so B will follow A and D.

Hence, the correct option is (A).

17. C is the opening sentence, since it introduces the subject, D describes what is said in C and thus will follow C. A will follow B, because the preposition 'for' will follow 'poses major challenge' and combines D and B, thus B follows.

Hence, the correct option is (B).

18. C is the opening part containing the subject because the conjunction at the end of C is but the following sentence must be opposite to R in intent, that is A. But the subject of A is in D so CDAB is the right sequence.

Hence, the correct option is (B).

19. The passage begins by introducing the topic at hand - the giant wall of the Dhauladhar range - then comes statement Q which further introduces the topic, it mentions that it has a modest altitude as compared to the Himalayan ranges, then comes statement S which talks about how despite being lower than the Himalayas, the mountain range sweeps 12,000 ft. This is followed by statement R which talks of another characteristic the mountain range has - a lifeline - and then comes statement P which talks about how the mountain range is a lifeline.

So, the correct sequence is QSRP.

Hence, the correct option is (C).

20. The passage begins with the topic at hand - the truth is far more important than the teacher. This is followed by statement R, which further explains how in order to be a good teacher one should have an understanding of themselves. Then comes statement Q, which explains how wisdom begins with self-knowledge. This is followed by statement P - this gives an example of how the lack of self-knowledge leads to destruction. The final statement is S - as shown by the adverb 'therefore' the seeker of through has to be a pupil or teacher.

So, the correct sequence is RQPS.

Hence, the correct option is (C).

21. The passage begins with an introduction to the topic at hand - the importance of discipline. This is followed by statement S which talks about how necessary discipline is in schools where there is 1 teacher for a 100 students, then comes statement R which talks about how when there are a 100 students a lack of discipline would mean complete chaos and then comes statement Q which talks about if there were 5-6 students in a class a teacher could give appropriate help and according to statement P, they could understand each child.

So, the correct sequence is SRQP.

Hence, the correct option is (B).

22. The passage begins with an introduction to the topic at hand - The Tolstoy Farm which was founded in 1910 - then comes statement R which talks about how this farm became the topic of multiple researches and according to statement Q - A Jewish architect Kallenbach was by the side of Gandhi the whole time. Then comes statement P which talks about how Kallenbach was rich and bought the farm. Finally came statement S which talks about how he put his social, moral and religious components in the doctrine.

So, the correct sequence is RQPS.

Hence, the correct option is (D).

23. The passage begins with an introduction to the topic at hand - decentralized planning. Then comes statement S which talks about how decentralized planning is implemented, this is followed by statement R - this talks about how individuals and small groups carry out their plans to achieve a common goal. Then according to statement P which talks about how decentralized planning operates from the bottom up and according to statement Q is more connected with capitalized economies.

So, the correct sequence is SRPQ.

Hence, the correct option is (D).

24. The passage starts with the introduction to the topic at hand - the doubt that if mankind has ever lived sustainably. This is followed by statement Q which mentions an exception. Then comes statement P which generalizes the issue- this is followed by statement S which talks about how this behaviour has accelerated after the Industrial Revolution and according to statement R, we have now reached a place where we are about to destroy ourselves and the Earth.

So, the correct sequence is QPSR.

Hence, the correct option is (B).

25. The passage starts with an introduction to the topic - measurement as an important concept in performance management. Then comes statement R, this talks about how measurement is the basis for generating and providing feedback. This is followed by statement Q which talks about the other functions of measurement - identifying where things are going well and then according to statement P where, where things are not going well. The final statement - S - talks about how measuring performance is easy for those who are responsible for achieving targets.

So, the correct sequence is RQPS.

Hence, the correct option is (A).

26. The passage starts with an introduction to the topic at hand - the equity theory - this is followed by statement R which talks about what is included in the equity theory - people are motivated better with equity - this is followed by statement S which states how equity is different from equality and then comes statement Q which talks about equity always being a comparative process. Finally there is statement P which talks about what is involved in being treated equitably.

So, the correct sequence is RSQP.

Hence, the correct option is (C).

27. The first statement introduces the passage to us - the power of rumours and prophecies, then comes statement Q which talks about how rumors originate and circulate, this is followed by statement S which talks about what constitutes a rumor - they reflect the minds of people. Then next comes statement P which gives an instance of a rumour - the ones in 1857, this instance is further elaborated in statement R - which talks about the rumors under the leadership of Governor General Lord William Bentick.

So, the correct sequence is QSPR.

Hence, the correct option is (B).

28. The passage begins with the topic at hand - the Constitution of India emerging through a process of intense debate. This is followed by statement R, this talks about how many provisions were decided by a process of give and take. Then comes statement Q which states an exception of the process, statement S explains the exception in detail - granting a vote to every Indian adult. Finally comes statement P which talks about how this decision itself was unprecedented.

So, the correct sequence is RQSP.

Hence, the correct option is (B).

29. The sentence 'A' starts the paragraph by pointing towards the North Indian Sculpture. Therefore, A is the first part.

The sentence 'C' completes the sentence 'A'. as the best-known example is the Sarnath. Therefore, C is the second part.

The pronoun 'It' mentioned in the sentence 'D' refers back to the noun 'Sarnath' mentioned in the sentence 'C'. Therefore, D follows C.

The sentence 'B' is concluding the paragraph. Therefore, it is the last part.

Thus, the correct sequence is: ACDB.

Hence, the correct option is (B).

30. The sentence 'D' is independent of any other sentence as it is giving general information about the noun "Shastriya Sangeet". Therefore, the sentence 'D' is the first part.

The pronoun 'It' mentioned in the sentence 'C' refers back to the noun 'Shastriya Sangeet' mentioned in the sentence 'D'. Therefore, D follows C.

The sentence 'B' haven't any subject, The pronoun 'It' mentioned in the sentence 'C' act as the subject for the sentence 'B'. Therefore, B is the third part.

The sentence 'A' is the concluding sentence. Therefore, it is the last part.

Thus, the correct sequence is: DCBA.

Hence, the correct option is (A).

31. Sentence C introduces us to the subject 'two cats'. It is the introductory sentence and will be put in the first place.

Sentence B tells us about the instance of the cats spotting a loaf of bread. It will be put in second place.

Sentence D tells us the reaction of the cats after seeing the loaf of bread. It will be put in third place.

The last sentence is A as it mentions the conviction of one of the cats that the loaf was hers as she first spotted it.

Thus, the correct sequence is: CBDA.

Hence, the correct option is (D).

32. The sentence 'B' is independent of any other sentences as it is giving general information about "Finding fault with others". Therefore, 'B' is the first part.

The pronoun "It" mentioned in the sentence 'A' refers back to 'finding fault with others' mentioned in the sentence 'B'. Therefore, 'A' follows 'B'.

The phrase "sit in idle groups and rail" mentioned in the sentence 'D' is linked with the "most popular pastimes" mentioned in the sentence 'A'. Therefore, 'D' follows 'A'.

The sentence 'C' is the concluding sentence. Therefore, 'C' is the last sentence.

Thus, the correct sequence is: BADC.

Hence, the correct option is (C).

33. The sentence 'B' is independent of any other sentences as it is giving general information about the noun "Martha". Therefore, 'B' is the first part.

The pronoun "She" mentioned in the sentence 'A' refers back to the noun 'Martha' mentioned in the sentence 'B'. Therefore, 'A' follows 'B'.

The pronoun "we" mentioned in the sentence 'D' refers back to the "author and Martha" mentioned in the sentence 'A'. Therefore, 'D' follows 'A'.

The sentence 'C' is the concluding sentence. Therefore, 'C' is the last sentence.

Thus, the correct sequence is: BADC.

Hence, the correct option is (A).

34. The first sentence will be R because here we have to talk about the issues mentioned in S1.

The second sentence will be Q because then we have to talk about what these gasses do.

The third sentence will be P because we have to talk about their functioning.

The fourth sentence will be S because this option has not been used yet.

Thus, the correct sequence is: RQPS

Hence, the correct option is (C).

35. The first sentence will be R because here we have to talk about the ones who value books.

The second sentence will be S because then we have to talk about what they feel about reading books.

The third sentence will be Q because we have to talk about what is the current trend.

The fourth sentence will be P because this option has not been used yet.

Thus, the correct sequence is: RSQP

Hence, the correct option is (C).

36. The first sentence will be P because here we have to talk about the importance of education.

The second sentence will be S because then we have to talk about the ways that are created with the help of education.

The third sentence will be Q because we have to talk about its positive effects.

The fourth sentence will be R because it has not been used yet.

Thus, the correct sequence is: PSQR

Hence, the correct option is (A).

37. The first sentence will be Q because here we have to talk about the economic benefits of educating women.

The second sentence will be P because then we have to talk about the dual role of a mother.

The third sentence will be S because we have to talk about the positive results that will come with both the parents earning.

The fourth sentence will be R because it has not been used yet.

Thus, the correct sequence is: QPSR

Hence, the correct option is (B).

38. The passage is in points about how the British rule has ruined the country.

The first line tells us that the rule is a curse as it destroys. It then explains about our non-violent battle and the intention of destroying the government. The last line sarcastically explains that our dharma is to see that the curse of this Government is blotted out.

The correct sequence is:

S1: The British rule in India has brought about moral, material, cultural and spiritual ruination of this great country.

P: I regard this rule as a curse.

S: I am out to destroy this system of Government.

Q: Sedition has become my religion.

R: Ours is a non-violent battle.

S6: We are not to kill anybody but it is our dharma to see that the curse of this Government is blotted out.

Hence, the correct option is (B).

39. Since the introductory part is already there, R will be the 1st statement as it takes the story forward by talking about the place where Mr. Sherlock Holmes and Doctor Watson were staying.

The next statement will be P as tells us about the visit by someone who was known to them.

Now the statement P must be followed by S as it narrates how Mr. Soames looked like.

And the concluding statement will be Q.

So the correct order will be: R-P-S-Q.

Hence, the correct option is (B).

40. Since the introductory part is already there, Q will be the 1st statement as it tells us more about the idea of exhaustion of sources of power.

The next statement will be P as it further states that the sources are exhaustible.

Now the statement P must be followed by R as it makes us explore other sources of power as well.

And the concluding statement will be S.

So the correct order will be: Q-P-R-S.

Hence, the correct option is (B).

41. Since the introductory part is already there, Q will be the 1st statement as it furthers the statement in S1.

The next statement will be R as it takes us to another aspect of body movement mentioned as 'breathing'.

Now the statement R must be followed by P as it talks about the idea of catalyst needed for an activity.

And the concluding statement will be S.

So the correct order will be: Q-R-P-S.

Hence, the correct option is (C).

42. Since the introductory part is already there, Q will be the 1st statement as it tells us more about the idea of exhaustion of sources of power.

The next statement will be P as it further states that the sources are exhaustible.

Now the statement P must be followed by R as it makes us explore other sources of power as well.

And the concluding statement will be S.

So the correct order will be: QPRS.

Hence, the correct option is (B).

43. Since the introductory part is already there, Q will be the 1st statement as it furthers the statement in S1.

The next statement will be R as it takes us to another aspect of body movement mentioned as 'breathing'.

Now the statement R must be followed by P as it talks about the idea of catalyst needed for an activity.

And the concluding statement will be S.

So the correct order will be: QRPS.

Hence, the correct option is (C).

44. The second sentence should have a direct reference to the 1st sentence and most certainly it should start with a pronoun referring to optimism. So, R follows 1. The author continues to define optimism. So Q is next. If we now read the two sentences that are left, we see that S starts with 'they' So it can't come next. So the next sentence is P followed by S.

Thus, the correct sequence is: RQPS

Hence, the correct option is (A).

45. The first sentence here should be C, as it introduces us to the idea of will mentioned in the paragraph.

Thus, we can eliminate option (A) and (C).

The next sentence should be B as it introduces the views of a lawyer.

Following B, should be A because it tells us the reason why lawyer suggested young people as witness.

The next sentence should be D as it tells us that it would be helpful if doctor is a witness.

The correct sequence is: CBADE.

Hence, the correct option is (B).

Ques (1-5):Direction: Read the following passage and answer the question which follows.

Even though globalization is one of the most discussed topics in the contemporary world. It is not altogether a well-defined concept. A multitude of global interactions is put under the broad heading of globalization, varying from the expansion of cultural and scientific influences across borders to the enlargement of economic and business relations throughout the world. A wholesale rejection of globalization would not only go against global business, but it would also cut out movements of ideas, understanding, and knowledge that can help all the people of the world, including the most disadvantaged members of the world population. A comprehensive rejection of globalization can thus be powerfully counterproductive. There is a strong need to separate out the different questions that appear merged together in the rhetoric of the antiglobalization protests. The globalization of knowledge deserves a particularly high profile recognition, despite all the good things that can be rightly said about the importance of "Local knowledge".

Globalization is often seen, both in journalistic discussions and in remarkably many academic writings, as a process of westernization. Indeed, some who take an upbeat view of the phenomenon even see it as a contribution of Western civilization to the world.

Q.1 According to the passage, globalization is perceived often by media and academia as:

A. Supporting local knowledge system
B. Detrimental to local knowledge system
C. A process of Westernisation
D. A process of facilitating global business

Q.2 The attempt of a author in the passage is:

A. Unconditioned advocacy of globalization
B. Unconditioned rejection of globalization
C. Unconditioned rejection of local know ledge systems
D. Unbiased evaluation of globalization

Q.3 According to the passage, which one of the following is not a well-defined concept?

A. Multiculturalism
C. Globalization

B. Identity
D. Local knowledge

Q.4 As per the passage a wholesale reduction of globalization would result in affecting:

(a) Global businesses
(b) Movement of Ideas
(c) Local knowledge systems
Choose the correct answer from the options given below:

A. (a) and (b) only
C. (c) and (b) only

B. (a) and (c) only
D. (a), (b) and (c)

Q.5 According to the passage, which one of the following is counterproductive?

A. Comprehensive support to globalization
B. Wholesale rejection of globalization
C. Comprehensive rejection of anti-globalization protests
D. Recognition of local knowledge systems

Ques (6-10):Direction: Read the following passage and answer the question which follows.

The first computer games were played in the arcades, amusement centers having time-consuming, coin-operated games. Young males traditionally visited these, and hence, were the first audience for games. When the first game console appeared in homes, everybody could play them. But due to the nature of the games, which were largely copied from the consoles, the prime audience remained young males. This continued when new generations of consoles appeared. When PC gaming started, computers were still primarily used by men. It was also difficult to install and play these games, which required knowledge of the operating system of the computers. Only a few women had this knowledge or an interest in it. However, the age range became a bit larger because computers were primarily owned by a bit older men. This changed when the Internet started to become popular. The so-called Casual Games that could be played on the Internet, directly in a web browser, did not require any installation and were very easy to play. Games often last only a few minutes, making it possible for women to play them at irregular intervals and briefly in between other tasks. This attracted a completely different audience, middle-aged women. Suddenly, the computer became the tool of everybody: young and old and male and female. The introduction of Social Gaming, through sites like Facebook, made it crucial that you have and maintain a large social network to help you in progressing in the game. Today, more than 70% of both men and women play games and they spend an average of over five hours a week on it, with women playing more than men. But the gaming industry continues to be dominated by men and still has trouble in creating enough interesting content for women.

Q.6 Unlike social gaming, casual games do not require:

A. The presence of internet
B. A social media account, such as Facebook
C. Computers
D. None of these

Q.7 Which of the following is not true of games in arcades?

A. Their content was interesting to women
B. They were designed for young males
C. They often lasted for a long time
D. They had to be played after inserting a coin

Q.8 Even when consoles appeared at homes, young males were the audience:

A. As special games were designed for these home-computers

B. As only young males knew how to play games having played in arcades

C. As women did not know how to program computers and play games

D. As older men were not interested in games

Q.9 Computers became the tool of everybody, when _____.

A. The internet made it easier for all to access computers for gaming

B. Homes became arcades and games and consoles came home

C. 70% of people started using computers to play games for at least 5 hours a week

D. Women learnt to use computers, and create games for themselves

Q.10 The passage sketches the history of the gaming-industry and discusses which of the following?

A. Creating content that can interest women is still a challenge for the male dominated gaming industry

B. Women will never be the owners of the industry as they lack the essential skills

C. The focus of the industry is still not on women as they are smaller in number

D. Women continue to be passive consumers though are equal in number to men

Ques (11-20):Direction: Read the following passage and answer the question which follows.

This story was told to me by a friend.

It is my destiny (said he) to buy in the **dearest** markets and to sell— if I succeed in selling at all— in the cheapest. Usually, indeed, having tired of a picture or decorative article, I have positively to give it away; almost to make its acceptance by another a personal favour to me. But the other day was marked by an exception to this rule so striking that I have been wondering if perhaps the luck has not changed and I am, after all, destined to be that most **enviable** thing, a successful dealer. It happened thus. In drifting about the old curiosity shops of a cathedral city I came upon a portfolio of water-colour drawings, among which was one that to my eye would have been a possible Turner, even if an earlier owner had not shared that opinion or hope and set the magic name with all its initials (so often placed in the wrong order) beneath it. "How much is this?" I asked scornfully.

"Well," said the dealer, "if it were a genuine Turner it would be worth anything. But let's say ten shillings. You can have it for that; but I don't mind if you don't, because I'm going to London next week and should take it with me to get an opinion." I pondered. "Mind you, I don't guarantee it," he added. I gave him the ten shillings. By what incredible means I found a purchaser for the drawing at fifty pounds there is no need to tell, for the point of this narrative resides not in bargaining with collectors, but in bargaining with my own soul. The astonishing fact remains that I achieved a profit of forty-nine pounds ten and was duly elated. I then began to think. The dealer (so my thoughts ran) in that little street by the cathedral west door, he ought to participate in this. He behaved very well to me and I ought to behave well to him. It would be only fair

to give him half. Thereupon I sat down and wrote a little note saying that the potential Turner drawing, which no doubt he recollected, had turned out to be authentic, and I had great pleasure in enclosing him half of the proceeds, as I considered that the only just and decent course. Having no stamps and the hour being late I did not post this, and went to bed.

At about 3.30 a.m. I woke widely up and, according to custom, began to review my life's errors, which are in no danger of ever suffering from loneliness. From these I reached, by way of mitigation, my recent successful piece of chaffering, and put the letter to the dealer under both examination and cross-examination. Why (so my thoughts ran) give him half? Why be Quixotic? This is no world for **Quixotry**. It was my eye that detected the probability of the drawing, not his. He had indeed failed; did not know his own business. Why put a premium on ineptitude? No, a present of, say, ten pounds at the most would more than adequately meet the case. Sleep still refusing to oblige me, I took a book of short stories and read one. Then I closed my eyes again, and again began to think about the dealer. Why (so my thoughts ran) send him ten pounds? It will only give him a wrong idea of his customers, none other of whom would be so fair, so sporting, as I. He will expect similar letters every day and be disappointed, and then he will become embittered and go down the vale of tears a miserable creature. He looked a nice old man too; a pity, nay a crime, to injure such a nature. No, ten pounds is absurd. Five would be plenty. Ten would put him above himself.

While I was dressing the next morning I thought about the dealer again. Why should I (so my thoughts ran), directly I had for the first time in my life brought off a financial coup, spoil it by giving a large part of the profit away? Was not that flying in the face of the Goddess of Business, whoever she may be? Was it not asking her to disregard me— only a day or so after we had at last got on terms? There is no fury like a woman scorned; it would probably be the end of me. City magnates are successful probably just because they don't do these foolish impulsive things. **Impulse is the negation of magnatism**. If I am to make any kind of figure in this new role of fine-art-speculator (so my thoughts continued) I must control my feelings. No, five pounds is absurd. A douceur of one pound will meet the case. It will be nothing to me—or, at any rate, nothing serious—but a gift of quail and manna from a clear sky to the dealer, without, however, doing him any harm. A pound will be ample, accompanied by a brief note. The note was to the effect that I had sold the drawing at a profit which enabled me to make him a present, because it was an old, and perhaps odd, belief of mine that one should do this kind of thing; good luck should be shared. I had the envelope in my pocket, containing the note and the cheque when I reached the club for lunch; and that afternoon I played bridge so disastrously that I was glad I had not posted it. After all (so my thoughts ran, as I destroyed the envelope and contents) such bargains are all part of the game. Buying and selling are a perfectly straightforward matter between dealer and customer. The dealer asks as much as he thinks he can extort, and the customer, having paid it, is under no obligation whatever to the dealer. The incident is closed.

Q.11 Whose experience has been shared in the given passage?

A. The narrator

B. Someone who has not been mentioned at all in the passage

C. The narrator's cousin

D. The narrator's friend

Q.12 Which of the following is most similar in meaning to the word '**dearest**' as used in the passage?

A. Beloved   **B.** Most Expensive

C. Sweetheart   **D.** Closest

Q.13 What according to the narrator's friend is his destiny?

A. To purchase and sell

B. To purchase from an expensive market and sell at a cheap one

C. To purchase at a very low price and sell at a higher price

D. To sell goods that are dear to him

Q.14 Which of the following can be considered as the most apt conclusion about the protagonist of the story?

A. He procrastinates until his thoughts change as time passes and he decides that he wont share the amount with the dealer.

B. The protagonist is too tired in the end to find out the seller and give away his share.

C. He is too generous to think that the seller should get a share and strives hard to deliver the amount to him.

D. He is a very manipulative person and deliberately fails to deliver the share of the seller.

Q.15 Which of the following is most opposite in meaning to the word '**enviable**' as given in the passage?

A. Abominable   **B.** Admirable

C. Intelligent   **D.** Unintelligent

Q.16 Which of the following can be inferred from the following statement: 'for the point of this narrative resides not in bargaining with collectors, but in bargaining with my own soul.'

A. Since the protagonist had bargained a lot while purchasing the painting and had earned an enormous profit, he decided to pay a fair share to the seller.

B. The protagonist's soul had to be bargained in order to pay the seller's share.

C. Since the protagonist sold the painting at an exceptionally high price than it was worth, he felt obliged to share it with the seller.

D. It was the question of the protagonist's moral judgement whether he would pay the seller's share which he deserved.

Q.17 Which of these is one of the excuses that the protagonist formulates in order to justify that he should not share half the profit with the dealer?

A. Since the painting was not authentic, and it was by chance that the protagonist had earned a huge profit. So it was not a good idea to offer a fifty percent share to the dealer.

B. The dealer was an inexperienced businessman as he had not confirmed the authentic price of the painting from other sellers.

C. It was the protagonist who realised the worth of the painting and the dealer was not competent enough in the business.

D. The dealer was a fool and deserved to be paid the least amount possible.

Q.18 Which of the following comes closest in meaning to the phrase '**impulse is the negation of magnatism**' as given in the passage?

A. Spontaneity is the key to success

B. One should act according to their impulse

C. Premeditate well before you act

D. Following one's instinct can eliminate the possibility of becoming rich

Q.19 Which of the following is most opposite in meaning to the word '**Quixotic**' as given in the passage?

A. Idealistic   **B.** Honourable

C. Satisfactory   **D.** Realistic

Q.20 Which of the following can be an apt title of the passage?

A. The Market Norms

B. The Gullible Dealer

C. The Fortunate Friend

D. Third Thoughts

Ques (21-25):Direction: Read the following passage and answer the question which follows.

One day in 1924, five men who were camping in the Cascade Mountains of Washington saw a group of huge apelike creatures coming out of the woods. They hurried back to their cabin and locked themselves inside. While they were in, the creatures attacked them by throwing rocks against the walls of the cabin. After several hours, these strange hairy giants went back into the woods.

After this incident the men returned to the town and told the people of their adventure. However, only a few people accepted their story. These were the people who remembered hearing tales about footprints of an animal that walked like a human being.

The five men, however, were not the first people to have seen these creatures called Bigfoot. Long before their experience, local Native Americans were certain that a race of apelike animals had been living in the neighboring mountain for centuries. They called these creatures Sasquatch.

In 1958, workmen, who were building a road through the jungles of Northern California often found huge footprints in the earth around their camp.

Then in 1967, Roger Patterson, a man who was interested in finding Bigfoot went into the northern California jungles with a friend. While riding, they were suddenly thrown off from their horses. Patterson saw a tall apelike animal standing not far away. He managed to shoot seven rolls of film of the hairy creature before the animal disappeared in the hushes. When Patterson's film was shown to the public, not many people believed his story.

In another incident, Richard Brown, a music teacher and also an experience hunter spotted a similar creature. He saw the animal clearly through the telescopic lens of his rifle. He said the creature looked more like a human than an animal.

Later many other people also found deep footprints in the same area. In spite of regular reports of sightings and footprints, most experts still do not believe that Bigfoot really exists.

Q.21 What did the five campers do when they saw a group of apelike creatures?

A. They ran into the woods and hid there for several hours.

B. They quickly ran back into their cabin and locked the cabin door.

C. They threw rocks against the walls of their cabin to frighten the creatures away.

D. They attacked the creatures by throwing rocks at them.

Q.22 Did the town people believe the story of the five men about their meeting with Bigfoot ?

A. No, not everyone believed their story

B. Only those who had heard the same tale the second time believed them

C. Some said the five men were making up their own story

D. All the people believed what they said

Q.23 Who were the first people to have seen these apelike creatures before the five campers?

A. The workers who built the road in the jungles of Northern California

B. Roger Patterson and his friend

C. The local Native Americans

D. Richard Brown, a music teacher and a hunter

Q.24 The word neighbouring would BEST be replaced with:

A. Far-off **B.** Nearby

C. Remote **D.** Far-away

Q.25 Who gave the name 'Sasquatch' to the apelike creatures?

A. The five campers

B. Roger Patterson

C. The local Native Americans

D. Richard Brown

Ques (26-30):Direction: Read the following passage carefully and answer the questions that follow.

After the backslapping bonhomie and high of Houston, it was time for a reality check in New York. Contrary to expectations that were consciously generated and managed by both sides, India and the United States failed to arrive at a limited trade deal that was to have been announced during this visit of Prime Minister Narendra Modi to the U.S. The deal stumbled over duties imposed by India on ICT (information and communication technology) products — the U.S. wanted the 20% duty on mobile phones and ethernet switches to be reduced or eliminated. America is also understood to have demanded greater access to the Indian market for medical devices such as stents and knee implants apart from its dairy and agricultural products. These are sensitive products politically for the Indian side as Mr. Modi has often taken credit for making them affordable. Loosening price controls now is not an option for India as that would push up the prices of these products in the country. For its part, India wanted the Generalised System of Preferences which gives preferential market access for its products in the U.S., restored. These are so

far as a "limited trade deal" goes; a full-scale trade agreement would pose bigger challenges on issues such as intellectual property, e-commerce and the ticklish subject of H1B visas.

Foreign Secretary Vijay Gokhale has said that the two sides "narrowed" down their differences and made "significant progress" but it is clear that there is still a wide gulf even assuming that India is willing to go more than half the way to strike a deal. That a deal could not be struck despite Commerce Minister Piyush Goyal winging his way to New York to lead negotiations tells the story. For U.S. President Trump, even a limited deal with India will be something to talk about as he approaches election year. This is especially because trade talks with China are going nowhere. China has not only taken Mr. Trump's punitive tariffs on its chin but has retaliated in kind, picking the products that could hurt his constituency and supporters. This explains the hectic, behind-the-scenes activity with India in the last few weeks. With its economy in the grip of a major slowdown, any concessions from India on imports of American products may not have gone down well both politically and in economic terms. Going by the limited information in the public domain, it appears that India has played tough and refused to yield to U.S. demands. Trade negotiations are never easy and for them to succeed, both sides have to believe in a policy of give and take. It does not help if one side tries to bulldoze the other into submitting totally to its interests. At this point in time it does seem that even a limited trade deal between India and the U.S. is some distance away.

Q.26 According to the above passage, what is important to secure a trade deal between the two countries?

A. One country will have to loosen up their price controls.

B. Politically sensitive products have to be made affordable.

C. The two countries will have to make mutual concessions and compromises.

D. One of the countries can intimidate the other into submitting totally to its interests.

Q.27 What is the main theme of the above passage?

A. Indian economy in the grip of a major economic slowdown.

B. India and U.S. agree that the first priorities for the future should be to manage current challenges and address those that were likely immediately ahead.

C. India and the United States redouble their efforts to go down a path of constructive engagement that can lead to a first ever bilateral trade agreement.

D. India's refusal to give in to the U.S.'s demands makes it impossible for the two to reach a limited trade deal.

Q.28 Why are certain medical devices politically "sensitive products" according to the above passage?

A. By raising the import duties on these products, the government gained the favor of Indian businessmen.

B. As India is one of the major exporters of these items to the US, the move has revenue implication of about USD 240.

C. These medical devices helped in the exclusion of India from the Generalised System of Preferences (GSP) scheme.

D. Slackening the price control on these products can push up their prices in the country.

Q.29 Which of the following words is the most appropriate synonym of "bonhomie" in the context of the passage?

A. Turpitude
B. Virtuoso
C. Semaphore
D. Conviviality

Q.30 Which of the following sentences conveys the correct meaning of "ticklish" in the given context of the above passage?

A. He was ticklish and found it annoying when people took advantage of it.

B. The transport system, already chaotic at best, was flung into ticklish confusion.

C. Since they are ticklish human beings, he implies, he does not have to engage them at that level.

D. Dalkin, executive director of the ABC, was a man in command when it came to handling the potentially ticklish issue.

Ques (31-35):Direction: Read the following passage carefully and answer the question given below it.

When it comes to structures that are both majestic and well-fortified, the classic European castle is the pinnacle of design. Across the ages castles changed, developed, and eventually fell out of use, but they still command the fascination of our culture. Castles were originally built in England by Norman invaders in 1066. As William the Conqueror advanced through England, he fortified key positions to secure the land he had taken. Castles also served as bases of operation for offensive attacks. Troops were summoned to, organized around, and deployed from castles.

In this way, castles served both offensive and defensive roles in military operations. Not limited to military purposes, castles also served as offices from which the lord would administer control over his fiefdom. They would address disputes, handle business, feast, and enjoy festivities. In this way, castles served as important social centers in medieval England. Castles also served as symbols of power.

The first castles constructed in England were made from earth and timber. Those who constructed them took advantage of natural features, such as hills and rivers, to increase defenses. Since these castles were constructed from wood, they were highly susceptible to attacks by fire. Wooden castles were gradually replaced by stone, which greatly increased the strength of these fortifications; however, being made from stone did not make these castles entirely fireproof. Attackers could hurl flaming objects into the castle through the windows or ignite the wooden doors. The demise of castles can ultimately be attributed to gunpowder. During the 15th century, artillery became powerful enough to break through stone walls.

This greatly undermined the military role of castles. Castles were then replaced by artillery forts that had no role in civil administration, and country houses that were indefensible. Though castles no longer serve their original purposes, remaining castles receive millions of visitors each year from those who wish to experience these majestic „vestiges: of a time long passed.

Q.31 Which one of the following is not a function of castles as expressed in the passage?

[CTET Paper - I, 2018]

A. Castles served both offensive and defensive purposes militarily.

B. Castles served as symbols of power.

C. Castles were important social centres in medieval England.

D. Castles were the places where knights would keep their best horses.

Q.32 Which one of the following best describes the main idea in Paragraph 2?

[CTET Paper - I, 2018]

A. It describes how and why William the Conqueror took control of England.

B. It explains why castles were first built in England and the military purposes they served.

C. It shows how Norman lords were often scared and frequently retreated.

D. It details all of the purposes that English castles served.

Q.33 Which one of the following best explains how gunpowder was the nemesis of traditional castles?

[CTET Paper - I, 2018]

A. Wars were fought with guns and hiding in castles was no longer necessary.

B. Artillery forts with large cannons became more stylish than traditional castles.

C. Defending castles grew difficult since attackers could just shoot castle defenders.

D. Cannons were able to knock down stone walls, so castles offered little protection.

Q.34 Choose a word from the given options which means almost the same as the word 'vestiges' used in.

[CTET Paper - I, 2018]

A. Reminder
B. Outskirts
C. Farrago
D. Creation

Q.35 Choose a word which serves as the antonym of the word 'pinnacle'.

[CTET Paper - I, 2018]

A. Nadir
B. Crest
C. Apex
D. Steeple

Ques (36-40):Direction: Read the passage given below and answer the questions that follow by selecting the correct most appropriate options.

1. Each drop represents a little bit of creation and of life itself. When the monsoon brings to northern India the first rains of summer, the parched earth opens its pores and quenches its thirst with a hiss of ecstasy. After baking in the sun for the last few months, the land looks cracked, dusty and tired. Now, almost overnight, new grass springs up, there is renewal everywhere, and the damp earth releases a fragrance sweeter than any devised by man.

2. Water brings joy to earth, grass, leaf bud, blossom, insect, bird, animal and the pounding heart of man. Small children run out of their homes to romp naked in the rain. Buffaloes, which

have spent the summer listlessly around lakes gone dry, now plunge into heaven of muddy water. Soon the lakes and rivers will overflow with the monsoon's generosity, Trekking in the Himalayan foothills, I recently walked for kilometres without encountering habitation. I was just scolding myself for not having brought along a water- bottle when I came across a patch of green on a rock face. I parted a curtain of tender maidenhair fern and discovered a tiny spring issuing from the rock-nectar for the thirsty traveller.

3. I stayed there for hours, watching the water descend, drop by drop, into a tiny casement in the rocks. Each drop reflected creation. That same spring, I later discovered, joined other springs to form a. swift, tumbling. stream, which went cascading down the hill into other streams until, in the plains, it became part of a river. And that river flowed into another mightier river that kilometres later emptied into the ocean. Be like water, taught Laotzu, philosopher 'and founder of Taoism. Soft and limpid, it finds its way through, over or under any obstacle. It does not quarrel; it simply moves on.

Q.36 Children respond to the first rains of summer by:

[CTET Paper - I, 2021]

A. Giving shouts of joy
B. Floating paper boats in the water
C. Running and playing in the rain
D. Singing songs

Q.37 The tiny spring issuing from the rock is hidden by:

[CTET Paper - I, 2021]

A. Thick moss **B.** Maiden hair fern
C. Bushes and creepers **D.** Tall grass

Q.38 To become part of a river, a tiny drop has to:

[CTET Paper - I, 2021]

A. Have a lot of strength
B. Depend on external forces
C. Suffer a lot
D. Merge its identity

Q.39 Which of the following words is most similar in meaning to the word 'pounding' as used in para 2 of the passage?

[CTET Paper - I, 2021]

A. Shaking **B.** Benumbing
C. Palpitating **D.** Sinking

Q.40 Which part of speech is the underlined word in the following sentence?

Almost overnight new grass spring up.

[CTET Paper - I, 2021]

A. Preposition **B.** Pronoun
C. Adjective **D.** Adverb

Ques (41-45):Direction: Read the passage carefully and answer the question that follows.

Moghal Garden is located in Rashtrapati Bhawan in New Delhi, and it is a garden that exceeds all other gardens in terms of loveliness and elegance. This garden is a feast for our noses and eyes, and it takes away all of life's worries and cares. Every year in February, this garden is open to the public. There, peacefulness and sublimity reign supreme. This garden has fascinated everyone's interest.

In February, I went to see the Moghal Garden with some colleagues. We arrived there in a really good mood. The weather was pleasant and sunny. Despite the lack of an entry ticket, the gate to Moghal Garden was not soon in sight. We felt as though we were in heaven when we entered the garden; pollution of any kind was unimaginable.

There were several different kinds of flowers all over. Their fragrant perfume spread all over the garden. The various types of coloured flowers produced a very pleasing appearance all over. There were bushes being cut into the shapes of different animals. There were rose flowers of different colours- red, pink, yellow, white and black of enormous size. There we saw Bara Dari. The path to that place was covered by creepers and blossoms. There was a circular tank with multi-coloured fragrant flowers.

There was a large grassy area. In the middle of that, there was a fountain having beautiful lotus flowers. They were swaying to the rhythm of the wind. We reluctantly left the garden now that it was evening.

Q.41 When did the author visit the Moghal Garden with some of his colleagues?
A. During a festival season
B. When he was invited
C. In February
D. When there was a pleasant weather

Q.42 How were the bushes in the garden designed?
A. They were being cut into the shape of an elephant.
B. They were being cut into the shapes of different animals.
C. They were of different colours and enormous size.
D. They were being arranged in a horizontal position.

Q.43 The path to which place was covered by creepers and blossoms?
A. Bara Dari **B.** Bara Bara
C. Moghal Garden **D.** Rashtrapati Bhawan

Q.44 Which of the following responded to the rhythm of the wind?
A. A fountain
B. The author and his colleagues
C. The beautiful lotus flowers
D. Rose flowers of different colours

Q.45 According to the given passage, which of the following is FALSE?
A. There was no pollution in the garden.
B. The weather was pleasant and sunny.
C. Moghal Garden is located in Rashtrapati Bhawan.
D. There is an entry ticket for the garden.

// Smart Answer Sheet //

Correct   Indicates percentage of students who answered questions correctly.

Skipped   Indicates percentage of students who skipped questions.

Q.	Ans.	Correct / Skipped
1	C	47.16 % / 36.07 %
2	D	41.57 % / 39.95 %
3	C	44.43 % / 31.23 %
4	A	47.46 % / 43.59 %
5	B	54.29 % / 31.33 %
6	B	43.87 % / 48.28 %
7	A	64.08 % / 34.86 %
8	B	59.97 % / 39.6 %
9	A	61.7 % / 31.57 %

Q.	Ans.	Correct / Skipped
10	A	41.21 % / 37.02 %
11	D	85.31 % / 13.63 %
12	B	80.57 % / 14.66 %
13	B	77.38 % / 10.13 %
14	A	89.79 % / 10.0 %
15	A	43.98 % / 46.23 %
16	D	86.7 % / 11.0 %
17	C	58.14 % / 36.15 %
18	D	62.93 % / 36.98 %

Q.	Ans.	Correct / Skipped
19	D	88.06 % / 10.69 %
20	D	79.64 % / 17.63 %
21	B	64.61 % / 30.38 %
22	A	66.32 % / 31.63 %
23	C	47.34 % / 41.53 %
24	B	89.91 % / 10.03 %
25	C	42.16 % / 45.23 %
26	C	58.55 % / 31.47 %
27	D	69.03 % / 30.09 %

Q.	Ans.	Correct / Skipped
28	D	13.83 % / 78.44 %
29	D	65.0 % / 30.74 %
30	D	68.58 % / 30.8 %
31	D	52.6 % / 43.56 %
32	D	57.5 % / 32.53 %
33	D	27.65 % / 67.75 %
34	A	41.2 % / 54.48 %
35	A	41.14 % / 50.08 %
36	C	49.97 % / 34.51 %

Q.	Ans.	Correct / Skipped
37	B	59.95 % / 30.25 %
38	D	56.11 % / 33.03 %
39	C	23.52 % / 68.58 %
40	D	56.6 % / 36.15 %
41	C	13.59 % / 75.65 %
42	B	45.21 % / 47.61 %
43	A	48.92 % / 42.7 %
44	C	58.75 % / 32.01 %
45	D	69.32 % / 30.32 %

Performance Analysis	
Avg. Score (%)	55.56%
Toppers Score (%)	60.0%
Your Score	

//Hints and Solutions//

1. "Globalization is often seen, both in journalistic discussions and in remarkably many academic writings, as a process of westernization."

Upon perusal of the above statement, it can be concluded that globalization is perceived often by media and academia as a process of Westernisation.

Hence, the correct option is (C).

2. "There is a strong need to separate out the different questions that appear merged together in the rhetoric of the antiglobalization protests. The globalization of knowledge deserves a particularly high profile recognition, despite all the good things that can be rightly said about the importance of "Local knowledge"."

Upon perusal of the above statement, it can be concluded that the author encourages an unbiased evaluation of globalization and not an unconditioned rejection of globalization.

Hence, the correct option is (D).

3. "Even though globalization is one of the most discussed topics in the contemporary world. It is not altogether a well-defined concept."

Upon perusal of the above statements, it can be concluded that globalization is not a well-defined concept.

Hence, the correct option is (C).

4. "A wholesale rejection of globalization would not only go against global business, but it would also cut out movements of ideas, understanding, and knowledge that can help all the people of the world, including the most disadvantaged members of the world population."

Upon perusal of the above statement, it can be concluded that only the statements (a) and (b) are correct.

Hence, the correct option is (A).

5. "A comprehensive rejection of globalization can thus be powerfully counterproductive."

Upon perusal of the above statement, it can be concluded that wholesale rejection of globalization is counterproductive.

Hence, the correct option is (B).

6. Computers and the presence of the internet are the basic requirements for both social and casual games.

The passage states that social gaming is games played on social media websites such as Facebook, which require a large social network to progress in games. So, social media gaming requires a social media account. However; as per the passage, casual gaming does not require social media accounts and can be played in short intervals.

Hence, the correct option is (B).

7. The first sentence of the passage talks about the nature of arcade games.

As per the passage, the arcade games were: designed for young males; coin-operated; time-consuming. It does not talk about its content being interesting to women.

Hence, the correct option is (A).

8. The passage states that the first computer games were in arcades, amusement centers. They were focused on young males as the audience.

The passage also mentions that the home console games were largely copied from the arcade games, so only the young males who had played them knew how to play on home consoles. None of the other options give an adequate reason for the question.

Hence, the correct option is (B).

9. The passage talks about computers becoming a tool for everyone after the internet started getting popular.

So, the correct answer must be that the internet made computers a tool for everyone. None of the other options correctly describe the reason for computers being everyone's tool.

Hence, the correct option is (A).

10. The last sentence of the passage states that the gaming industry is having trouble creating interesting content for women.

This is the only option that is correct, given the context of the passage. Other options talk about a smaller number of women, or women being passive consumers or lacking skills. This is not really the focus of the passage.

Hence, the correct option is (A).

11. The first sentence of the passage mentions, 'This story was told to me by a friend.'

The second line which mentions '(said he)' confirms that the story told by the narrator is about himself and not a third person. Hence, the correct option is (D).

12. Dearest, in this context, is the superlative degree adjective of 'dear'.

Dear: expensive

The meaning of the other words-

Beloved: dearly loved

Sweetheart: means the same as beloved

Closest: most near and dear to someone
Hence, the correct option is (B).

13. According to the passage, It is my destiny (said he) to buy in the dearest markets and to sell— if I succeed in selling at all— in the cheapest.
Hence, the correct option is (B).

14. In the given story, the protagonist, having earned a huge profit decides to share the amount with the dealer. However, he dwells upon the idea and as time passes he intends on giving a lesser amount and ends up giving nothing at all. To 'procrastinate' means to 'delay or postpone action'.

Hence, the correct option is (A).

15. Enviable: arousing or likely to arouse envy, something so good that it makes you feel jealous.

Abominable: causing moral revulsion, very bad, terrible.

Thus we can see that Abominable is the antonym of Enviable. Hence, the correct option is (A).

16. By the expression 'bargaining with my soul' the protagonist means that having made a huge profit by selling the painting he bought from the dealer in ten shillings, his conscience was put to test.

The protagonist had to make a moral judgement whether he would be rightful enough to give a fair share to the dealer or not. Hence, the correct option is (D).

17. The passage mentions four justifications in total which the protagonist puts forth himself to reason out why he should share the minimum amount possible with the dealer. From the following statement, it is clear that option (C) is the correct answer.

Hence, the correct option is (C).

18. In the context where the given phrase has been mentioned, the protagonist says that City magnates are successful probably just because they don't do these foolish impulsive things. Magnates are tycoons or merchants who are very rich. An 'impulse' is an instinctive urge/ passionate urge to act spontaneously. It means that if the protagonist is driven by passion and gives away a share to the dealer, he will never become a successful magnate.
Hence, the correct option is (D).

19. Quixotic: extremely idealistic, unrealistic and impractical.

Realistic: having or showing a sensible and practical idea of what can be achieved or expected.

Thus we can see that Realistic is the antonym of Quixotic.
Hence, the correct option is (D).

20. The gist of the passage is how if an idea is kept with oneself for an ample duration of time and pondered over constantly, there is a possibility that we cite various reasons and change the initial decision altogether. A third thought is what happens when you take a second thought and build on it even further, creating a whole new thought.

Thus, option (D) can be the best title of the passage as it encloses the main idea.
Hence, the correct option is (D).

21. Five men who were camping in the Cascade Mountains of Washington saw a group of huge apelike creatures coming out of the woods. They hurried back to their cabin and locked themselves inside.

Hence, the correct option is (B).

22. After the incident when five men saw the big foots they returned to the town and told the people of their adventure. However, only a few people accepted their story.

Hence, the correct option is (A).

23. Then in 1967, Roger Patterson, a man who was interested in finding Bigfoot went into the northern California jungles with a friend. While riding, they were suddenly thrown off from their horses. Patterson saw a tall apelike animal standing not far away. Therefore the first people to have seen these apelike creatures before the five campers was Roger Patterson and his friend.

Hence, the correct option is (C).

24. Neighbouring means: a person or place which is adjacent with the given person of place. Therefore nearby will be correct option which can replace the word 'neighbouring'

Hence, the correct option is (B).

25. Local Native Americans were certain that a race of apelike animals had been living in the neighboring mountain for centuries. They called these creatures Sasquatch.

Hence, the correct option is (C).

26. It is stated towards the end of the above passage that trade negotiations are never easy and for them to succeed, both sides have to believe in a policy of give and take, that is, make concessions and compromises.

It does not help if one side tries to bulldoze the other into submitting totally to its interests. A limited deal between India and America was not possible because both the countries refused to yield to the others' demands.

Hence, the correct option is (C).

27. The above passage is mainly about how India and the U.S. failed to secure even a limited trade deal. The U.S. wanted the 20% duty on mobile phones and ethernet switches to be reduced or eliminated among other demands, and India wanted the GSP to be restored. It is stated in the passage- Going by the limited information in the public domain, it appears that India has played tough and refused to yield to U.S. demands.

Hence, the correct option is (D).

28. It is said in the above passage that America demanded greater access to the Indian market for medical devices such as stents and knee implants apart from its dairy and agricultural products.

These are sensitive products politically for the Indian side as Mr. Modi has often taken credit for making them affordable.

Loosening price controls now is not an option for India as that would push up the prices of these products in the country.

Hence, the correct option is (D).

29. Bonhomie means cheerful friendliness; geniality.

The word that is a synonym of this is Conviviality: the quality of being friendly and lively; friendliness.

The meanings of the rest of the words are:

- Turpitude: a corrupt or depraved or degenerate act or practice
- Virtuoso: someone who is dazzlingly skilled in any field
- Semaphore: an apparatus for visual signalling

Hence, the correct option is (D).

30. The meaning of ticklish, in the above context, is (of a situation or problem) difficult or tricky and requires careful handling.

In the above passage, the subject of H1B visas is called ticklish. Its other meaning is sensitive to being tickled.

Hence, the correct option is (D).

31. According to the passage, "In this way castles served both offensive and defensive roles in military operations. In this way, castles served as important social centres in medieval England. Castles also served as symbols of power."

So, "castles were the places where knights would keep their best horses" is not a function of castles as expressed in the passage.

Hence, the correct option is (D).

32. According to the passage, "In this way, castles served both offensive and defensive roles in military operations. Not limited to military purposes, castles also served as offices from which the lord would administer control over his fiefdom. They would address disputes, handle business, feast, and enjoy festivities. In this way, castles served as important social centers in medieval England. Castles also served as symbols of power."

The whole passage describes all the purposes that English castles served.

Hence, the correct option is (D).

33. According to the passage, "Attackers could hurl flaming objects into the castle through the windows or ignite the wooden doors. The demise of castles can ultimately be attributed to gunpowder."

The nemesis of traditional castles was brought because cannons were able to knock down stone walls, thus, castles offered little protection.

Hence, the correct option is (D).

34. The meaning of the given words:

Vestiges mean a trace or remnant of something that is disappearing or no longer exists.

Reminder means a thing that causes someone to remember something.

Hence, the correct option is (A).

35. The meaning of the given words:

Pinnacle means the most successful point; the culmination.

Nadir means the lowest or most unsuccessful point in a situation.

Hence, the correct option is (A).

36. Children respond to the first rains of summer by running and playing in the rain.

According to the passage, 'Small children run out of their homes to romp naked in the rain.'

Romp means to play in a rough, excited, and noisy way. It can be concluded that the children played excitedly in the rain.

Hence, the correct option is (C).

37. According to the passage, 'I parted a curtain of tender maidenhair fern and discovered a tiny spring issuing from the rock-nectar for the thirsty traveller.'

Upon the perusal of the above statement, it can be concluded that the tiny spring issuing from the rock is hidden by maidenhair fern.

Hence, the correct option is (B).

38. According to the passage, 'I stayed there for hours, watching the water descend, drop by drop, into a tiny casement in the rocks.'

From the lines, it is evident that every drop of rain has its own identity which it represents and to become a part of the river it has to merge its identity.

Hence, the correct option is (D).

39. The meaning of given words:

Pounding means the sound, feeling, or action of something beating repeatedly.

Palpitating means (of the heart) beating rapidly and strongly.

Hence, the correct option is (C).

40. Almost is an adverb here. Almost means 'nearly', 'not quite' or 'not completely'.

An adverb is a word that is used to change, modify or qualify several types of words including an adjective, a verb, a clause, another adverb, or any other type of word or phrase, with the exception of determiners and adjectives, that directly modify nouns.

Hence, the correct option is (D).

41. Let's refer to the passage, "In February, I went to see the Moghal Garden with some colleagues".

From the given lines, it can be understood that the author went to the Moghal Garden in the month of February.

Hence, the correct option is (C).

42. Let's refer to the passage, "There were bushes being cut into the shapes of different animals."

From the given lines, it can be understood that the bushes in the garden were cut into the shapes of different animals.

Hence, the correct option is (B).

43. Let's refer to the passage, "There were rose flowers of different colours- red, pink, yellow, white and black of enormous size. There we saw Bara Dari. The path to that place was covered by creepers and blossoms."

Hence, the correct option is (A).

44. Let's refer to the passage, "There was a large grassy area. In the middle of that, there was a fountain having beautiful lotus flowers. They were swaying to the rhythm of the wind."

From the given lines, it can be understood that as the wind blew, the beautiful lotus flowers in the fountain moved slowly or rhythmically backwards and forwards or from side to side.

Hence, the correct option is (C).

45. Let's refer to the passage, "Despite the lack of an entry ticket, the gate to Moghal Garden was not soon in sight."

From the given lines, it can be understood that despite the fact that there was no entry ticket, the gate to Moghal Garden was not soon in view.

Hence, the correct option is (D).

Q.1 Direction: Arrange the sentences P, Q, R between S1 and S5 such that they will form a meaningful passage.

S1: Rain is a beautiful gift of nature to mankind.

S5: It makes people dance with joy and sing sweet songs.

P - In summer, when the heat is intense, rain is a blessing.

Q - Therefore, it is welcomed by all.

R - It provides great relief from the scorching heat of the sun.

Choose from the options given below:

A. QPR   **B.** PRQ   **C.** PQR   **D.** QRP

Ques (2-10):Directions: The following items consist of a sentence, parts of which have been jumbled. These parts have been labelled as (P), (Q), (R), and (S). You are required to re-arrange the jumbled parts of the sentence and mark your response accordingly.

Q.2 life is considered (P) / the origin of (Q) / the history of universe (R) / a unique event in (S)

The correct sequence should be:

[Indian Military Academy (IMA), 2020], [Officers Training Academy (OTA), 2020]

A. (Q), (P), (S), (R)   **B.** (P), (S), (Q), (R)
C. (S), (Q), (P), (R)   **D.** (R), (S), (P), (Q)

Q.3 productive resources is (P) / how we manage (Q) / and competitiveness (R) / critical to strategic growth (S)

The correct sequence should be:

[Indian Military Academy (IMA), 2020], [Officers Training Academy (OTA), 2020]

A. (P), (Q), (R), (S)   **B.** (R), (S), (P), (Q)
C. (S), (R), (P), (Q)   **D.** (Q), (P), (S), (R)

Q.4 in service firms (P) / operations strategy (Q) / from the corporate strategy (R) / is generally inseparable (S)

The correct sequence should be:

[Indian Military Academy (IMA), 2020], [Officers Training Academy (OTA), 2020]

A. (S), (R), (Q), (P)   **B.** (Q), (P), (S), (R)
C. (R), (S), (P), (Q)   **D.** (P), (S), (Q), (R)

Q.5 are travelling, (P) / a recent survey has revealed (Q) / that they are worried about their safety (R) / even as more and more Indians (S)

The correct sequence should be:

[Indian Military Academy (IMA), 2020], [Officers Training Academy (OTA), 2020]

A. (S), (P), (Q), (R)   **B.** (Q), (S), (R), (P)
C. (P), (R), (S), (Q)   **D.** (R), (P), (S), (Q)

Q.6 the imagination of children (P) / stories can exercise (Q) / more than the stories (R) / because they tell (S)

The correct sequence should be:

[Indian Military Academy (IMA), 2020], [Officers Training Academy (OTA), 2020]

A. (Q), (R), (S), (P)   **B.** (S), (P), (Q), (R)
C. (Q), (P), (S), (R)   **D.** (R), (S), (Q), (P)

Q.7 as a record of (P) / and suffering of humans (Q) / the achievements, experiments (R) / history is considered (S)

The correct sequence should be:

[Indian Military Academy (IMA), 2020], [Officers Training Academy (OTA), 2020]

A. (S), (P), (R), (Q)   **B.** (R), (Q), (S), (P)
C. (P), (Q), (R), (S)   **D.** (Q), (R), (S), (P)

Q.8 can be invented (P) / it appears (Q) / has been invented (R) / that all that (S)

The correct sequence should be:

[Indian Military Academy (IMA), 2020], [Officers Training Academy (OTA), 2020]

A. (Q), (S), (P), (R)   **B.** (Q), (R), (S), (P)
C. (R), (S), (Q), (P)   **D.** (S), (P), (Q), (R)

Q.9 during the last century (P) / Indian social, political and cultural life (Q) / as a testimony of (R) / Indian cinema stands (S)

The correct sequence should be:

[Indian Military Academy (IMA), 2020], [Officers Training Academy (OTA), 2020]

A. (S), (P), (Q), (R)   **B.** (Q), (R), (S), (P)
C. (P), (Q), (R), (S)   **D.** (S), (R), (Q), (P)

Q.10 of all searches for knowledge (P) / should be the beginning (Q) / an exploration into truth (R) / and experiments of life (S)

The correct sequence should be:

[Indian Military Academy (IMA), 2020], [Officers Training Academy (OTA), 2020]

A. (R), (Q), (P), (S)   **B.** (S), (P), (Q), (R)
C. (R), (S), (P), (Q)   **D.** (Q), (R), (S), (P)

Ques (11-20):Direction: In the following question, parts of a sentence have been jumbled and labeled as P, Q, R and S. You are required to rearrange the jumbled parts of the sentence and mark your response accordingly by selecting the correct option.

Q.11 consideration for others /(P) for self-gratification /(Q) freedom does not mean the opportunity /(R) or the setting aside of /(S).

[Officers Training Academy (OTA), 2021], [Indian Military Academy (IMA), 2021]

A. S P Q R   **B.** Q S P R   **C.** R P Q S   **D.** R Q S P

Q.12 of any kind (P)/ to freedom and intelligence (Q)/ domination or compulsion (R) /is a direct hindrance (S)/.

[Officers Training Academy (OTA), 2021], [Indian Military Academy (IMA), 2021]

A. R P S Q   **B.** R Q P S   **C.** S P Q R   **D.** Q R S P

Q.13 enough potassium, /(P) banana provides /(Q) from various sugars /(R) and sustained energy /(S).
[Officers Training Academy (OTA), 2021], [Indian Military Academy (IMA), 2021]

A. P Q R S **B.** R S Q P **C.** S Q R P **D.** Q P S R

Q.14 of great trouble /(P) this is a time /(Q) the world to the maximum /(R) as one virus threatens /(S).
[Officers Training Academy (OTA), 2021], [Indian Military Academy (IMA), 2021]

A. P Q S R **B.** R S P Q **C.** S R Q P **D.** Q P S R

Q.15 are of the opinion /(P) some archaeologists /(Q) and that everybody enjoyed equal status /(R) that Harappan society had no rulers, /(S).
[Officers Training Academy (OTA), 2021], [Indian Military Academy (IMA), 2021]

A. S P Q R **B.** Q S R P **C.** Q P S R **D.** R P S Q

Q.16 in the same locality /(P) marriage within a unit /(Q) endogamy refers to /(R) or a group living /(S).
[Officers Training Academy (OTA), 2021], [Indian Military Academy (IMA), 2021]

A. Q R S P **B.** R S P Q **C.** Q P S R **D.** R Q S P

Q.17 when steam engines /(P) dominated industrialization /(Q) coal was the main source /(R) of energy in the initial stages, /(S).
[Officers Training Academy (OTA), 2021], [Indian Military Academy (IMA), 2021]

A. S P R Q **B.** R S P Q **C.** P Q R S **D.** Q R S P

Q.18 from the scientists? /(P) is the information /(Q) that comes /(R) how important /(S).
[Officers Training Academy (OTA), 2021], [Indian Military Academy (IMA), 2021]

A. Q S P R **B.** Q R S P **C.** S Q R P **D.** S P Q R

Q.19 brought on by destructive pests /(P) humans have suffered /(Q) frustration and food losses /(R) since earliest times /(S).
[Officers Training Academy (OTA), 2021], [Indian Military Academy (IMA), 2021]

A. S P Q R **B.** Q R S P **C.** S Q R P **D.** R S Q P

Q.20 most spectacular gold coins /(P) some of the /(Q) the Gupta rulers in India /(R) were issued by /(S).
[Officers Training Academy (OTA), 2021], [Indian Military Academy (IMA), 2021]

A. R S P Q **B.** Q P S R **C.** P Q R S **D.** S P Q R

Ques (21-28):Direction: In the following question, the 1st and the last part of the sentence/passage are numbered 1 and 6. The rest of the sentence/ passage is split into four parts and named P, Q, R, and S. These four parts are not given in their proper order. Read the sentence/passage and find out which of the four combinations is correct.

Q.21 1. The next morning I found myself somewhat refreshed but very hungry.
P. I asked him to let me help unload the vessel.
Q. I noticed I was near a large ship.
R. I went at once to the captain.
S. It was unloading a cargo of pig iron.
6. I wanted to earn money for food.

A. PQRS **B.** QSRP **C.** PRSQ **D.** SRPQ

Q.22 1. The salmon fish pushed themselves
P. to return to their spawning grounds
Q. and fertilized them
R. but once they laid their eggs
S. to their limits
6. they died.

A. SQPR **B.** RSQP **C.** SPRQ **D.** RPSQ

Q.23 1. One of my friends Krishnan went to live in a village.
P. But it was a very slow animal.
Q. So Krishnan bought a donkey for 200 rupees.
R. One day his new neighbor told him that he must buy a donkey.
S. Every family there had a donkey to carry things for them.
6. It did not like to work.

A. SQPR **B.** RSQP **C.** QPRS **D.** PRSQ

Q.24 1. The only choice
P. university will be to
Q. tuition fees to meet
R. left before the Indian
S. substantially raise the
6. the rising expenditure.

A. RPSQ **B.** PQSR **C.** SQRP **D.** QPSR

Q.25 1. Osteoarthritis in the knee is a problem that affects millions of people.
P. And so it reduces disability and improves the quality of life.
Q. Due to muscle flexibility there is less pain.
R. Knee exercises are done sitting in a chair or lying on one's back.
S. Knee exercises help prevent joint stiffness and strengthen muscles around the joint.
6. Exercises that help thigh muscles without involving weight-bearing are safe and effective.

A. QSRP **B.** SQRP **C.** RQPS **D.** RSPQ

Q.26 1. Another way for people to economize at an amusement park is to bring their own food.
P. Also, instead of filling up on soft drinks, they should bring a thermos of iced tea.
Q. Instead they should pack a nourishing, well-balanced lunch of cold chicken, carrot sticks, and fruit.
R. They will also save on calories.
S. They will avoid having to pay high prices for hamburgers and hot dogs.
6. Every dollar that is not spent at the refreshment stand is one that can be spent on another ride.

A. QSRP **B.** SQPR **C.** RSPQ **D.** PRSQ

Q.27 1. The vegetable bin of my refrigerator contained an assortment of weird-looking items.

P. The carrots dropped into U shapes as I picked them up with the tips of my fingers.

Q. To the right of the oranges was a bunch of carrots that had begun to sprout points, spikes, and tendrils.

R. Near the carrots was a net bag of onions.

S. Next to a shriveled, white-coated lemon were two oranges covered with blue fuzz.

6. Each onion had sent curling shoots through the net until the whole thing resembled a man of green spaghetti.

A. SQPR   **B.** QSRP   **C.** PRSQ   **D.** RSQP

Q.28 1. One reason for studying Psychology is to help you deal with your children.

P. Offer her a choice of staying up till 7:30 with you or going upstairs and playing until 8:00.

Q. A little knowledge of Psychology comes in handy.

R. Since she gets to make the choice, she does not feel so powerless and will not resist.

S. Perhaps your daughter refuses to go to bed when you want her to and bursts into tears at the mention of lights out.

6. Psychology is also useful in rewarding a child for a job well done.

A. RPSQ   **B.** PQSR   **C.** SQPR   **D.** QPSR

Ques (29-37):Direction: Give below, each item consists of six sentences of a passage. The first and sixth sentences are given in the beginning as S1 and S6. The middle four sentences have been jumbled up and labelled as P, Q, R and S. You are required to find the proper sequence of the four sentences and choose the correct option accordingly.

Q.29 S1: The master always says, "Refuse to be miserable".

S6: This is the art of right contact in life.

P: Before you fall into self-pity and blame games, remember that responsibility comes to only those who feel responsible.

Q: Challenges are faced by the strong and courageous, and if life brings you such opportunities, then turn failures into success.

R: Life can be painful, but it need not be sorrowful.

S: If you want to be happy, find occasions to be cheerful.

The correct sequence should be:

[Officers Training Academy (OTA), 2019], [Indian Military Academy (IMA), 2019]

A. RSPQ   **B.** QRSP   **C.** SQPR   **D.** RQSP

Q.30 S1 : Gandhiji reached Newcastle and took charge of the agitation.

S6 : The treatment that was meted out to these brave men and women in jail included starvation and whipping, and being forced to work in the mines by mounted military police.

P: During the course of the march, Gandhiji was arrested twice, released, arrested a third time and sent to jail.

Q: The employers retaliated by cutting off water and electricity to the workers' quarters, thus forcing them to leave their homes.

R: Gandhiji decided to march this army of over two thousand men, women and children over the border and thus see them lodged in Transvaal jails.

S: The morale of the workers, however, was very high and they continued to march till they were prosecuted and sent to jail.

The correct sequence should be:

[Officers Training Academy (OTA), 2019], [Indian Military Academy (IMA), 2019]

A. QRPS   **B.** SRQP   **C.** QPSR   **D.** RQSP

Q.31 S1: One of the most important forces in the modem world, socialism was a direct result of the Industrial Revolution.

S6: This is how socialism as a theory and practice came into being.

P: Socialism was a direct challenge to capitalism and sought to put an end to such an exploitative economic structure.

Q: The gulf between the 'haves' and the 'have nots' continued to increase and out of this gap between the rich and poor sprang disputes.

R: It generated new wealth but as this new wealth only went to a minority, it could not solve the question of distribution.

S: The Industrial Revolution solved the question of production.

The correct sequence should be:

[Officers Training Academy (OTA), 2019], [Indian Military Academy (IMA), 2019]

A. PQRS   **B.** SRQP   **C.** SRPQ   **D.** RQSP

Q.32 S1 : Institutions define and play a regulatory role with regard to human behaviour.

S6 : It shows how important it is for a nation to build institutions for nurturing democracy.

P: Once established, institutions set a dynamic relationship with the members constituting them and they mutually affect each other.

Q: They shape preferences, power and privilege.

R: At the same time, institutions themselves can be transformed by the politics they produce and such transformation can affect social norms and behaviours.

S: They also provide a sense of order and predictability.

The correct sequence should be:

[Officers Training Academy (OTA), 2019], [Indian Military Academy (IMA), 2019]

A. RPQS   **B.** QRSP   **C.** PSRQ   **D.** QSRP

Q.33 S1: Idioms are a colourful and fascinating aspect of language.

S6: Idioms may also suggest a particular attitude of the person using them, for example, disapproval, humour, exasperation or admiration, so you must use them carefully.

P: Your language skills will increase rapidly if you can understand idioms and use them confidently and correctly.

Q: They are commonly used in all types of language, informal and formal, spoken and written.

R: In addition, idioms often have a stronger meaning than non-idiomatic phrases.

S: One of the main problems students have with idioms is that it is often impossible to guess the meaning of an idiom from the words it contains.

The correct sequence should be:

[Officers Training Academy (OTA), 2019], [Indian Military Academy (IMA), 2019]

A. RQPS **B.** SRQP **C.** RSPQ **D.** QPSR

Q.34 S1: Each organism is adapted to its environment.

S6: What can be taken in and broken down depends on the body design and functioning.

P: There is a range of strategies by which the food is taken in and used by the organism.

Q: For example, whether the food source is stationary (such as grass) or mobile (such as deer), would allow for differences in how the food is accessed and what is nutritive apparatus used by a cow or a lion.

R: The form of nutrition differs depending on the type and availability of food material as well as how it is obtained by an organism.

S: Some organisms break down the food material outside the body and then absorb it and others take in the whole material and break it down inside their bodies.

The correct sequence should be:

[Officers Training Academy (OTA), 2019], [Indian Military Academy (IMA), 2019]

A. RQPS **B.** QPSR **C.** SQPR **D.** QPRS

Q.35 S1: "When I was alive and had a human heart," answered the statue, "I did not know what tears were, for I lived in the Palace of Sans-Souci where sorrow is not allowed to enter.

S6: And now that I am dead they have set me up here so high that I can see all the ugliness and all the misery of my city, and though my heart is made of lead yet I cannot choose but weep."

P: So I lived, and so I died.

Q: Round the garden ran a very lofty wall, but I never cared to ask what lay beyond it, everything about me was so beautiful.

R: My courtiers called me the Happy Prince, and happy indeed I was, if pleasure be happiness.

S: In the daytime I played with my companions in the garden, and in the evening I led the dance in the Great Hall.

The correct sequence should be:

[Officers Training Academy (OTA), 2019], [Indian Military Academy (IMA), 2019]

A. QSRP **B.** PQRS **C.** PRQS **D.** RPQS

Q.36 S1: One day her mother, having made some cakes, said to her, "Go, my dear, and see how your grandmother is doing, for I hear she has been very ill. Take her a cake, and this little pot of butter."

S6: "Does she live far off?" said the wolf.

P: He asked her where she was going.

Q: The poor child, who did not know that it was dangerous to stay and talk to a wolf, said to him, "I am going to see my grandmother and carry her a cake and a little pot of butter from my mother."

R: As she was going through the wood, she met with a wolf, who had a very great mind to eat her up, but he dared not, because of some woodcutters working nearby in the forest.

S: She set out immediately to go to her grandmother, who lived in another village.

The correct sequence should be:

[Officers Training Academy (OTA), 2019], [Indian Military Academy (IMA), 2019]

A. PRQS **B.** SRPQ **C.** PRSQ **D.** RPQS

Q.37 S1: I had spent many nights in the jungle looking for game, but this was the first time I had ever spent a night looking for a man-eater.

S6: It was in this position·my men an hour later found me fast asleep; of the tiger, I had neither heard nor seen anything.

P: I bitterly regretted the impulse that had induced me to place myself at the man-eater's mercy.

Q: The length of road immediately in front of me was brilliantly lit by the moon, but to right and left the overhanging trees cast dark shadows, and when the night wind agitated the branches and the shadows moved, I saw a dozen tigers advancing on me.

R: As the grey dawn was lighting up the snowy range which I was facing, I rested my head on my drawn-up knees.

S: I lacked the courage to return to the village and admit I was too frightened to carry out my self-imposed task, and with teeth chattering, as much from fear as from cold, I sat out the long night.

The correct sequence should be:

[Officers Training Academy (OTA), 2019], [Indian Military Academy (IMA), 2019]

A. QPSR **B.** PRSQ **C.** SRPQ **D.** RPQS

Ques (38-45):Direction: Given are four sentence-paragraphs (S1-S4). S1 and S4 are given. From the given options (P, Q, R), choose two sentences which can be S2 and S3.

Q.38 S1: Indian movies include Bollywood, Tollywood, and other regional movies and documentaries based on India.

S2: ______

S3: ______

S4: in Mumbai to be more exact.

P: Indian Film Industry is largely known as Bollywood.

Q: Bollywood is the name for India's film industry, and it is indeed located in India –

R: India's cultural and traditional outfit is now replaced with western dresses.

A. PQ **B.** QR **C.** RP **D.** QP

Q.39 S1: Time was running out to save dozens of people trapped inside a tunnel three days after a devastating flash flood likely caused by

S2: ______

S3: ______

S4: sweeping away bridges and roads and hitting two hydroelectric plants.

P: a glacier burst in India's Himalayan north, officials said on Wednesday (Feb 10).

Q: More than 170 people were still missing after a barrage of water and debris hurtled with terrifying speed and power down a valley on Sunday morning,

R: "As time passes, the chances of finding them are reducing. But miracles do happen,"

A. PQ   **B.** QR   **C.** RP   **D.** RQ

Q.40 S1: It may take days for more bodies to be recovered under the tonnes of rocks and other debris and the thick blanket of grey mud.

S2: ______

S3: ______

S4: other parts of India whose whereabouts at the time of the disaster may not be known.

P: Twenty-five of the bodies were yet to be identified.

Q: is a tunnel near a severely damaged hydroelectric plant that was under construction at Tapovan in Uttarakhand state.

R: Many of the victims are poor workers from hundreds of miles away in.

A. QP   **B.** RP   **C.** QR   **D.** PR

Q.41 S1: She said the Security Council's fundamental role must be:

S2: ______

S3: ______

S4: along with a call for the immediate release of all those detained.

P: "ensuring democracy is expeditiously restored and the country does not fall back into isolation."

Q: Diplomats said that was the key element of a draft statement for the council to release,

R: The U.N. envoy for Myanmar, Christine Schraner Burgener, urged the U.N. Security Council "to collectively send a clear signal in support of democracy in Myanmar."

A. PQ   **B.** QR   **C.** RP   **D.** PR

Q.42 S1: Parks went to her first Montgomery NAACP meeting in December 1943,

S2: ____________

S3: ____________

S4: Theoharis and historian Martha S. Jones' latest book on Black women's voting rights Vanguard.

P: Back then, only 31 out of several thousand of the city's Black residents were registered to vote, according to

Q: where she was elected secretary of the chapter.

R: and during her second attempt, Parks was thwarted by a difficult questionnaire, another Jim Crow-era voter suppression tactic to keep Black people off voter rolls.

A. PQ   **B.** RQ   **C.** QP   **D.** RP

Q.43 S1: Once the oppositely charged ions form, they are attracted by their positive and negative charges creating an ionic bond and thus forming an ionic compound.

S2: __________

S3: __________

S4: The creation of an ionic bond between a metal atom (sodium) and a nonmetal (fluorine) is an example of this.

Options:

P. This difference causes an unequal sharing of electrons such that one atom completely loses one or more electrons and the other atom gains one or more electrons.

Q. Ionic bonds are also formed when there is a large electronegativity difference between two atoms.

R. The octet rule states that an atom is most stable when there are eight electrons in its valence shell.

A. PQ   **B.** RQ   **C.** QP   **D.** RP

Q.44 S1: The majority of migration is from developing to developed countries.

S2: __________

S3: __________

S4: This translates into a loss of considerable resources when these people migrate, with the direct benefit accruing to the recipient states who have not forked out the cost of educating them.

Options:

P. These countries have invested in the education and training of young health professionals.

Q. This is of growing concern worldwide because of its impact on the health systems in developing countries.

R. Brain drain is the migration of skilled human resources for trade, education, etc.

A. QP   **B.** RP   **C.** QR   **D.** PQ

Q.45 S1: Moral stories offer several benefits for children of all ages.

S2: __________

S3: __________

S4: However, the best moral stories will also teach a truth to your child.

Options:

P: Short moral stories work well at getting your child's attention, keeping them focused during the length of the story.

Q: The more you read the same moral stories, the more your child will familiarize with the story and the moral lesson.

R: They work to engage your child's imagination, are entertaining, and can make your little one smile.

A. RP   **B.** PR   **C.** QP   **D.** PQ

// Smart Answer Sheet //

| Correct | Indicates percentage of students who answered questions correctly. |

| Skipped | Indicates percentage of students who skipped questions. |

Q.	Ans.	Correct / Skipped	Q.	Ans.	Correct / Skipped	Q.	Ans.	Correct / Skipped	Q.	Ans.	Correct / Skipped	Q.	Ans.	Correct / Skipped
1	B	54.55 % / 33.53 %	10	A	12.78 % / 69.92 %	19	C	47.56 % / 39.64 %	28	C	55.86 % / 30.41 %	37	A	52.73 % / 39.43 %
2	A	81.56 % / 13.72 %	11	D	65.78 % / 30.86 %	20	B	43.67 % / 48.26 %	29	B	19.17 % / 67.47 %	38	A	59.19 % / 33.09 %
3	D	30.26 % / 67.6 %	12	A	49.57 % / 34.77 %	21	B	59.96 % / 32.29 %	30	A	50.43 % / 32.42 %	39	A	56.54 % / 35.97 %
4	B	49.1 % / 46.28 %	13	D	54.45 % / 31.26 %	22	C	64.56 % / 34.67 %	31	B	42.68 % / 49.05 %	40	D	13.92 % / 77.34 %
5	A	19.68 % / 78.31 %	14	D	46.19 % / 33.34 %	23	B	65.29 % / 33.86 %	32	A	31.1 % / 68.86 %	41	A	14.78 % / 70.24 %
6	C	81.85 % / 16.8 %	15	C	45.02 % / 43.55 %	24	A	69.12 % / 30.65 %	33	D	89.44 % / 10.16 %	42	C	42.54 % / 44.2 %
7	A	55.85 % / 31.94 %	16	D	69.53 % / 30.36 %	25	B	58.83 % / 33.97 %	34	A	66.37 % / 33.28 %	43	C	46.84 % / 47.35 %
8	A	61.56 % / 31.32 %	17	B	61.63 % / 36.58 %	26	B	40.95 % / 55.71 %	35	A	51.69 % / 34.1 %	44	A	16.91 % / 81.47 %
9	D	40.05 % / 46.2 %	18	C	56.71 % / 34.47 %	27	A	57.49 % / 34.21 %	36	B	62.05 % / 36.35 %	45	A	20.0 % / 72.33 %

Performance Analysis	
Avg. Score (%)	57.78%
Toppers Score (%)	62.22%
Your Score	

//Hints and Solutions//

1. The first statement in the sequence should be the one that introduces a new topic. It should not be a continuation or extension of a topic.

P is first in the sequence: S1 starts by saying that rain is a beautiful gift of nature. P starts by providing support to S1's claim. It says that rain is a blessing in the intense heat of summer.

P is followed by R: R continues P's point. It explains that rain provides relief from the scorching heat of the sun.

R is followed by Q: Q infers from R. It says that as it provides relief it is welcomed by all. S5 continues this point by saying that people dance and sing with joy on its arrival.

Thus, the correct sequence is PRQ.

Hence, the correct option is (B).

2. While arranging the parts of the passage, we should find some grammatical or contextual connections between them-

- Sentence Q starts with the topic 'The origin'. Thus, it will be put in the first place.
- Sentence P further tells us about the segment the origin (of life) is concerned with. It will be put in second place.
- Sentence S further tells about the above-mentioned event being a distinctive one. Therefore, it will be the the third sentence.
- The last sentence is R as it provides the concluding part.

Therefore, the sentence will be:

The origin of life is considered a unique event in the history of the universe.

Hence, the correct option is (A).

3. While arranging the parts of the passage, we should find some grammatical or contextual connections between them-

- Sentence Q starts with the interrogative tone regarding one's management skills. Thus, it will be put in the first place.
- Sentence P further tells us about the segment in which the above-mentioned skills are required. It will be put in second place.
- Sentence S initiates the purpose of managing productive resources. Therefore, it will be the third sentence.
- The last sentence is R as it provides the concluding part.

Therefore, the sentence will be:

How we manage productive resources is critical to strategic growth and competitiveness.

Hence, the correct option is (D).

4. While arranging the parts of the passage, we should find some grammatical or contextual connections between them-

- The given sentence follows the assertive sentence structure.
- Now the sentence must begin with the part starting with the noun or the pronoun ('Operations strategy' in this case).
- Therefore the sentence must begin with part Q.
- The given structure is followed only in the second option.
- The rest of the alternatives start with a preposition. Therefore, they are eliminated.

Therefore, the sentence will be:

Operations strategy in service firms is generally inseparable from the corporate strategy.

Hence, the correct option is (B).

5. While arranging the parts of the passage, we should find some grammatical or contextual connections between them-

- Sentence S starts with the topic 'Indian people'. Thus, it will be put in the first place.
- Sentence P further tells us about the activity that the people are following. It will be put in second place.
- Sentence Q initiates a recently concluded survey. Therefore, it will be the third sentence.
- The last sentence is R as it provides the concluding part of the above-mentioned survey.

Therefore, the sentence will be:

Even as more and more Indians are travelling, a recent survey has revealed that they are worried about their safety.

Hence, the correct option is (A).

6. While arranging the parts of the passage, we should find some grammatical or contextual connections between them-

- Sentence Q starts with the topic 'Stories'. Thus, it will be put in the first place.
- Sentence P further tells us about the effect that the stories have on the children. It will be put in second place.
- Sentence S initiates the reason behind the stories being quite effective. Therefore, it will be the third sentence.
- The last sentence is R as it provides the concluding part.

Therefore, the sentence will be:

Stories can exercise the imagination of children because they tell more than the stories.

Hence, the correct option is (C).

7. While arranging the parts of the passage, we should find some grammatical or contextual connections between them-

- The given sentence follows the assertive sentence structure.
- Now the sentence must begin with the part starting with the noun or the pronoun ('History' in this case).
- Therefore, the sentence must begin with part S.
- The given structure is followed only in the first option.

Therefore, the sentence will be:

"History is considered as a record of the achievements, experiments and suffering of humans."

Hence, the correct option is (A).

8. While arranging the parts of the passage, we should find some grammatical or contextual connections between them-

- The given sentence follows the assertive sentence structure.
- Now the sentence must begin with the part starting with the noun or the pronoun ('It' in this case).
- Therefore, the sentence must begin with part Q.
- The second part must be S as it introduces another/complementary clause with the conjunction 'that'.
- The given structure is followed only in the first option.

Therefore, the sentence will be:

It appears that all that can be invented has been invented.

Hence, the correct option is (A).

9. While arranging the parts of the passage, we should find some grammatical or contextual connections between them-

- Part S starts with the topic 'Indian cinema'. Therefore, it will be put in the first place.
- Part R further initiates the statement of what the cinema reflects. It will be put in second place.
- Part Q concludes the above-mentioned statement regarding Indian cinema. Therefore, it will be the third sentence.
- The last part is P as it provides the concluding part.

Therefore, the sentence will be:

Indian cinema stands as a testimony of Indian social, political and cultural life during the last century.

Hence, the correct option is (D).

10. While arranging the parts of the passage, we should find some grammatical or contextual connections between them-

- Sentence R starts with the topic 'The search for truth'. Thus, it will be put in the first place.
- Sentence Q further presents the above-mentioned search as the start of something. It will be put in second place.
- Sentence P initiates the purpose of the search for truth. Therefore, it will be the third sentence.
- The last sentence is S as it provides the concluding part.

Therefore, the sentence will be:

An exploration into truth should be the beginning of all searches for knowledge and experiments of life.

Hence, the correct option is (A).

11. The correct answer is- **RQSP**.

The correct sentence is, "Freedom does not mean the opportunity for self-gratification or the setting aside of consideration for others."

While arranging the parts of the passage, we should find some grammatical or contextual connections between them-

- Sentence R contains the phrase 'freedom'. Hence it will be put in the first place.
- Sentence Q further tells us about what the noun 'opportunity' is all about. It will be put in second place.
- Sentence S is in continuation (initiates another aspect of freedom) of the previous sentence. Hence it will be the 3rd sentence.
- The last sentence is P as it mentions the conclusion of another aspect of freedom (lack of consideration for others).

Hence, the correct option is (D).

12. The correct order is **RPSQ**.

The correct sentence is, "Domination or compulsion of any kind is a direct hindrance to freedom and intelligence"

While arranging the parts of the passage, we should find some grammatical or contextual connections between them-

- Sentence R contains the phrase 'domination/compulsion'. Thus, it will be put in the first place.
- Sentence P further tells us about the type of domination/compulsion. It will be put in second place.
- Sentence S is in continuation (further defines the above-mentioned nouns) of the previous sentence. Hence it will be the 3rd sentence.
- The last sentence is Q as it mentions the conclusion of the nouns (an obstruction to freedom and intelligence).

Hence, the correct option is (A).

13. The correct order is **QPSR**.

The correct sentence is, "Banana provides enough potassium and sustained energy from various sugars."

While arranging the parts of the passage, we should find some grammatical or contextual connections between them:

- Sentence Q introduces us to the noun 'Banana'. Thus, it will be put in the first place.
- Sentence P further tells us about the particular nutrient (potassium) provided by a banana. It will be put in second place.

- Sentence S is in continuation (mentions an additional point related to the provision of energy) of the previous sentence. Hence it will be the 3rd sentence.

The last sentence is R as it mentions the conclusion (the role of sugars in bananas).

Hence, the correct option is (D).

14. The correct order is **QPSR**.

The correct sentence is, "This is a time of great trouble as one virus threatens the world to the maximum."

While arranging the parts of the passage, we should find some grammatical or contextual connections between them-

- Sentence Q contains the pronoun 'this'. Hence it will be put in the first place.

- Sentence P further tells us about how the situation is at present. It will be put in second place.

- Sentence S is in continuation (mentions the reason behind the present situation) of the previous sentence. Hence it will be the 3rd sentence.

- The last sentence is R as it mentions the conclusion (the degree of the effect of the virus).

Hence, the correct option is (D).

15. The correct order is **QPSR**.

The correct sentence is, "Some archaeologists are of the opinion that Harappan society had no rules and that everybody enjoyed equal status."

While arranging the parts of the passage, we should find some grammatical or contextual connections between them-

- Sentence Q starts with the noun 'archaeologists'. So it will be put in the first place.

- Sentence P further tells us about the opinion of the above-mentioned archaeologists. It will be put in second place.

- Sentence S is in continuation (mentions the first opinion about the Harappan society) of the previous sentence.

- The last sentence is R as it mentions the conclusion (mentions the opinion regarding the status of the people living in Harappan society).

Hence, the correct option is (C).

16. The correct order is **RQSP**.

The correct sentence is, "Endogamy refers to marriage within a unit or a group living in the same locality."

While arranging the parts of the passage, we should find some grammatical or contextual connections between them-

- Sentence R contains the phrase 'endogamy'. Hence it will be put in the first place.

- Sentence Q further tells us what the above-mentioned phrase is all about. It will be put in second place.

- Sentence S is in continuation (initiates another aspect of endogamy) of the previous sentence.

- The last sentence is P as it mentions the conclusion of another aspect of endogamy (marriage within the group from the same locality).

Hence, the correct option is (D).

17. The correct order is **RSPQ**.

The correct sentence is, "Coal was the main source of energy in the initial stages when steam engines dominated industrialization."

While arranging the parts of the passage, we should find some grammatical or contextual connections between them-

- Sentence R contains the noun 'coal'. Hence it will be put in the first place.

- Sentence S further tells us about coal being the primary source of energy. It will be put in second place.

- Sentence P is in continuation (tells about the major recipient of energy produced from coal) of the previous sentence.

- The last sentence is Q as it mentions the conclusion by mentioning the event 'industrialization'.

Hence, the correct option is (B).

18. The correct order is **SQRP**.

The correct sentence is, "How important is the information that comes from the scientists?"

While arranging the parts of the passage, we should find some grammatical or contextual connections between them-

- The given sentence follows the interrogative sentence structure as indicated by the use of the question mark in the 'P' part.

- Now the sentence must begin with an interrogative word (what, which, whose, etc.) and end with the question mark.

- So the 'S' part will be the beginning part and 'P' will be the concluding part.

- The given structure is followed only in the option (C).

Hence, the correct option is (C).

19. The correct order is **SQRP**.

The correct sentence is, "Since earliest times humans have suffered frustration and food losses brought on by destructive pests."

While arranging the parts of the passage, we should find some grammatical or contextual connections between them-

- Sentence S contains the adverb 'since' denoting the timeline. Hence it will be put in the first place.

- Sentence Q further tells us about the humans going through something. It will be put in second place.

- Sentence R is in continuation (frustration accompanied by food losses) of the previous sentence.

- The last sentence is P as it mentions the conclusion by telling about the agent (harmful pests) of the food losses.

Hence, the correct option is (C).

20. The correct order is **QPSR**.

The correct sentence is, "Some of the most spectacular gold coins were issued by the Gupta rulers in India."

While arranging the parts of the passage, we should find some grammatical or contextual connections between them-

- The given sentence follows the passive voice structure as indicated by the use of the preposition 'by' in the 'S' part.
- Now the part 'S' must be followed by the part containing the subject i.e. the Gupta rulers.
- Hence the 'R' part will come immediately after the part 'S'.
- The given structure is followed only in the option (B).

Hence, the correct option is (B).

21. As we can see that the order QSRP is connected. The process was successive that the person was hungry then he saw a ship that was unloading a cargo of pig iron. He went to the captain and ask him to let him do the job in order to earn money for food.

Hence, the correct option is (B).

22. The correct order is "SPRQ" which is producing some meaning when put in an order.

The salmon fish pushed themselves to their limits to return to their spawning grounds but once they laid their eggs and fertilized them they died.

Hence, the correct option is (C).

23. The correct order is "RSQP" as it makes some sense when put in such an order. After combining in the given order, sentences seem to be connected.

One of my friends Krishnan went to live in a village. One day his new neighbor told him that he must buy a donkey. So Krishnan bought a donkey for 200 rupees. But it was very slow. It did not like to work.

Hence, the correct option is (B).

24. When the order "RPSQ" is followed, the sentence formed will be:

"The only choice left before the Indian University will be to substantially raise the tuition fees to meet the rising expenditure."

We can see that the sentence conveys some meaning and is complete.

Hence, the correct option is (A).

25. When the order "SQPR" is followed, the sentence formed will be:

Osteoarthritis in the knee is a problem that affects millions of people. Knee exercises help prevent joint stiffness and strengthen muscles around the joint. Due to muscle flexibility, there is less pain. And so it reduces disability and improves the quality of life. Knee exercises are done sitting in a chair or lying on one's back. Exercises that help thigh muscles without involving weight-bearing are safe and effective.

Hence, the correct option is (B).

26. When the order "SQPR" is followed, the sentence formed will be:

Another way for people to economize at an amusement park is to bring their own food. They will avoid having to pay high prices for hamburgers and hot dogs. Instead, they should pack a nourishing, well-balanced lunch of cold chicken, carrot sticks, and fruit. Also, instead of filling up on soft drinks, they should bring a thermos of iced tea. They will also save on calories. Every dollar that is not spent at the refreshment stand is one that can be spent on another ride.

Hence, the correct option is (B).

27. When the order "SQPR" is followed, the sentence formed will be:

The vegetable bin of my refrigerator contained an assortment of weird-looking items. Next to a shriveled, white-coated lemon were two oranges covered with blue fuzz. To the right of the oranges was a bunch of carrots that had begun to sprout points, spikes, and tendrils. The carrots dropped into U shapes as I picked them up with the tips of my fingers. Near the carrots was a net bag of onions. Each onion had sent curling shoots through the net until the whole thing resembled a man of green spaghetti.

Hence, the correct option is (A).

28. When the order "SQPR" is followed, the sentence formed will be:

One reason for studying Psychology is to help you deal with your children. Perhaps your daughter refuses to go to bed when you want her to and bursts into tears at the mention of lights out. A little knowledge of Psychology comes in handy. Offer her a choice of staying up till 7:30 with you or going upstairs and playing until 8:00. Since she gets to make the choice, she does not feel so powerless and will not resist. Psychology is also useful in rewarding a child for a job well done.

Hence, the correct option is (C).

29. The correct sequence is 'QRSP'.

Sentence 1 is an introduction mantra statement stating "Refuse to be miserable".

Q follows S1 which talks about challenges and opportunities and tells about how one can turn failures into success.

RS as a pair follows Q, as these talk about two aspects of life - painful or sorrowful and to be happy one needs to find occasions to be cheerful.

P at the end follows S. It gives a learning statement to the readers, stating that responsibility comes to those who feel responsible.

S6 thus is the conclusion that this is the art of right contact in life.

Thus the correct sentence order after rearrangement is "The master always says, "Refuse to be miserable". Challenges are faced by the strong and courageous, and if life brings you such opportunities, then turn failures into success. Life can be painful, but it need not be sorrowful. If you want to be happy, find occasions to be cheerful. Before you fall into self-pity and blame games, remember that responsibility comes to only those who feel responsible. This is the art of right contact in life."

Hence, the correct option is (B).

30. The correct sequence is 'QRSP'.

The given para jumble talks about Gandhiji's agitation and his actions during the agitation.

S1 is an introduction stating that Gandhiji had reached Newcastle and took charge of agitation.

Q further talks about the statement about how the employers retaliated and left their home.

R then follows, where Gandhiji marched over the army of over 2000 people with the intention of seeing them in jail.

P follows R, which mentions about the action taken against Gandhiji wherein he was arrested twice and sent to jail.

S talks about high morals of the workers where they continued the march and sent to jail.

S6 thus is a fitting conclusion about the treatment given to the retaliators.

Thus the correct sentence order after rearrangement is "Gandhiji reached Newcastle and took charge of the agitation. The employers retaliated by cutting off water and electricity to the workers' quarters, thus forcing them to leave their homes. Gandhiji decided to march this army of over two thousand men, women and children over the border and thus see them lodged in Transvaal jails. During the course of the march, Gandhiji was arrested twice, released, arrested a third time and sent to jail. The morale of the workers, however, was very high and they continued to march till they were prosecuted and sent to jail. The treatment that was meted out to these brave men and women in jail included starvation and whipping, and being forced to work in the mines by mounted military police."

Hence, the correct option is (A).

31. The correct sequence is 'SRQP'.

S1 gives an introduction about how socialism resulted in the industrial revolution.

S tells about how the Industrial Revolution solved the question of production.

R follows S stating that the solved question of production created a new wealth that went only to a minority and how it couldn't solve the question of distribution.

Q elaborates on how the question of distribution created the gulf between the 'haves' and the 'have not' that continued to increase and how disputes sprang out of this gap.

P explains how socialism was a direct challenge to this divide creating capitalism and how it sought to end such an exploitative economic structure.

S6 gives a fitting conclusion stating how socialism came into being.

Thus the correct sentence order after rearrangement is "One of the most important forces in the modem world, socialism was a direct result of the Industrial Revolution. The Industrial Revolution solved the question of production. It generated new wealth but as this new wealth only went to a minority, it could not solve the question of distribution. The gulf between the 'haves' and the 'have nots' continued to increase and out of this gap between the rich and poor sprang disputes. Socialism was a direct challenge to capitalism and sought to put an end to such an exploitative economic structure. This is how socialism as a theory and practice came into being."

Hence, the correct option is (B).

32. The correct sequence is 'RPQS'.

The para jumble highlights the role of institutions for humans and society in general.

S1 gives an introduction to the role of institutions with regard to human behaviour.

R follows immediately which connects the power and privilege and states that it can be transformed by politics produced by them, thus affecting the social norms.

P further tells us that the institutions set a relationship between their members and themselves.

Q that it shapes preferences and power.

S states that it provides a sense of order and predictability.

S6 thus concludes the idea and shows its importance to nurture democracy.

Thus the correct sentence order after rearrangement is "Institutions define and play a regulatory role with regard to human behaviour. At the same time, institutions themselves can be transformed by the politics they produce and such transformation can affect social norms and behaviours. Once established, institutions set a dynamic relationship with the members constituting them and they mutually affect each other. They shape preferences, power and privilege. They also provide a sense of order and predictability. It shows how important it is for a nation to build institutions for nurturing democracy."

Hence, the correct option is (A).

33. The correct sequence is 'QPSR'.

The given para jumble gives information about idioms and their usage and meaning.

S1 is an introduction to the idea of idioms and that it is a fascinating aspect of a language.

Q states that it is used in languages and also when one communicates through various mediums - formal or informal, written or spoken.

P tells how one's language skills improve when they understand idioms and use them confidently.

S throws light on the fact, that sometimes the words of the idioms might be difficult to decipher the meaning.

R strongly states that idioms carry a strong meaning than non-idiomatic expressions.

S6 concludes and suggests that the attitude of people can be determined.

Thus the correct sentence order after rearrangement is "Idioms are a colourful and fascinating aspect of language. They are commonly used in all types of language, informal and formal, spoken and written. Your language skills will increase rapidly if you can understand idioms and use them confidently and correctly. One of the main problems students have with idioms is that it is often impossible to guess the meaning of an idiom from the words it contains. In addition, idioms often have a stronger meaning than non-idiomatic phrases. Idioms may also suggest a particular attitude of the person using them, for example, disapproval, humour, exasperation or admiration, so you must use them carefully."

Hence, the correct option is (D).

34. The correct sequence is 'RQPS'.

The para jumble talks about organisms and it's adaptability in the environment.

S1 is an introduction to the topic.

R gives information about how nutrition differs depending on the availability of food material.

Q gives an instance of the idea talked about in a sentence P.

P says that there is a range of strategies on how food is taken.

S gives information about types of organisms and their system of the breakdown of food

S6 as a fitting conclusion states that it is all dependent on the design and functioning.

Thus the correct sentence order after rearrangement is "Each organism is adapted to its environment. The form of nutrition differs depending on the type and availability of food material as well as how it is obtained by an organism. For example, whether the food source is stationary (such as grass) or mobile (such as deer), would allow for differences in how the food is accessed and what is nutritive apparatus used by a cow or a lion. There is a range of strategies by which the food is taken in and used by the organism. Some organisms break down the food material outside the body and then absorb it and others take in the whole material and break it down inside their bodies. What can be taken in and broken down depends on the body design and functioning.

Hence, the correct option is (A).

35. The correct sequence is 'QSRP'.

S1 are introductory lines by statue and his history.

Q elaborates about the place where the statue lived.

S gives details about the activities throughout the day.

R is a further extension of sentence S and tells why he was called Happy Prince.

P gives information about how he died.

S6 thus is a conclusion given by the statute himself. He witnesses the reality of ugliness and miseries and says that his heart weeps though it is made of lead.

Thus the correct sentence order after rearrangement is "When I was alive and had a human heart," answered the statue, "I did not know what tears were, for I lived in the Palace of Sans-Souci where sorrow is not allowed to enter. Round the garden ran a very lofty wall, but I never cared to ask what lay beyond it, everything about me was so beautiful. In the daytime I played with my companions in the garden, and in the evening I led the dance in the Great Hall. My courtiers called me the Happy Prince, and happy indeed I was, if pleasure be happiness. So I lived, and so I died. And now that I am dead they have set me up here so high that I can see all the ugliness and all the misery of my city, and though my heart is made of lead yet I cannot choose but weep."

Hence, the correct option is (A).

36. The correct sequence is 'SRPQ'.

The para jumble is a short conversation between the wolf and a little girl.

S1 is an introduction to where the mother asks her daughter to pay a visit to her grandmother.

S gives information about the daughter's immediate step to visit her grandmother

R informs that she encounters a wolf who was determined to eat her.

PQ is a dialogue between the wolf and the grand-daughter and she explains where she is going and what she had with her.

S6 is an interrogative statement by the wolf. Thus it ends here.

Thus the correct sentence order after rearrangement is "One day her mother, having made some cakes, said to her, "Go, my dear, and see how your grandmother is doing, for I hear she has been very ill. Take her a cake, and this little pot of butter." She set out immediately to go to her grandmother, who lived in another village. As she was going through the wood, she met with a wolf, who had a very great mind to eat her up, but he dared not, because of some woodcutters working nearby in the forest. He asked her where she was going. The poor child, who did not know that it was dangerous to stay and talk to a wolf, said to him, "I am going to see my grandmother and carry her a cake and a little pot of butter from my mother." "Does she live far off?" said the wolf."

Hence, the correct option is (B).

37. The correct sequence is 'QPSR'.

S1 introduces the topic of the author's wish/quench to look for a man-eater.

Q further describes the jungle scene and the road nearby where he saw tigers moving towards him.

P is a fitting line where the author regrets his impulse at the man-eater's mercy.

SR describes the scene where the author was and that he lacked the courage to return home and was frightened too.

S6 concludes and tells about how the men found him which also shows that the author was too scared.

Thus the correct sentence order after rearrangement is "I had spent many nights in the jungle looking for game, but this was the first time I had ever spent a night looking for a man-eater. The length of road immediately in front of me was brilliantly lit by the moon, but to right and left the overhanging trees cast dark shadows, and when the night wind agitated the branches and the shadows moved, I saw a dozen tigers advancing on me. I bitterly regretted the impulse that had induced me to place myself at the man-eater's mercy. I lacked the courage to return to the village and admit I was too frightened to carry out my self-imposed task, and with teeth chattering, as much from fear as from cold, I sat out the long night. As the grey dawn was lighting up the snowy range which I was facing, I rested my head on my drawn-up knees. It was in this position·my men an hour later found me fast asleep; of the tiger, I had neither heard nor seen anything.

Hence, the correct option is (A).

38. The correct answer is **'PQ'.**

In order to arrange the parts of the paragraph, we will have to establish grammatical connections between the given statements.

Let's see how the parts of the paragraph can be arranged properly.

Sentence 'S1' establishes the subject matter.

Sentence 'R' is clearly out of context with the given passage as the passage is talking about the Indian film industry whereas sentence 'R' speaks about outfits of India.

'S4' is the ending of a sentence.

The only sentence that will fit 'S3' is 'Q' as then only the sentence 'S4' will make sense.

So, 'Q' will be 'S3'.

Of the remaining alternatives, the sentence 'P' is the only statement left and it is evident that it further tells the reader about 'S1'.

So, the sentence 'P' will be 'S2'

Thus, the correct order is **S1PQS4'**

S1: Indian movies include Bollywood, Tollywood, and other regional movies and documentaries based on India.

S2: Indian Film Industry is largely known as Bollywood.

S3: Bollywood is the name for India's film industry, and it is indeed located in India –

S4: in Mumbai to be more exact.

Hence, the correct option is (A).

39. The correct answer is **'PQ'.**

In order to arrange the parts of the paragraph, we will have to establish grammatical connections between the given statements.

Let's see how the parts of the paragraph can be arranged properly.

Sentence 'S1' establishes the subject matter.

Sentence 'P' will follow 'S1' because it is in further continuation of S1.

The statement is further telling what likely caused the devastating flash flood

Thus, the sentence 'P' will be 'S2'.

Of the remaining alternatives, sentence 'Q' will precede 'S4' as it is the beginning of the statement 'S4'.

So, the sentence 'Q' will be 'S3'

The sentence 'R' is not in context with the given paragraph.

Thus, the correct order is **'S1PQS4'**

S1: Time was running out to save dozens of people trapped inside a tunnel three days after a devastating flash flood likely caused by

S2: a glacier burst in India's Himalayan north, officials said on Wednesday (Feb 10).

S3: More than 170 people were still missing after a barrage of water and debris hurtled with terrifying speed and power down a valley on Sunday morning,

S4: sweeping away bridges and roads and hitting two hydroelectric plants.

Hence, the correct option is (A).

40. The correct answer is **'PR'.**

In order to arrange the parts of the paragraph, we will have to establish grammatical connections between the given statements.

Let's see how the parts of the paragraph can be arranged properly.

Sentence 'S1' establishes the subject matter.

Sentence 'R' will precede 'S4' because it is clearly evident that it is the first half of 'S4'.

Thus, the sentence 'R' will be 'S3'.

Of the remaining alternatives, the sentence 'Q' is not in context with the given paragraph as it is an incomplete statement the beginning of which is unknown.

The sentence 'P' will follow 'S1' as it is giving further information about the event.

So, the sentence 'P' will be 'S2'

Thus, the correct order is '**S1PRS4**'

S1: It may take days for more bodies to be recovered under the tonnes of rocks and other debris and the thick blanket of grey mud.

S2: Twenty-five of the bodies were yet to be identified.

S3: Many of the victims are poor workers from hundreds of miles away

S4: other parts of India whose whereabouts at the time of the disaster may not be known.

Hence, the correct option is (D).

41. The correct answer is '**PQ**'.

In order to arrange the parts of the paragraph, we will have to establish grammatical connections between the given statements.

Let's see how the parts of the paragraph can be arranged properly.

Sentence 'S1' establishes the subject matter.

Sentence 'P' will follow 'S1' because it is in further continuation of S1.

The statement is further telling what the Security Council's fundamental role must be.

Thus, the sentence 'P' will be 'S2'.

Of the remaining alternatives, sentence 'Q' will precede 'S4' as it is the beginning of the statement 'S4'.

So, the sentence 'Q' will be 'S3'

The sentence 'R' is not in context with the given paragraph.

Thus, the correct order is '**S1PQS4**'

S1: She said the Security Council's fundamental role must be

S2: "ensuring democracy is expeditiously restored and the country does not fall back into isolation."

S3: Diplomats said that was the key element of a draft statement for the council to release,

S4: along with a call for the immediate release of all those detained.

Hence, the correct option is (A).

42. The correct answer is '**QP**'.

In order to arrange the parts of the paragraph, we will have to establish grammatical connections between the given statements.

Let's see how the parts of the paragraph can be arranged properly.

Sentence 'S1' establishes the subject matter.

Sentence 'Q' will follow 'S1' because it is in further continuation of S1.

The statement is further telling about Park's Montgomery NAACP meeting in December 1943

Thus, the sentence 'Q' will be 'S2'.

Of the remaining alternatives, sentence 'P' will precede 'S4' as it is the beginning of the statement 'S4'.

So, the sentence 'P' will be 'S3'

The sentence 'R' is not in context with the given paragraph as it is talking about her second attempt whereas the first attempt is not mentioned anywhere in the paragraph.

Thus, the correct order is '**S1QPS4**

S1: Parks went to her first Montgomery NAACP meeting in December 1943,

S2: where she was elected secretary of the chapter.

S3: Back then, only 31 out of several thousand of the city's Black residents were registered to vote, according to

S4: Theoharis and historian Martha S. Jones' latest book on Black women's voting rights Vanguard.

Hence, the correct option is (C).

43. The correct answer is '**QP**'.

The paragraph is about how an ionic bond is formed.

S1 starts the paragraph and tells the first method of forming an ionic bond.

Q follows S1 as Q mentions another method of forming ionic bond. It's clear from adverb 'also'.

In sentence 'Q' a term 'difference' is used which is further described in sentence P. So, P follows Q.

S4 concludes the paragraph.

It's clear that 'QP' is the correct order.

Hence, the correct option is (C).

44. The correct answer is '**QP**'.

The paragraph is about migration of young talents to foreign countries.

S1 is the starter which introduces the topic that the migration is from developing to developed countries.

Q follows S1 as it says that the migration is a cause of concern of developing countries.

P follows R as it explains the reason why these developing countries should be concerned of the matter.

S4 concludes the paragraph.

It's clear that 'QP' is the correct order of sentences.

Hence, the correct option is (A).

45. The correct answer is '**RP**'.

The paragraph is about moral stories.

S1 is the starter and will be followed by 'R' as it contains pronoun 'they' referring to noun phrase 'moral stories'.

R is followed by 'P' as it introduces a type of moral stories; i.e. 'short moral stories'. These stories are interesting and attracts child's attention.

S4 concludes the paragraph by contrasting 'P' that 'best moral stories are truth teaching stories'.

It's clear that 'RP' is the correct order of sentences.

Hence, the correct option is (A).

Ques (1-8):Direction: In the following question, a sentence has been given in Direct/Indirect Speech. Out of the four alternatives suggested, select the one which best expresses the same sentence in Indirect/Direct Speech.

Q.1 Tom said to me, "I shall meet you at the station".

A. Tom told me that he would meet me at the station.

B. Tom told me that he will meet me at the station.

C. Tom told me that I would meet me at the station.

D. Tom told me that he would have met me at the station.

Q.2 Ram says to me, "You are smart".

A. Ram tells me that I am smart.

B. Ram tells me that you are smart.

C. Ram tells me that I was smart.

D. Ram told me that I am smart.

Q.3 The boss said to her secretary, "Did you discuss this matter with the manager"?

A. The boss asked her secretary whether she discussed that matter with the manager.

B. The boss asked her secretary if you have discussed that matter with the manager.

C. The boss asked her secretary if she had discussed that matter with the manager.

D. The boss asked her secretary whether she has discussed that matter with the manager.

Q.4 The robber said to Alexander, "I am your captive".

A. The robber told Alexander that he is his captive.

B. The robber told Alexander that he was your captive.

C. The robber told to Alexander that he was his captive.

D. The robber told Alexander that he was his captive.

Q.5 The holy prophet said, "God helps those who help others".

A. The holy prophet said that God helped those who helped others.

B. The holy prophet said that God helps those who help others.

C. The holy prophet said that God helps people who help others.

D. The holy prophet said that God helps those people who help others.

Q.6 She asked her brother if he could give her some money then.

A. She said to her brother, "Could I give you some money now?"

B. She said to her brother, "Can you give me some money then?"

C. She said to her brother, "Can you give me some money now?"

D. She asked her brother, "Give me some money now."

Q.7 He said, "I will return tomorrow".

A. He said that he will return tomorrow.

B. He said that he would return tomorrow.

C. He said that he would return the next day.

D. He said that I would return the next day.

Q.8 'Why has the clock stopped?' thought Peter.

A. Peter wondered why the clock had stopped.

B. Peter wanted to know why the clock had stopped.

C. Peter asked why the clock had stopped.

D. Peter was thinking why the clock had stopped.

Ques (9-20):Direction: Rewrite the sentence in the indirect speech.

Q.9 Kumar said, "I am unwell."
[SSC Sub Inspector (CPO), 2018], [SSC Sub Inspector (CPO), 2017]

A. Kumar said that he had been unwell.

B. Kumar said that he is unwell.

C. Kumar said that he has been unwell.

D. Kumar said that he was unwell.

Q.10 Anbu said to Suresh, "Priya is playing in the garden."
[SSC Sub Inspector (CPO), 2018], [SSC Sub Inspector (CPO), 2017]

A. Anbu told Suresh that Priya was playing in the garden.

B. Anbu told Suresh that Priya played in the garden.

C. Anbu told Suresh that Priya plays in the garden.

D. Anbu told Suresh that Priya play in the garden.

Q.11 Vasanth said to Praveen, "I have eaten three apples."
[SSC Sub Inspector (CPO), 2018], [SSC Sub Inspector (CPO), 2017]

A. Vasanth told Praveen that he ate three apples.

B. Vasanth told Praveen that he has eaten three apples.

C. Vasanth told Praveen that he had eaten three apples.

D. Vasanth told Praveen that he eats three apples.

Q.12 Sunder said, "I will go to my sister's house today."
[SSC Sub Inspector (CPO), 2018], [SSC Sub Inspector (CPO), 2017]

A. Sunder said that he went to his sister's house that day.

B. Sunder said that he has to go to his sister's house that day.

C. Sunder said that he goes to his sister's house that day.

D. Sunder said that he would go to his sister's house that day.

Q.13 Nisha said to Sunil, "I will not be going for the class."
[SSC Sub Inspector (CPO), 2018], [SSC Sub Inspector (CPO), 2017]

A. Nisha told Sunil that she will not have gone for the class.

B. Nisha told Sunil that she does not go for the class.

C. Nisha told Sunil that she would not be going for the class.

D. Nisha told Sunil that she had not been going for the class.

Q.14 Rahim said, "I will have completed my project."
[SSC Sub Inspector (CPO), 2018], [SSC Sub Inspector (CPO), 2017]

A. Rahim said that he would complete his project.

B. Rahim said that he would have completed his project.

C. Rahim said that he had completed his project.

D. Rahim said that he has completed his project.

Q.15 Prabha said to Prabhu, "Prem was playing cards."
[SSC Sub Inspector (CPO), 2018], [SSC Sub Inspector (CPO), 2017]

A. Prabha told Prabhu that Prem had been playing cards.
B. Prabha told Prabhu that Prem has been playing cards.
C. Prabha told Prabhu that Prem playing cards.
D. Prabha told Prabhu that Prem plays cards.

Q.16 "Where do you live?", said the stranger.
[SSC Sub Inspector (CPO), 2018], [SSC Sub Inspector (CPO), 2017]

A. The stranger enquired where I lived.
B. The stranger enquires where I lived.
C. The stranger enquired where I had been living.
D. The stranger enquires where I have been living.

Q.17 "Call the first witness," said the judge.
[SSC Sub Inspector (CPO), 2017]

A. The judge commands to call the first witness.
B. The judge pleaded to call the first witness.
C. The judge commanded to called the first witness.
D. The judge commanded to call the first witness.

Q.18 Siva said, "I have read the novel Pride and Prejudice."
[SSC Sub Inspector (CPO), 2018], [SSC Sub Inspector (CPO), 2017]

A. Siva said that he have read the novel Pride and Prejudice.
B. Siva said that he reads the novel Pride and Prejudice.
C. Siva said that he had read the novel Pride and Prejudice.
D. Siva said that he read the novel Pride and Prejudice.

Q.19 He said to him, "Is your name not Krishna?"
[SSC Sub Inspector (CPO), 2017]

A. He inquired him whether his name was not Krishna.
B. He inquired him whether my name was not Krishna.
C. He inquires him whether his name was not Krishna.
D. He inquired him whether his name is not Krishna.

Q.20 Suresh said to me, "I have been dancing for two hours".
[SSC Sub Inspector (CPO), 2018], [SSC Sub Inspector (CPO), 2017]

A. Suresh told me that he has been dancing for two hours.
B. Suresh told me that he had been dancing for two hours.
C. Suresh told me that he is dancing for two hours.
D. Suresh told me that he was dancing for two hours.

Q.21 Choose the option that is the indirect form of the sentence.
Vandana said, "I'm being dropped to office today''.
[SSC Sub Inspector (CPO), 2019]

A. Vandana said that she should be dropped to office today.
B. Vandana said that I am being dropped to office on that day.
C. Vandana said that she was being dropped to office that day.
D. Vandana said she was dropped to office today.

Q.22 Choose the option that is the indirect form of the sentence.

Akshay said, "I am making biryani today."
[SSC Sub Inspector (CPO), 2019]

A. Akshay said that he made biryani today.
B. Akshay said that he would be making biryani on the next day.
C. Akshay said that he is making biryani today.
D. Akshay said that he was making biryani on that day.

Q.23 Choose the option that is the indirect form of the sentence.
Jaya told me "I've been waiting for you since 4 pm."
[SSC Sub Inspector (CPO), 2019]

A. Jaya told me that she had been waiting for me since 4 pm.
B. Jaya told me that she will be waiting for me since 4 pm.
C. Jaya told me she was waiting for you since 4 pm.
D. Jaya said me that she has been waiting for me since 4 pm.

Q.24 Choose the option that is the indirect form of the sentence.
Lokesh said, "I am very busy this week".
[SSC Sub Inspector (CPO), 2019]

A. Lokesh said that I am very busy this week.
B. Lokesh said that I am very busy that week.
C. Lokesh said that he was very busy that week.
D. Lokesh said that he are very busy this week.

Q.25 Choose the option that is the indirect form of the sentence.
"We are going to Tirupati next week," Deepa told her friends.
[SSC Sub Inspector (CPO), 2019]

A. Deepa told her friends that they will go to Tirupati next week.
B. Deepa told to her friends that she is going to Tirupati following week.
C. Deepa told her friends that we were going to Tirupati the following week.
D. Deepa told her friends that they were going to Tirupati the following week.

Q.26 Choose the option that is the direct form of the sentence.
The Principal said to them that he did not want to see any one to return with a complaint against them.
[SSC Sub Inspector (CPO), 2019]

A. The Principal said to them, "I did not want to saw any one to return with a complaint against them."
B. The Principal said to them, "I do not want to see any one to return with a complaint against you."
C. The Principal said to them, "I do not wanted to see any of them to be returning with a complaint."
D. The Principal said to them, "I do not want to see any one to returns with a complaint against you."

Q.27 Choose the option that is the indirect form of the sentence.
"Please bring me a cup of coffee," Shakila said to the waiter.
[SSC Sub Inspector (CPO), 2019]

A. Shakila told the waiter to bring her a cup of coffee.

B. Shakila said to the waiter he should bring her a cup of coffee.

C. Shakila told to the waiter that he should brought her a cup of coffee.

D. Shakila said to the waiter you bring me a cup of coffee.

Q.28 Choose the option that is the direct form of the sentence.

I told them to be quiet.

[SSC Sub Inspector (CPO), 2019]

A. I said to them "Be you quiet!"

B. I told to them, "You must be quiet."

C. I said to them, "Be quiet!"

D. I said them, "You be quiet."

Q.29 Choose the option that is the direct form of the sentence.

My neighbour enquired how my father was.

[SSC Sub Inspector (CPO), 2019]

A. My neighbour asked, "What about your father's welfare?"

B. My neighbour enquired, "How is your father?"

C. My neighbour asked, "How my father was?"

D. My neighbour enquired, "How is my father?"

Q.30 Choose the option that is the direct form of the sentence.

He exclaimed sadly that it was a pity that so many lives had been lost in the floods.

[SSC Sub Inspector (CPO), 2019]

A. He said sadly, "It is a pity that so many lives had been lost in the floods."

B. He said sadly, "What a pity that so many lives are being lost in the floods!"

C. He said sadly, "What a pity that so many lives have been lost in the floods."

D. He said sadly, "It was a pity that so many lives were loss in the floods."

Q.31 Choose the option that is the indirect form of the sentence.

The judge said to Jia, "Stand in the witness box."

[SSC Sub Inspector (CPO), 2019]

A. The judge told Jia you are standing in the witness box.

B. The judge told Jia to stand in the witness box.

C. The judge told to Jia stand in the witness box.

D. The judge told Jia you will stand in the witness box.

Q.32 Choose the option that is the direct form of the sentence.

The teacher asked the students if they had understood her question.

[SSC Sub Inspector (CPO), 2019]

A. The teacher asked the students, "Have you understood her question?"

B. The teacher asking the students, "If you have understood my question?"

C. The teacher asked the students, "Have you understood my question?"

D. The teacher asks the students, "whether you understand my question?"

Q.33 Choose the option that is the indirect form of the sentence.

"I have joined computer classes" Rudra said.

[SSC Sub Inspector (CPO), 2019]

A. Rudra said that he had joined computer classes.

B. Rudra said that I am joining computer classes.

C. Rudra said that I joined computer classes.

D. Rudra said that I join computer classes.

Q.34 Choose the option that is the direct form of the sentence.

Vikas said to Navin that he hadn't met him since February the previous year.

[SSC Sub Inspector (CPO), 2019]

A. Vikas told Navin, "You haven't meeting me since February last year."

B. Vikas said to Navin, "I haven't met you since February last year."

C. Vikas told to Navin, "I haven't met him since February last year."

D. Vikas said, "Navin, I haven't meet you since February last year."

Q.35 Choose the option that is the direct form of the sentence.

The counter clerk asked me what my mobile number was.

[SSC Sub Inspector (CPO), 2019]

A. The counter clerk asked to me, "What was your mobile number?"

B. The counter clerk asked me, "What is your mobile number?"

C. The counter clerk enquired me, "What is your mobile number?"

D. The counter clerk asks me, "What is your mobile number?"

Q.36 Choose the option that is the direct form of the sentence.

He asked me to wait there until I got my turn.

[SSC Sub Inspector (CPO), 2019]

A. He said to me, "Wait here until you get your turn."

B. He told to me "Wait here until you get your turn."

C. He said to me, "You are wait here until you get your turn."

D. He asked me to "wait there until you get my turn."

Q.37 Choose the option that is the direct form of the sentence.

Jai said that he wanted to be a soldier.

[SSC Sub Inspector (CPO), 2019]

A. Jai said, "I wanted to be a soldier."

B. Jai said that, "I wanted to become a soldier."

C. Jai said, "I want to be a soldier."

D. Jai said, "He wants to become a soldier."

Q.38 Choose the option that is the indirect form of the sentence.

She said to him, "I don't want to go there."

[SSC Sub Inspector (CPO), 2019]

A. She said he didn't want to go there.

B. She told him that she didn't want to go there.

C. He said to her that she didn't want to go there.

D. She said to him that you do not want to go there.

Q.39 Choose the option that is the indirect form of the sentence.

"Get out of this room", the officer shouted at the cadet.

A. The officer shouted at the cadet and asked him to get out of that room.

B. The officer shouted at the cadet and asked him to get out of this room.

C. The officer shouts at the cadet and asks him to go out of that room.

D. The officer shouting at the cadet and asking him to go out of the room.

Q.40 Choose the option that is the indirect form of the sentence.

"Have you got a blue scarf"? The customer asked the assistant.
[SSC Sub Inspector (CPO), 2019]

A. The customer asked the assistant if he have a blue scarf.

B. The customer asked the assistant he has a blue scarf.

C. The customer asking the assistant if he is having a blue scarf.

D. The customer asked the assistant if he had a blue scarf.

Q.41 Choose the option that is the direct form of the sentence.

The policeman enquired where his helmet was.
[SSC Sub Inspector (CPO), 2019]

A. The policeman asked him, "Where is your helmet?"

B. The policeman enquired, "Where his helmet was?"

C. The policeman enquired, "Where your helmet is?"

D. The policeman asked him, "Where his helmet is?"

Q.42 Choose the option that is the direct form of the sentence.

Devi replied that she was sorry but she could not go.
[SSC Sub Inspector (CPO), 2019]

A. Devi replied, " She was sorry I could not go."

B. Devi replied, "Sorry she could not go."

C. Devi replied, "I'm sorry but I cannot go."

D. Devi replies, "I could not went but sorry."

Q.43 Choose the option that is the direct form of the sentence.

Abdul said that he had seen that film the day before.
[SSC Sub Inspector (CPO), 2019]

A. Abdul said, "I had seen this film the day before."

B. Abdul said, "I saw this film yesterday."

C. Abdul said, "I saw that film yesterday."

D. Abdul said, "I see this film on the previous day."

Q.44 Choose the option that is the indirect form of the sentence.

Kishore said "I'm leaving now."
[SSC Sub Inspector (CPO), 2019]

A. Kishore said that he was leaving then.

B. Kishore said that he left then.

C. Kishore says that I am leaving now.

D. Kishore said that he had to leaving then.

Q.45 Choose the option that is the indirect form of the sentence.

"I'm hungry" said the child to his mother.
[SSC Sub Inspector (CPO), 2019]

A. The child said his mother that he is hungry.

B. The child said to his mother that I am hungry.

C. The child told his mother that she was hungry.

D. The child told his mother that he was hungry.

// Smart Answer Sheet //

Correct — Indicates percentage of students who answered questions correctly.

Skipped — Indicates percentage of students who skipped questions.

Q.	Ans.	Correct	Skipped
1	A	62.18 %	34.82 %
2	A	62.72 %	32.47 %
3	C	44.89 %	34.42 %
4	D	48.61 %	41.93 %
5	B	44.75 %	43.43 %
6	C	58.44 %	36.45 %
7	C	64.97 %	30.76 %
8	A	29.92 %	67.3 %
9	D	69.89 %	30.05 %

Q.	Ans.	Correct	Skipped
10	A	27.7 %	71.66 %
11	C	56.02 %	36.26 %
12	D	86.77 %	10.94 %
13	C	63.39 %	34.54 %
14	B	48.4 %	34.06 %
15	A	55.83 %	43.08 %
16	A	76.29 %	13.04 %
17	D	48.9 %	50.01 %
18	C	58.18 %	37.35 %

Q.	Ans.	Correct	Skipped
19	A	87.26 %	11.69 %
20	B	51.6 %	47.33 %
21	C	40.49 %	45.47 %
22	D	69.13 %	30.61 %
23	A	56.81 %	36.02 %
24	C	14.99 %	72.64 %
25	D	68.14 %	31.25 %
26	B	26.39 %	68.26 %
27	A	40.87 %	54.11 %

Q.	Ans.	Correct	Skipped
28	C	82.88 %	14.6 %
29	B	28.01 %	68.91 %
30	C	59.15 %	34.91 %
31	B	77.77 %	20.21 %
32	C	65.93 %	32.53 %
33	A	66.48 %	31.78 %
34	B	19.85 %	78.87 %
35	B	31.57 %	68.07 %
36	A	53.35 %	40.81 %

Q.	Ans.	Correct	Skipped
37	C	67.49 %	30.59 %
38	B	16.07 %	82.12 %
39	A	27.32 %	70.61 %
40	D	57.24 %	33.69 %
41	A	45.32 %	47.77 %
42	C	53.21 %	43.84 %
43	B	48.3 %	35.53 %
44	A	54.82 %	35.78 %
45	D	78.28 %	21.27 %

Performance Analysis	
Avg. Score (%)	60.0%
Toppers Score (%)	71.11%
Your Score	

//Hints and Solutions//

1. Tom told me that he would meet me at the station.

The given sentence is of direct speech. "Said to" will change to "told". Since the reporting verb is in the past tense, changes will be made to the reported verb. "Shall" will change to "would" as the pronoun "I" will change to "he". Option (A) follows the rules correctly, so, it is the correct answer.

Hence, the correct option is (A).

2. We know that if the reporting verb is in the present or future tense, no changes are made to the verb/tense of the reported speech.

For the given sentence, "says to" will change to "tells". "You" will change to "I". As we can see that option (A) follows the rules correctly, so it is the correct answer.

Hence, the correct option is (A).

3. The given sentence is in interrogative form. To convert such sentences into the indirect narration, the below rules are followed:

Say/Said is changed to ask/asked/wonder/wondered/enquire of/enquired of etc as per the sense of the sentence.

If the reported speech is in the form of WH-Question (who/what/why/how/where/when/which etc), no conjunction is used before the question word. The question word itself works as conjunction.

So, the correct answer will be:

The boss asked her secretary if she had discussed that matter with the manager.

Hence, the correct option is (C).

4. The robber told Alexander that he was his captive.

The given sentence is indirect speech. To convert it into indirect speech, we'll convert "said to" into "told". The tense of the reported speech is simple present which will change to simple past. The pronoun "I" is the first-person pronoun. First-person pronoun changes according to the subject of the reporting speech which is "robber" in the sentence. So, "I" will change to "he" in indirect speech. "Your" is a second-person pronoun. Second-person pronoun changes according to the object of the reporting verb which is Alexander in the sentence. So, "your" will change to "his". Option (D) follows these rules correctly, so it is the answer.

Hence, the correct option is (D).

5. The holy prophet said that God helps those who help others.

The given sentence is in direct speech. Since the reporting verb "said" is not being followed by any object here, it will remain the same in indirect speech. Inverted commas will be replaced by the conjunction "that". The reported speech consists of a proverb and in this case, we do not change the tense of the reported speech. So, it will be written the same in indirect speech. Option (B) is the correct answer as it follows these rules.

Hence, the correct option is (B).

6. She said to her brother, "Can you give me some money now?"

The given sentence is the direct speech of an interrogative sentence. So, "asked to" will change back to "said to". The conjunction "if" will be removed and the part ahead of it will be quoted in inverted commas. Since the modal verb here is "could" which is the past of "can", we'll use "can" to start the reported speech. "Her" will change to "me" and the word "then" will change to "now". Option (C) adheres to these rules, so it is the correct answer.

Hence, the correct option is (C).

7. He said that he would return the next day.

The given sentence is in direct speech. The reporting verb "said" is not being followed by any object. So, "said" will not change to "told" and will remain the same. The verb "will" would change to its past form "would" and the word "tomorrow" will change to "the next day". The pronoun "I" is the first-person pronoun. First-person pronoun changes according to the subject of the reporting verb which is "he" here. Thus, "I" will change to "he". Option (C) adheres to these rules, so it is the correct answer.

Hence, the correct option is (C).

8. The given sentence is in interrogative form. Below are the steps to convert the sentence into indirect speech:

"thought" is an indication of wondering about something. So, it will change to "wondered".

The reported speech is in the form of WH-Question, so no conjunction is used before the question word. The question word itself works as a conjunction.

The reported verb is made assertive; i.e. it is kept in the order of subject + verb.

The tense of the reported speech will change from present perfect tense to past perfect tense.

Option (A) is the correct answer as it follows these rules.

Hence, the correct option is (A).

9. Kumar said that he was unwell.

While changing the narration of an assertive sentence, we need to follow the given steps-

- The conjunction 'that' should be used in place of a comma (,) and inverted commas (" ").
- 'Said' remains unchanged.
- The simple present tense (am) is changed into the simple past tense (was).
- The first-person (I) is changed into the third-person (he) i.e. subject of the reporting verb. (Kumar)

Hence, the correct option is (D).

10. Anbu told Suresh that Priya was playing in the garden.

While changing the narration of an assertive sentence, we need to follow the given steps-

- The conjunction 'that' should be used in place of a comma (,) and inverted commas (" ").

- 'Said to' is changed into 'told'.

- The present continuous tense (is playing) is changed into the past continuous tense (was playing).

Hence, the correct option is (A).

11. Vasanth told Praveen that he had eaten three apples.

While changing the narration of an assertive sentence, we need to follow the given steps-

- The conjunction 'that' should be used in place of a comma (,) and inverted commas (" ").

- 'Said to' is changed into 'told'.

- The present perfect tense (have eaten) is changed into the past perfect tense (had eaten).

- The first-person (I) is changed into the third-person (he) i.e. subject of the reporting verb. (Vasanth)

Hence, the correct option is (C).

12. Sunder said that he would go to his sister's house that day.

While changing the narration of an assertive sentence, we need to follow the given steps-

- The conjunction 'that' should be used in place of a comma (,) and inverted commas (" ").

- 'Said' remains unchanged.

- 'Will' is changed into 'would'.

- The first person (I/my) is changed into the third-person (he/his) i.e. subject of the reporting verb. (Sunder)

- 'Today' is changed into 'that day'.

Hence, the correct option is (D).

13. Nisha told Sunil that she would not be going for the class.

While changing the narration of an assertive sentence, we need to follow the given steps-

- The conjunction 'that' should be used in place of a comma (,) and inverted commas (" ").

- 'Said to' is changed into 'told'.

- 'Will' is changed into 'would'.

- The first-person (I) is changed into the third-person (she) i.e. subject of the reporting verb. (Nisha)

Hence, the correct option is (C).

14. Rahim said that he would have completed his project.

While changing the narration of an assertive sentence, we need to follow the given steps-

- The conjunction 'that' should be used in place of a comma (,) and inverted commas (" ").

- 'Said' remains unchanged.

- 'Will' is changed into 'would'.

- The first-person (I) is changed into the third-person (he) i.e. subject of the reporting verb. (Rahim)

Hence, the correct option is (B).

15. Prabha told Prabhu that Prem had been playing cards.

While changing the narration of an assertive sentence, we need to follow the given steps-

- The conjunction 'that' should be used in place of a comma (,) and inverted commas (" ").

- 'Said to' is changed into 'told'.

- The past continuous tense (was playing) is changed into the past perfect continuous tense (had been playing).

Hence, the correct option is (A).

16. The stranger enquired where I lived.

While changing the narration of an interrogative sentence, we need to follow the given steps-

- A conjunction is not used in the sentence of wh-family words (what, where, who, whom, why, etc.).

- 'Question mark (?)' is changed to full stop (.).

- 'Said' will be changed into 'asked/ enquired'.

- 'Do + v1 (live)' is changed into 'v2' (lived) in indirect speech.

- 2nd person (you) is changed into (I).

Hence, the correct option is (A).

17. The judge commanded to call the first witness.

While changing the narration of an imperative sentence, we need to follow the given steps-

- 'Said' is changed into 'ordered/commanded/ requested/ advised'.

- The conjunction 'to' should be used in place of a comma (,) and inverted commas (" ").

- At last line up the remaining sentence.

Hence, the correct option is (D).

18. Siva said that he had read the novel Pride and Prejudice.

While changing the narration of an assertive sentence, we need to follow the given steps-

- The conjunction 'that' should be used in place of a comma (,) and inverted commas (" ").

- 'Said' remains unchanged.

- The present perfect tense (have read) is changed into the past perfect tense (had read).

- The first-person (I) is changed into the third-person (he) i.e. subject of the reporting verb. (Siva)

Hence, the correct option is (C).

19. He inquired him whether his name was not Krishna.

While changing the narration of an interrogative sentence, we need to follow the given steps-

- The conjunction 'whether/if' should be used in place of a comma (,) and inverted commas (" ").
- 'Question mark (?)' is changed to full stop (.).
- 'Said to' will be changed into 'asked/ inquired'.
- The simple present tense (is) is changed into the simple past tense (was).
- The second-person (your) is changed into his i.e. according to the object of the reporting verb (him).

Hence, the correct option is (A).

20. Suresh told me that he had been dancing for two hours.

While changing the narration of an assertive sentence, we need to follow the given steps-

- The conjunction 'that' should be used in place of a comma (,) and inverted commas (" ").
- 'Said to' is changed into 'told'.
- The present perfect continuous tense (have been dancing) is changed into the past perfect continuous tense (had been dancing).
- The first-person (I) is changed into the third-person (he) i.e. subject of the reporting verb. (Suresh)

Hence, the correct option is (B).

21. The correct sentence is: Vandana said that she was being dropped to office that day.

In the indirect form, 'today' changes to 'that day'. So, we can reject option (A) and (D).

The first person pronoun i.e., 'I' changes to third person i.e., 'she'.

The direct form is in present continuous form as indicated by (being dropped). So, the indirect form will be in past continuous form (was being dropped). Therefore, option (B) can also be rejected.

The only option which shows the structure of past continuous form is option (C).

Hence, the correct option is (C).

22. The correct answer is:

Akshay said that he was making biryani on that day.

The given sentence is in present continuous tense (am making) so the indirect form will be in past continuous tense (was making).

The first person 'I' will be changed to third person 'He'.

The only option which follows the structure (past continuous tense) is Option (D).

Option (A) is in simple past tense (made).

Option (B) is in future perfect continuous tense (would be making).

Option (C) is in present continuous tense (is making).

Hence, the correct option is (D).

23. The correct answer of the given direct form is:

"Jaya told me that she had been waiting for me since 4 pm."

The given sentence is in present perfect continuous tense so the indirect form will be in past perfect continuous tense.

The first person 'I' changes to third person 'she'.

Thus, the option which follows the correct structure (past perfect continuous) is option (A).

Option (B) is in future continuous tense (will be waiting).

Option (C) is in past continuous tense (was waiting).

Option (D) is in present perfect continuous tense (has been waiting).

Hence, the correct option is (A).

24. The correct answer is Lokesh said that he was very busy that week.

In the indirect form, first person changes to third person. So, 'I' will change to 'he'. We can reject options (A) and (B). 'He' is singular so it cannot be followed by 'are'. Option (D) is incorrect. The present tense form will be changed to past tense.

Hence, the correct option is (C).

25. The correct answer is:

Deepa told her friends that they were going to Tirupati the following week.

In the indirect form, the first person changes to the third person.

So, 'we' will change to 'they'.

Also, 'next week' changes to 'the following week'.

The given sentence is in present continuous form (are going).

Thus, it will change to past continuous form (were going).

The rest of the sentence remains the same.

Hence, the correct option is (D).

26. The correct answer is:

The Principal said to them, "I do not want to see any one to return with a complaint against you."

In the direct form, the second person changes to first person.

So, 'he' will change to 'I' as it is referring to the principal and 'them' will change to 'you' as it refers to the object i.e., them.

'Did' changes to 'do' in the direct form.

The sentence is in simple present tense so the direct form will also be in the simple present tense.

Hence, the correct option is (B).

27. The correct answer is:

Shakila told the waiter to bring her a cup of coffee.

Said is used when the speaker is making a statement and told is used when the speaker is giving an order.

So, here 'told' should be used. We are left with options (A) and (C).

The statement is in the simple present tense so the indirect form will be in the present tense.

Option (C) is grammatically incorrect as 'should' cannot be used with the past tense form of the verb.

Hence, the correct option is (A).

28. The correct answer is:

I said to them, "Be quiet!".

The given sentence is an order given by the speaker. In the direct form, it will be simple transformed to "Be quiet!".

All the other options are incorrect as they use 'you' which is incorrect as the speaker is not referring to a particular person.

Hence, the correct option is (C).

29. The correct answer is:

My neighbour enquired, "How is your father?"

Since the neighbor is enquiring, the direct form will be a question. The indirect form is in simple past tense as indicated by 'was'. So, the direct form will be in the simple present tense. 'Was' will be changed to 'is'. Also, the first person pronoun (my) will be changed to second person (your) in the direct form.

Hence, the correct option is (B).

30. The word 'exclaimed' states that the direct form will be an exclamation. The indirect form is in past perfect tense as indicated by the words 'had been'. So, the direct form will be in the present perfect tense.

Option (A) is in the past perfect tense.

Option (B) is in the present continuous tense.

Option (D) is grammatically incorrect as it uses 'loss' with 'were'.

Hence, the correct option is (C).

31. The correct answer is:

"The judge told Jia to stand in the witness box."

The sentence is in the simple present tense. So the indirect form will be in the present tense.

Option (A) is in the present continuous tense.

Option (C) is incorrect as the preposition 'to' is incorrectly used.

Option (D) is incorrect as the second person pronoun 'you' cannot be used in the indirect form.

Hence, the correct option is (B).

32. The correct answer is:

The teacher asked the students, "Have you understood my question?"

The given statement is in the past perfect tense as observed by the words 'had understood'. So, the direct form will be in present perfect tense i.e., it will contain 'have'. We can reject options (B) and (D).

In the sentence, 'her' refers to the speaker which is the teacher so in the direct form it will be changed to 'my'. Thus, option (A) can be eliminated as well.

Hence, the correct option is (C).

33. The correct answer is:

Rudra said that he had joined computer classes.

The given sentence is in present perfect tense as indicated by the words 'have joined'. So, the indirect form will be in past perfect tense. In indirect form, 'I' changes to second person pronoun. In this case it will be 'he'.

Option (B) is present continuous form.

Option (C) is in past tense.

Option (D) is in simple present tense.

Hence, the correct option is (A).

34. The correct answer is:

Vikas said to Navin, "I haven't met you since February last year."

The given sentence is in the indirect form. When we convert it to the direct mode of narration, we have to make the following changes:

The verb must change its form. Past perfect becomes present perfect.

'The previous year' becomes 'last year'.

The third person pronoun 'he' is changed into the second person pronoun 'you'.

'Him' is changed into the personal pronoun 'me'.

Hence, the correct option is (B).

35. The correct answer is:

The counter clerk asked me, "What is your mobile number?"

When we convert a sentence from indirect to direct speech, we make the following changes:

Quotation marks are added and the sentence ends with a full stop, comma or interrogation mark depending on the tone of the reported speech.

The tense of the verb, in the reported speech involving any order, request and instruction does not undergo any change during the conversion from indirect to direct mode. This is also true if the statement is a universal truth.

If the reporting verb is in the present tense, it does not undergo any change.

We omit the word 'to' before the verb if the verb is in bare infinitive.

When the reporting or principal verb is in the past tense, all past tenses of the indirect are changed into the corresponding present tenses.

Words expressing distance are generally converted into 'into' words expressing nearness in time or place. For eg. then becomes now, that day becomes today, that becomes this etc.

In reporting commands and requests, the verb expressing command or request is omitted and the infinitive is changed into the imperative.

In reporting questions the verbs like asked, inquired are omitted and replaced by 'said to'.

In reporting exclamations and wishes, the verb expressing exclamation or wish is omitted and simply replaced by 'said'.

Option (B) follows all the proper rules of sentence transformation.

Hence, the correct option is (B).

36. The correct answer is:

He said to me, "Wait here until you get your turn."

When we convert a sentence from indirect to direct speech, we make the following changes:

Quotation marks are added and the sentence ends with a full stop, comma or interrogation mark depending on the tone of the reported speech.

The tense of the verb, in the reported speech involving any order, request and instruction does not undergo any change during the conversion from indirect to direct mode. This is also true if the statement is a universal truth.

If the reporting verb is in the present tense, it does not undergo any change.

We omit the word 'to' before the verb if the verb is in bare infinitive.

When the reporting or principal verb is in the past tense, all past tenses of the indirect are changed into the corresponding present tenses.

Words expressing distance are generally converted into 'into' words expressing nearness in time or place. For eg. then becomes now, that day becomes today, that becomes this etc.

In reporting commands and requests, the verb expressing command or request is omitted and the infinitive is changed into the imperative.

In reporting questions the verbs like asked, inquired are omitted and replaced by 'said to'.

In reporting exclamations and wishes, the verb expressing exclamation or wish is omitted and simply replaced by 'said'

Option (A) follows all the proper rules for sentence transformation.

Hence, the correct option is (A).

37. The correct answer is:

Jai said, "I want to be a soldier."

The given sentence is in indirect mode and the verb in the reported speech is in the simple present tense and the reporting verb is in the simple past tense.

When we change a sentence from indirect to direct speech, we make the following changes:

Quotation marks are added and the sentence ends with a full stop, comma or interrogation mark depending on the tone of the reported speech.

The tense of the verb, in the reported speech involving any order, request and instruction does not undergo any change during the conversion from indirect to direct mode. This is also true if the statement is a universal truth.

If the reporting verb is in the present tense, it does not undergo any change.

We omit the word 'to' before the verb if the verb is in bare infinitive.

When the reporting or principal verb is in the past tense, all past tenses of the indirect are changed into the corresponding present tenses.

Words expressing distance are generally converted into 'into' words expressing nearness in time or place. For eg. then becomes now, that day becomes today, that becomes this etc.

In reporting commands and requests, the verb expressing command or request is omitted and the infinitive is changed into the imperative.

In reporting questions the verbs like asked, inquired are omitted and replaced by 'said to'.

In reporting exclamations and wishes, the verb expressing exclamation or wish is omitted and simply replaced by 'said'.

Option (C) satisfies all the criteria and is the answer.

Hence, the correct option is (C).

38. The correct answer is:

She told him that she didn't want to go there.

The sentence in question is in indirect mode of narration and the reporting verb is in the simple past tense. The verb in the reported speech is in simple present tense.

When we change a sentence from indirect to direct mode, we make the following changes:

Quotation marks are added and the sentence ends with a full stop, comma or interrogation mark depending on the tone of the reported speech.

The tense of the verb, in the reported speech involving any order, request and instruction does not undergo any change during the conversion from indirect to direct mode. This is also true if the statement is a universal truth.

If the reporting verb is in the present tense, it does not undergo any change.

We omit the word 'to' before the verb if the verb is in bare infinitive.

When the reporting or principal verb is in the past tense, all past tenses of the indirect are changed into the corresponding present tenses.

Words expressing distance are generally converted into 'into' words expressing nearness in time or place. For eg. then becomes now, that day becomes today, that becomes this etc.

In reporting commands and requests, the verb expressing command or request is omitted and the infinitive is changed into the imperative.

In reporting questions the verbs like asked, inquired are omitted and replaced by 'said to'.

In reporting exclamations and wishes, the verb expressing exclamation or wish is omitted and simply replaced by 'said'.

Option (B) follows all the proper rules of sentence transformation.

Hence, the correct option is (B).

39. The correct answer is:

"The officer shouted at the cadet and asked him to get out of that room."

The sentence in question is in the direct mode of narration.

The reporting verb is in the past tense.

The verb in the reported speech is in the present tense.

When we change a sentence from direct to indirect mode, we make the following changes:

Quotation marks are omitted and the sentence ends with a full stop.

The tense of the verb, in the reported speech involving any order, request and instruction does not undergo any change during the conversion from direct to indirect mode. This is also true if the statement is a universal truth.

If the reporting verb is in the present tense, it does not undergo any change.

We add the word 'to' before the verb if the verb is in the bare infinitive.

When the reporting or principal verb is in the present tense, all present tenses of the direct are changed into the corresponding past tenses.

Words expressing nearness in time or place are generally converted into 'into' words expressing distance. For eg. now becomes then, today becomes that day, yesterday becomes the previous day, this becomes that, etc.

In reporting commands and requests, the verb expressing command or request is added and the imperative is changed into the infinitive.

In reporting questions the verbs like asked and inquired are added

In reporting exclamations and wishes, the verbs expressing exclamation or wish are added

When we convert a sentence from the direct to the indirect mode(especially for a sentence ending with a mark of interrogation), we reverse the subject-verb placement. In direct sentences, we have the verb before the subject; while in indirect, the verb follows the subject.

Hence, the correct option is (A).

40. The correct answer is:

"The customer asked the assistant if he had a blue scarf."

We make changes in tenses of reported speech only when the reporting verb is in the past tense.

When the reported speech is an interrogative sentence we follow these steps-

Reporting verb 'said' is changed into 'asked'.

connector 'if' or 'whether' is used in place of commas.

Change the sentence, given in the reported speech, from interrogative to assertive.

The tense of reported speech is changed accordingly. (in above sentence- 'have' changes into 'had')

personal Pronouns of reported speech are changed as per subject and object of reporting verb. Here, the second person- 'You' will change into 'he' as per object - 'assistant'.

By following these steps we get the final sentence - " The customer asked the assistant if he had a blue scarf."

Hence, the correct option is (D).

41. The correct answer is:

"The policeman asked him, "Where is your helmet?"

The sentence in question is in the indirect mode of narration. The reporting verb is in the simple past tense. The verb in the reported speech is in the simple present tense.

When we convert a sentence from indirect to direct speech, we make the following changes:

- Quotation marks are added and the sentence ends with a full stop, comma, or interrogation mark depending on the tone of the reported speech.

- The tense of the verb, in the reported speech involving any order, request and instruction does not undergo any change during the conversion from indirect to direct mode. This is also true if the statement is a universal truth.

- If the reporting verb is in the present tense, it does not undergo any change.

- We omit the word 'to' before the verb if the verb is in the bare infinitive.

- When the reporting or principal verb is in the past tense, all past tenses of the indirect are changed into the corresponding present tenses.

- Words expressing distance are generally converted into words expressing nearness in time or place. For eg. then becomes now, that day becomes today, that becomes this, etc.

- In reporting commands and requests, the verb expressing command or request is omitted and the infinitive is changed into the imperative.
- In reporting questions the verbs like asked, inquired are omitted and replaced by 'said to'.
- In reporting exclamations and wishes, the verb expressing exclamation or wish is omitted and simply replaced by 'said'.

Hence, the correct option is (A).

42. The correct answer is:

Devi replied, "I'm sorry but I cannot go."

In the direct form, 'she' changes to 'I'. So, we are left with option (C) and (D). The given sentence is in simple past tense, which means the direct form will be in simple present tense. So, 'was' will be replaced by 'am' and 'could not' will be replaced with 'cannot'.

Hence, the correct option is (C).

43. The correct answer is:

Abdul said, "I saw this film yesterday."

In the direct form 'the day before' is changed to 'yesterday'. We are left with options (B) and (C). The indirect form is is past perfect tense which means the direct form will be in past tense. 'That' changes to 'this' in the direct form.

Hence, the correct option is (B).

44. The correct answer is:

Kishore said that he was leaving then.

The given statement is in the present continuous tense. So, the indirect form will be in the past continuous tense. In indirect form, 'now' changes to 'then'.

Option (B) is in the simple past tense.

Option (C) is in the present continuous tense.

Option (D) is grammatically incorrect.

Hence, the correct option is (A).

45. The correct answer is:

The child told his mother that he was hungry.

The child is telling something to his mother. So, 'told' should be used. We are left with option (C) and (D). The statement is in simple present tense, so the indirect form will be in simple past tense. Also, in the sentence 'his' is used which means the child is a male.

Hence, the correct option is (D).

Q.1 Direction: Out of the following options, select the word that best substitutes the given sentence:

Something that becomes outdated

A. old   **B.** obsolete   **C.** ancient   **D.** useless

Q.2 Direction: Which of the given words describe Yashpal's state most appropriately?

"I am feeling under the weather, today," said Yashpal.

A. Brightness   **B.** Hardness
C. Wellness   **D.** Illness

Q.3 Direction: Out of the following options, select the word that best substitutes the given sentence:

"Official prohibition or order to stop something"

A. Ban   **B.** Bane   **C.** Curse   **D.** Ruin

Q.4 Direction: Out of the following options, select the word that best substitutes the given sentence:

Choose the option that is closest in meaning to the word 'Quagmire'.

A. Buffoon   **B.** A traitor
C. An admirer   **D.** A predicament

Q.5 To kill someone for political reasons

A. homicide   **B.** murder
C. assassination   **D.** genocide

Q.6 Direction: Substitute the phrase in bold italics with the appropriate option:

Usually, no one gives a job to someone who runs away from the law.

[Allahabad High Court Review Officer (RO), 2019]

A. a fugitive   **B.** a persistent
C. a juvenile   **D.** None of the above

Q.7 Direction: In the following question, out of the given alternatives, choose the one which can be substituted for the given words/sentence.

A metal flame on which meat etc. is cooked over an open fire.

A. Chef   **B.** Barberian
C. Barbecue   **D.** Vendor

Q.8 Direction: Choose the correct meaning of the given proverb:

Killing of one's own brother

A. murder   **B.** matricide
C. fratricide   **D.** genocide

Q.9 Direction: In the following question, out of the given alternatives, choose the one which can be substituted for the given words/sentence.

A person who eats too much

A. glutton   **B.** reveller

C. sensualist   **D.** omnivore

Q.10 Direction: In the following question, out of the given alternatives, choose the one which can be substituted for the given words/sentence.

Something that is real or actual, rather than imaginary.

A. Vague   **B.** Elusive
C. Tangible   **D.** Imperceptible

Q.11 Direction: Select the word which means the same as the group of words given.

A contest between two people to settle a point of honour:

A. Dual   **B.** Duel   **C.** Duo   **D.** Duet

Q.12 Direction: Select the word which means the same as the group of words given.

A speech made to oneself:

A. Soliloquy   **B.** Solitary
C. Eloquent   **D.** Dialogue

Q.13 Direction: Select the word which means the same as the group of words given.

An area of grassland where animals graze:

[SSC MTS, 2019]

A. Forest   **B.** Park   **C.** Meadow   **D.** Garden

Ques (14-18):Direction: Select the word which means the same as the group of words given.

Q.14 "Being afraid of water or being near water"
[SSC Sub Inspector (CPO), 2018], [SSC Sub Inspector (CPO), 2017]

A. Xenophobia   **B.** Autophobia
C. Monophobia   **D.** Aquaphobia

Q.15 "To express your thoughts clearly in words"
[SSC Sub Inspector (CPO), 2018], [SSC Sub Inspector (CPO), 2017]

A. Articulate   **B.** Archive
C. Ambivalent   **D.** Equivocal

Q.16 "One who does not believe in God"
[SSC Sub Inspector (CPO), 2018], [SSC Sub Inspector (CPO), 2017]

A. Devotee   **B.** Theist
C. Atheist   **D.** Anarchist

Q.17 "Difficult or impossible to reach or to get"
[SSC Sub Inspector (CPO), 2018], [SSC Sub Inspector (CPO), 2017]

A. Illegible   **B.** Inevitable
C. Inaudible   **D.** Inaccessible

Q.18 "The scientific study of the mind"
[SSC Sub Inspector (CPO), 2018], [SSC Sub Inspector (CPO), 2017]

A. Philology   **B.** Psychology
C. Sociology   **D.** Anthropology

Ques (19-23):Direction: Select the most appropriate one-word substitution for the given group of words.

Q.19 The dates when days and nights are of equal length.
[SSC Sub Inspector (CPO), 2020]

A. Equinox   **B.** Solstice   **C.** Eclipse   **D.** Stellar

Q.20 Something which is considered to be very important.
A. Cardinal   **B.** Scanty
C. Meager   **D.** Supplementary

Q.21 A Kennel is a place where:
[Haryana Primary Teacher (PRT), 2020]

A. Horses are kept   **B.** Dogs are kept
C. Pigs are kept   **D.** Cats are kept

Q.22 The life history of a person written by himself.
A. Essay   **B.** Biography
C. Travelogue   **D.** Autobiography

Q.23 A person of evil reputation.
A. Renowned   **B.** Famous
C. Notorious   **D.** Icon

Q.24 Direction: In the question given below out of four alternatives, choose the one which can be substituted for the given sentence.

A person who renounces the world and practices self-discipline in order to attain salvation
A. Sceptic   **B.** Ascetic
C. Devotee   **D.** Antiquarian

Q.25 Direction: Select the word which means the same as the group of words given.

One who plans the steps and moves in a dance
[SSC Sub Inspector (CPO), 2019]

A. Composer   **B.** Choreographer
C. Producer   **D.** Director

Q.26 Direction: Select the word which means the same as the group of words given.

An arrangement of events or dates in the order of their occurrence.
A. Chronometry   **B.** Charter
C. Chronology   **D.** Calendar

Q.27 Direction: Select the word which means the same as the group of words given.

A solution for all difficulties or diseases.
[SSC Sub Inspector (CPO), 2019]

A. Medication   **B.** Treatment
C. Remedy   **D.** Panacea

Q.28 Direction: Select the word which means the same as the group of words given.

Branch of physics dealing with the properties of sound.
A. Mechanics   **B.** Radiation
C. Acoustics   **D.** Audition

Q.29 Direction: Select the word which means the same as the group of words given.

Sound of horses
A. Grunt   **B.** Screech   **C.** Squeak   **D.** Neigh

Q.30 Direction: Select the word which means the same as the group of words given.

An underground hole dug by a small animal as a dwelling.
A. Drain   **B.** Pit   **C.** Cave   **D.** Burrow

Q.31 Direction: Select the word which means the same as the group of words given.

The study of plants.
A. Geology   **B.** Botany
C. Lexicography   **D.** Philology

Q.32 Direction: Select the word which means the same as the group of words given.

A large number of fish swimming together.
A. Herd   **B.** Shoal   **C.** Brood   **D.** Cache

Q.33 Direction: Select the word which means the same as the group of words given.

A room or building with equipment for doing physical exercise.
A. Dormitory   **B.** Convent
C. Infirmary   **D.** Gymnasium

Q.34 Direction: Select the word which means the same as the group of words given.

Extreme fear of confined places.
A. Cellophobia   **B.** Claustrophobia
C. Chronophobia   **D.** Centrophobia

Ques (35-39):Direction: Select the word which means the same as the group of words given.

Q.35 Critical judge of any art and craft
A. Comrade   **B.** Curator
C. Connoisseur   **D.** Crusader

Q.36 A fault that may be forgiven
A. Veteran   **B.** Versatile   **C.** Venial   **D.** Virgin

Q.37 A group of worshippers
A. Congregation   **B.** Cortege
C. Caravan   **D.** Crusade

Q.38 Something causing shock or dismay
A. Mischievous   **B.** Remarkable
C. Frivolous   **D.** Appalling

Q.39 A person who delays or puts things off like work, chores, or other actions.
A. Diligent   **B.** Procrastinator
C. Persevere   **D.** Assiduous

Ques (40-45):Directions: In each of the following questions, choose the most suitable word for the given expression.

Q.40 One who is present everywhere.

A. Omnipresent   B. Omnipotent
C. Omnivorous   D. Eternal

Q.41 Killing of one person by another
A. Henpeck   B. Homicide
C. Arboreal   D. Patricide

Q.42 One who has a long experience of any occupation.
[NCHM JEE (Hotel Mgmt & Catering), 2018]

A. Amateur   B. Versatile
C. Veteran   D. Philanderer

Q.43 A place where dead bodies are kept for identification.
[NCHM JEE (Hotel Mgmt & Catering), 2018]

A. Sanatorium   B. Infirmary
C. Auditorium   D. Morgue

Q.44 Holding office without any remuneration.
[NCHM JEE (Hotel Mgmt & Catering), 2018]

A. tertiary   B. Honorary
C. Salutary   D. Potable

Q.45 A list of headings of the business to be transacted at a meeting.
[NCHM JEE (Hotel Mgmt & Catering), 2018]

A. Minutes   B. Propoganda
C. Agenda   D. Points

// Smart Answer Sheet //

Correct — Indicates percentage of students who answered questions correctly.

Skipped — Indicates percentage of students who skipped questions.

Q.	Ans.	Correct / Skipped	Q.	Ans.	Correct / Skipped	Q.	Ans.	Correct / Skipped	Q.	Ans.	Correct / Skipped	Q.	Ans.	Correct / Skipped
1	C	86.38 % / 10.79 %	10	C	64.65 % / 33.31 %	19	A	51.93 % / 35.1 %	28	C	66.52 % / 33.09 %	37	A	81.39 % / 11.54 %
2	D	69.81 % / 30.12 %	11	B	49.01 % / 38.6 %	20	A	42.98 % / 34.55 %	29	D	83.59 % / 15.17 %	38	D	81.82 % / 13.97 %
3	A	54.29 % / 45.59 %	12	A	63.12 % / 30.6 %	21	B	51.97 % / 34.74 %	30	D	13.99 % / 80.21 %	39	B	52.81 % / 30.68 %
4	D	59.31 % / 40.24 %	13	C	48.2 % / 38.18 %	22	D	61.52 % / 33.14 %	31	B	76.32 % / 15.28 %	40	A	76.75 % / 17.28 %
5	C	83.27 % / 14.57 %	14	D	60.06 % / 36.76 %	23	C	50.15 % / 33.94 %	32	B	12.91 % / 79.99 %	41	B	56.38 % / 39.46 %
6	A	19.81 % / 76.09 %	15	A	46.42 % / 33.31 %	24	B	51.33 % / 36.09 %	33	D	85.33 % / 11.18 %	42	C	63.58 % / 34.51 %
7	C	15.75 % / 77.09 %	16	C	83.66 % / 16.11 %	25	B	85.75 % / 11.2 %	34	B	51.84 % / 32.67 %	43	D	67.15 % / 31.37 %
8	C	84.32 % / 10.24 %	17	D	48.69 % / 45.46 %	26	C	24.29 % / 74.98 %	35	C	53.93 % / 38.76 %	44	B	53.27 % / 30.18 %
9	A	59.29 % / 40.58 %	18	B	86.46 % / 10.57 %	27	D	19.74 % / 70.49 %	36	C	46.26 % / 45.65 %	45	C	59.89 % / 37.94 %

Performance Analysis

Avg. Score (%)	55.56%
Toppers Score (%)	60.0%
Your Score	

//Hints and Solutions//

1. Ancient means belonging to the distant past, especially to the period in history before the end of the Roman Empire.

They believed ancient Greece and Rome were vital sources of learning.

Hence, the correct option is (C).

2. Illness means if someone is or feels under the weather, they feel ill.

For example: I'm feeling a bit under the weather - I think I'm getting a cold.

Therefore, the word that describes Yashpal's state most appropriately is illness.

Hence, the correct option is (D).

3. The correct answer is Ban.

Ban: an official order that prevents something from happening.

Bane: a cause of continuous trouble or unhappiness.

Curse: magic words that are intended to bring bad luck to someone.

Ruin: the process or state of being spoiled or destroyed.

Therefore, the word that best substitutes the given sentence is 'Ban.'

Hence, the correct option is (A).

4. Predicament (noun): An unpleasant situation that is difficult to get out of.

Quagmire (noun): An area of soft, wet ground that you sink into if you try to walk on it.

For example:

1. At the end of the game, the pitch was a real quagmire.
2. She is hoping to get a loan from her bank to help her out of her financial predicament.

Therefore, the word Predicament is the most appropriate synonym for Quagmire.

Hence, the correct option is (D).

5. Assassination means the murder of someone famous or important.

For example-

Assassinate is defined as the act of killing someone (usually a famous person) deliberately, or the act of killing someone after being hired to do so. An example of assassinate is pulling the trigger on a gun to kill a President.

Hence, the correct option is (C).

6. Someone who runs away from the law is a fugitive.

Fugitive: A person who is running away or hiding from the police or a dangerous situation.

For example:

- Thousands of fugitives are fleeing from the war-torn area.
- Butch Cassidy and the Sundance Kid were fugitives from justice.

Hence, the correct option is (A).

7. barbecue means to roast or broil (food, such as meat) on a rack or revolving spit over or before a source of heat (such as hot coals or a gas flame)

Hence, the correct option is (C).

8. Fratricide (from Latin: fratricidium, from the Latin words frater "brother" and the assimilated root of caedere "to kill, to cut down") is the act of killing one's brother. It can either be done directly or via the use of either a hired or an indoctrinated intermediary (an assassin).

for example-

The prince engaged in fratricide so he could eliminate his brothers and ascend to the throne.

Hence, the correct option is (C).

9. Glutton means- one that has a great capacity for accepting or enduring something

For example-

I can't control my eating. It's hard when people don't understand and call you a glutton.

Hence, the correct option is (A).

10. Tangible means something that is real or actual, rather than imaginary.

Vague means which is not clear.

Elusive means difficult to describe.

Imperceptible means difficult to perceive by mind or senses.

Hence, the correct option is (C).

11. Duel = combat between two persons specifically.

Dual = consisting of two parts, elements, or aspects.

Duo = a pair of people or things, especially in music or entertainment

Duet = a performance by two singers, instrumentalists, or dancers.

Hence, the correct option is (B).

12. Soliloquy = an act of speaking one's thoughts aloud when by oneself or regardless of any hearers, especially by a character in a play.

Solitary = done or existing alone.

Eloquent = fluent or persuasive in speaking or writing.

Dialogue = a conversation between two or more people as a feature of a book, play, or film.

Hence, the correct option is (A).

13. Meadow = an area of land with grass and other wild plants in it.

Forest = a large area of land covered with trees and plants, usually larger than wood, or the trees and plants themselves.

Park = a large area of land with grass and trees which is maintained for the pleasure of the public.

Garden = a piece of land, usually in a yard next to a house, where you grow flowers and vegetables

Meadow is a natural grassland, used for grazing animals.

Hence, the correct option is (C).

14. Let's explore the marked option:

- The word 'Aquaphobia' means 'an abnormal fear of water.'
    - Example: She has aquaphobia so she didn't go near the swimming pool.
- The root word 'phobia' means 'an irrational fear of something that's unlikely to cause harm' and the root word 'aqua' means 'water'.

Hence, the correct option is (D).

15. The word 'articulate' means 'having or showing the ability to speak fluently and coherently.'

- Examples,
    - She is an intelligent and highly articulate young woman.
    - She impressed the audience with her articulate speech.
- According to the meaning and examples that are given above, option (A) is the correct answer.

Hence, the correct option is (A).

16. The word 'Atheist' means 'someone who does not believe in any God.'

- Examples,
    - As an atheist, I do not accept this religious argument.
    - Although I am an atheist, I don't just automatically hate religion or dismiss other people's faith.
- According to the meaning and examples that are given above, 'atheist' is the correct answer.

Hence, the correct option is (C).

17. The word 'inaccessible' means 'very difficult or impossible to travel to or reach or obtain'.

- Examples,
    - This is one of the most inaccessible places in the world.
    - Some of the houses on the hillside are inaccessible to cars.
- According to the meaning and examples that are given above, 'inaccessible' is the correct answer.

Hence, the correct option is (D).

18. The word 'Psychology' means 'the scientific study of the human mind and its functions, especially those affecting behavior in a given context.'

- Eg. She had an undergraduate degree in psychology.
- Therefore, according to the meaning and example, 'psychology' is the correct answer.

Hence, the correct option is (B).

19. Let's look at the meaning of the marked option:

- Equinox- the time or date (twice each year) at which the sun crosses the celestial equator, when day and night are of approximately equal length (about September 22 and March 20)

Let's look at the meanings of the other given options:

- Solstice- the time or date (twice each year) at which the sun reaches its maximum or minimum declination, marked by the longest and shortest days (about June 21 and December 22)
- Eclipse- an obscuring of the light from one celestial body by the passage of another between it and the observer or between it and its source of illumination
- Stellar- relating to a star or stars

So, from the given meanings, we find that equinox is the correct one-word substitute.

Hence, the correct option is (A).

20. The most appropriate one-word for the given group of words is 'Cardinal'.

Word	Meaning	Example
Cardinal	of great importance	*Finding food was a **cardinal** concern.*
Scanty	smaller in size or amount than is considered necessary or is hoped for	*Evidence of such an association is, however, **scanty** in children of pre-school age.*
Meager	(of amounts or numbers) very small or not enough	*The prisoners existed on a **meager** diet.*
Supplementary	added to something else in order to improve it or complete	*Teachers often create **supplementary** materials for their classes.*

	it	

Hence, the correct option is (A).

21. Kennel - a small, usually wooden, shelter for a dog to sleep in outside. Plural: Kennels

Let's look at the places where other animals are kept:

Stable	A place where **horses** are kept
Sty/ pigsty	A place where **pigs** are kept
Cattery	A place where **cats** are kept

Hence, the correct option is (B).

22. Let's look at the meaning of the marked option:

Autobiography- an account of a person's life written by that person

Let's look at the meanings of the other given options:

- Essay- a short piece of writing on a particular subject
- Biography- an account of someone's life written by someone else
- Travelogue- a movie, book, or illustrated lecture about the places visited and experiences encountered by a traveler

So, from the given meanings, we find that Autobiography is the correct one-word substitute.

Hence, the correct option is (D).

23. Let's look at the meaning of the marked option:

Notorious- famous or well known, typically for some bad quality or deed

Let's look at the meanings of the other given options:

- Renowned- known or talked about by many people; famous
- Icon- a person or thing regarded as a representative symbol or as worthy of veneration

So, from the given meanings, we find that notorious is the correct one-word substitute.

Hence, the correct option is (C).

24. One word substitution is Ascetic.

Ascetic: Characterized by severe self-discipline and abstention from all forms of indulgence, typically for religious reasons.

Sceptic: A person inclined to question or doubt accepted opinions.

Devotee: A person who is very interested in and enthusiastic about someone or something.

Antiquarian: Relating to or dealing in antiques or rare books.

Hence, the correct option is (B).

25. Choreographer - one who plans the steps and moves in a dance. For Example: Lea Anderson is a choreographer who believes in making dance accessible.

Let's look at the meaning of the other options:

Composer: a person who writes music, especially as a professional occupation. For Example: The composer expresses his sorrow in his music.

Producer: a person, company, or country that makes, grows, or supplies goods or commodities for sale. For Example: a film producer.

Director: a person who is in charge of an activity, department, or organization. For Example: The director resigned in protest at the decision.

Hence, the correct option is (B).

26. Chronology is an arrangement of events or dates in the order of their occurrence.

Let's look at the meaning of the other options:

Chronometry - the science of accurate time measurement. For Example - An analogue to mineral chronometry is O isotope geothermometry.

Charter- a written grant by the sovereign or legislative power of a country, by which a body such as a city, company, or university is founded or its rights and privileges defined. For Example - This new law amounts to a tax evader's charter.

Calendar- a chart or series of pages showing the days, weeks, and months of a particular year, or giving particular seasonal information. For Example - Do you have next year's calendar?

Hence, the correct option is (C).

27. Let's look at the meaning of the correct answer:

Panacea - a solution or remedy for all difficulties or diseases. For Example - There is no panacea for the country's economic problems.

Let's look at the meaning of the other options:-

Medication - a drug or other form of medicine that is used to treat or prevent disease. For Example - The medication should ease the suffering.

Treatment - medical care given to a patient for an illness or injury. For Example - She is responding well to treatment.

Remedy - medicine or treatment for a disease or injury. For Example - The remedy is worse than the disease.

Hence, the correct option is (D).

28. Acoustics is the correct answer.

Acoustics means the branch of physics concerned with the properties of sound.

Mechanics means the branch of applied mathematics dealing with motion and forces producing motion.

Radiation means the emission of energy as electromagnetic waves or as moving subatomic particles, especially high-energy particles which cause ionization.

Audition means an interview for a role or job as a singer, actor, dancer, or musician, consisting of a practical demonstration of the candidate's suitability and skill.

Hence, the correct option is (C).

29. Let's look at the meaning of the correct answer:

Neigh - the sound of horses. For Example: With a wild neigh of terror the animal fell bodily into the pit, drawing the buggy and its occupants after him.

Hence, the correct option is (D).

30. The correct one word for the given descriptive sentence/words is Burrow.

Let's look at the meaning of the correct answer:

Burrow: An underground hole dug by a small animal as a dwelling. For Example: Two burrows were randomly selected for the addition of water to the sand.

Hence, the correct option is (D).

31. Let's look at the meaning of the correct answer:

Botany, :branch of biology that deals with the study of plants, including their structure, properties, and biochemical processes. Also included are plant classification and the study of plant diseases and of interactions with the environment.

Example: Her interests in plants motivated her to pursue this course in Botany.

Hence, the correct option is (B).

32. Let's look at the meaning of the correct answer:

Shoal (noun) - a group of fish or a large number of fish swimming together. For Example: There was a shoal of mackerel in the area.

Hence, the correct option is (B).

33. The correct answer is gymnasium.

A gymnasium is a room or building with equipment for doing exercise.

A dormitory is a large bedroom for a number of people in a school or institution.

A convent is either a community of priests, religious brothers, religious sisters, monks or nuns; or the building used by the community.

An infirmary is a place in a large institution to take care of those who are ill.

Hence, the correct option is (D).

34. Let's look at the meaning of the correct answer:

Claustrophobia (noun): fear of being in closed spaces. For Example: He suffers from claustrophobia so he never travels on underground trains.

Hence, the correct option is (B).

35. Connoisseur means a person who has a great deal of knowledge about the fine arts, cuisines, or an expert judge in matters of taste.

For example, He was a man of wide knowledge, a connoisseur in art and music.

Comrade- a colleague or a fellow member of an organization.

Curator- a person in charge of a museum.

Crusader- a person who campaigns vigorously for political, social, or religious change; a campaigner.
Hence, the correct option is (C).

36. Venial means a fault that may be forgiven.

Veteran means one, who has a long experience in any occupation.

Versatile means interested in and clever at many different things.

Virgin means a woman who has no sexual experience.
Hence, the correct option is (C).

37. Congregation: A group of people assembled for religious worship.

Cortege: A solemn procession, especially for a funeral.

Caravan: A group of people, typically with vehicles or animals travelling together.

Crusade: A vigorous campaign for political, social, or religious change.
Hence, the correct option is (A).

38. Appalling means something causing shock or dismay.

For example: She suffered appalling injuries in the accident.

Mischievous means causing or showing a fondness for causing trouble in a playful way.

Remarkable means worthy of attention; striking.

Frivolous means not having any serious purpose or value.
Hence, the correct option is (D).

39. A Procrastinator is a person who habitually puts off doing things.

For example, A person who delays or puts things off — like work, chores, or other actions" is a Procrastinator.

A Diligent is one who is having or showing care and conscientiousness in one's work or duties.

A Persevere is one who continues in a course of action even in the face of difficulty or with little or no indication of success.

An Assiduous is one who is showing great care and perseverance.
Hence, the correct option is (B).

40. Omnipresent means ubiquitous refer to the quality of being everywhere.

For example: Omnipresent emphasizes in a lofty or dignified way the power, usually divine, of being present everywhere at the same time, as though all-enveloping.

Hence,the correct option is (A).

41. Homicide means the killing of one human being by another. Homicide is a general term and may refer to a noncriminal act as well as the criminal act of murder.

Hence, the correct option is (B).

42. Veteran means a person who has had long service or experience in an occupation, office, or the like.

Hence, the correct option is (C).

43. A morgue or mortuary (in a hospital or elsewhere) means a place used for the storage of human corpses awaiting identification (ID), removal for autopsy, respectful burial, cremation or other methods of disposal.

Hence, the correct option is (D).

44. Honorary means (of an office or its holder) unpaid or given as an honour (without the person needing the usual certificates, etc.)

For example-

He was awarded an honorary degree. He's an honorary member of the club. He is the honorary president of the commission.

Hence, the correct option is (B).

45. Agenda means a list of items to be discussed at a formal meeting.

For example-

An agenda should include a few basic elements. Agenda items example include: A short meeting agenda lists the ultimate meeting goal.

Hence, the correct option is (C).

Q.1 Direction: Replace the phrase in bold with the correct option given below.

I am **looking up** my keys but I am unable to find them

[TISS NET, 2017]

A. looking into
B. looking for
C. looking after
D. no correction

Q.2 Direction: Replace the phrase in bold with the correct option given below.

There are very few **people in the world that doesn't** like ice cream.

[TISS NET, 2017]

A. people whom don't
B. people who don't
C. people which don't
D. No correction

Q.3 Direction: Replace the phrase in bold with the correct option given below.

No sooner **do the bell ring** than the students ran out of their classes.

[TISS NET, 2017]

A. Did the bell ring
B. Did the bells ring
C. Do the bell rang
D. No correction

Q.4 Direction: Select the most appropriate option to substitute the underlined segment in the given sentence. If there is no need to substitute it, select 'No Replacement required'.

What **should the goals** of a vaccination policy during a global pandemic?

A. should be the goals
B. has to been the goals
C. shall be a goals
D. No Replacement required

Ques (5-12):Direction: In the following sentence, a part of the sentence is underlined. There are some alternatives to the underlined part which may improve the sentence. Choose the correct alternative. In case no improvement is needed to choose 'No improvement' as your answer.

Q.5 Every year billions of Tulips are cultivated, a majority of which are grown and <u>to export</u> from Holland.

A. have exported
B. export
C. exported
D. No improvement

Q.6 Reporters say that Ajith had been a genius <u>from</u> childhood.

A. for
B. though
C. since
D. No improvement

Q.7 Experts <u>had say</u> that people (adults) need at least 6 hours of sleep every night.

A. have been saying
B. say
C. saying
D. No improvement

Q.8 He is <u>of the opinion</u> that education should be made more accessible to the differently abled students.

A. For the opinion
B. With the opinion
C. By the opinion
D. No improvement

Q.9 POSHAN Abhiyaan or the National Nutrition Mission is playing a major role in improving nutrition indicators <u>under India</u>.

A. Along India
B. Overall India
C. Across India
D. No improvement

Q.10 While every fifth child under the age five is vitamin A deficient, one in every third baby has vitamin B12 deficiency and two out of every five children <u>is anemic</u>.

A. Are anemic
B. Is anemia
C. Are anemia
D. No improvement

Q.11 In its report, The State of the World's Children 2019, UNICEF said that every second child in that age group <u>is affected</u> by some form of malnutrition.

A. are affected
B. is effected
C. is effect
D. No improvement

Q.12 Nowadays rent for a two-room house can run <u>as high to</u> Rs. 40,000/ in Mumbai.

A. so high so
B. so high to
C. as high as
D. No improvement

Ques (13-15):Direction: In the following sentence, a part of the sentence is underlined. Below are given alternatives to the underlined part, which may improve the sentence. Choose the correct alternative. In case no improvement is needed, choose the option that indicates 'No improvement'.

Q.13 Cryptozoology is not a recognized branch of zoology but a pseudoscience because it <u>relied heavily upon</u> anecdotal evidence, stories and alleged sightings.

A. It has been relying heavily upon

B. It relies heavily upon

C. It relied heavily on

D. It rely heavily upon

A. B, C and D
B. A and B
C. Only B
D. No improvement

Q.14 When Benjamin Franklin invented the lightning-rod, the clergy condemned it as an impious attempt <u>for defeat of God's will</u>.

A. To defeat God's will

B. At defeat of God's will

C. At defeating the will of God

D. In defeating God's will

A. Only C
B. Only D
C. A and B
D. No improvement

Q.15 However, third-party experts doubted North Korea's claims and <u>contends that the</u> device was probably a less destructive fission bomb.

A. Contend that the

B. Contended that the

C. Contending that the

D. Avowed that the

A. Only A **B.** A and D **C.** C and D **D.** B and D

Q.16 Direction: Which of the following phrases (A), (B), (C), (D) given below in the statement should replace the phrase printed in bold in the sentence to make it grammatically correct? If the sentence is correct as it is given and 'No Correction is required', mark (D) as the answer.

The 'Solitary Reaper' is **one of the good** poems composed by William Wordsworth.

A. One of the better

B. A better

C. One of the best

D. No correction required

Q.17 Direction: In the following question, out of four alternatives, select the word which can replace the underlined word given in the question. In case no replacement is needed, select 'None of these'.

Since the early 20th century, tiger populations have lost at least 93% of their historic range and have been <u>extirpated</u> in Western and Central Asia, from the islands of Java and Bali, and in large areas of Southeast and South Asia and China.

A. Ameliorated **B.** Improved

C. Eradicated **D.** None of these

Ques (18-19):Direction: In the given question, a word in the sentence is printed in bold. Below the sentence, alternatives to the emboldened part are given which may help improve the sentence. Choose the correct alternative out of the given options.

Q.18 The economic **slander** has grown rapidly in the era of globalization.

A. Variety **B.** Indigence

C. Raid **D.** Disparity

Q.19 Elderly people need time and **compassion** from their physicians.

A. Inconceivable **B.** Plausible

C. Indestructible **D.** Empathy

Ques (20-21):Direction: Phrases in the sentences given below are underlined. Choose the option which you feel can replace all of the underlined phrases. If there is no improvement needed, please click on "No improvement required.

Q.20 1. I <u>waited on</u> the important points.

2. You should have <u>ran</u> me <u>across</u> when you were in London.

3. I <u>ran down</u> the story.

A. Looked up

B. Showed up

C. Ran away

D. No improvement needed

Q.21 1. I will <u>take on</u> all the letters.

2. <u>Take for</u> the trash and come here.

3. He will <u>take up</u> the old furniture.

A. Think back

B. Took off

C. Take out

D. No improvement needed

Ques (22-24):Direction: A sentence is given by a portion (a phrase or a group of words) marked in bold. Choose the best replacement for the part in bold, as per the options given below, to make the sentence meaningful and grammatically correct.

Q.22 Kiran was **wistful** after seeing her old school and childhood pictures.

I. Cynical

II.Nostalgic

III.Cutesy

A. Only I **B.** Only II

C. Only I and II **D.** No improvements

Q.23 Rajesh had his plans fixed for his weekend but **out of the blue** he had to go to office even on weekends.

I. Zemblanity

II. Misfortune

III. Serendipitous

A. Only II **B.** Only I

C. Only III **D.** Only II and III

Q.24 Reena was happy to do the work **at the drop of a hat**.

I. Promptly

II. Grudgingly

III. Unwillingly

A. Only III **B.** Only I

C. Only II **D.** No improvements

Ques (25-37):Direction: Phrases in the sentences given below are underlined. Choose the option which you feel can replace all of the underlined phrases. If there is no improvement needed, please click on "No improvement required".

Q.25 1. The <u>got in</u> had occurred just before midnight.

2. The two robbers had an alibi for the time period of the <u>run up.</u>

3. The would-be thieves had smashed the door lock in an attempt to <u>turn in</u>.

A. Break in

B. Broke in

C. Got in

D. No improvement required

Q.26 1. Work can get difficult but you just need to <u>hand over</u>.

2. The second half of the movie was so horrible but we just had to <u>hang out</u>.

3. You need to <u>hand down</u> till the driver returns.

A. Hang up

B. Hold onto

C. Hang in there

D. No improvement needed

Q.27 1. <u>Call for</u> this item from the list.

2. He tried to <u>cut on</u> sweets.

3. The floods <u>count up</u> all communication.

A. Cut off

B. Cut into

C. Cut in

D. No improvement needed

Q.28 1. The story does, however, <u>abound upon</u> felicities; the physical descriptions of the planet, for example, are superb.

2. While other ions <u>abound upon</u> cytoplasm in their millimoles, liberal estimates of free Ca concentrations run around 0.1 micromolar, maximum.

3. Examples <u>flutter up</u> the professions, for example, the question of auditors and joint-stock companies, or solicitors and conveyancing.

A. Abound in

B. Abound on

C. Abound

D. No improvement required

Q.29 1. People are <u>reaching for</u> new jobs at hedge funds, corporate buyout shops, boutique banks and startups.

2. They were <u>adding on</u> several tickets to the automobile exhibition show.

3. He's been <u>adding for</u> an invitation, but I don't want him to come.

A. Beating down

B. Angling for

C. Holding off

D. No improvement required

Q.30 1. We will <u>crack up</u> to pay his bills.

2. I will <u>check through</u> to collect money for the campaign.

3. He will <u>check with</u> to serve the meal.

A. Came across

B. Chip in

C. Come apart

D. No improvement needed

Q.31 1. The police will <u>ask in</u> the tip and catch the gang red-handed.

2. It had previously relied on other banks to <u>act upon</u> its behalf on an agency basis.

3. Seventeen years later a British government chose to <u>back on</u> that suggestion and dispatch the fleet.

A. Ask after

B. Back in

C. Act on

D. No improvement required

Q.32 1. She promised to <u>get through</u> me after she finishes her work.

2. I don't know when I am going to <u>get out of</u> reading.

3. Can you <u>get ahead</u> me with the figures?

A. Get back to

B. Get back at

C. Grow up

D. No improvement needed

Q.33 1. He suddenly <u>backed up</u> saying, 'It's a lie'.

2. 'Hey', she <u>bore up</u>, 'I'm just trying to help.'

3. We <u>bawled out</u> but we weren't able to find him.

A. Break out

B. Called on

C. Broke in

D. No improvement needed

Q.34 1. He had to <u>ask out</u> for some food.

2. You need to <u>back up</u> for your car.

3. We will have to <u>blow up</u> for help.

A. Ask around

B. Added up

C. Broke down

D. No improvement needed

Q.35 1. The top and bottom <u>come up</u> if you pull hard enough.

2. My whole life had <u>get apart</u> at the seams.

3. After the first act, the play begins to <u>get upon</u> at the seams

A. Come in

B. Come upon

C. Come apart

D. No improvement required

Q.36 1. He always <u>blew</u> people <u>out</u> in the meetings.

2. Her mother <u>bore</u> her <u>up</u> for forgetting the meeting.

3. When he heard the news, he <u>blew over</u>.

A. Blew in

B. Bawled out

C. Broke into

D. No improvement needed

Q.37 1. We decided to <u>eat out</u> today.

2. Let's <u>do away with</u> these clothes.

3. I am <u>counting on</u> you to take care of him.

A. Catch up

B. Check out

C. Break into

D. No improvement needed

Q.38 Which of the phrases given below the sentence should replace the word/phrase that is given in bold in the sentence to make it grammatically correct? If the sentence is correct as it is given and no correction is required, mark 'No correction required' as the answer.

John Snow **has returned** to Castle Black one month ago.

A. returned

B. have returned

C. has been returned

D. No correction required

Ques (39-41):Direction: A sentence/part of the sentence is emboldened. Five alternatives are given to the embolden part which will improve the sentence. Choose the correct alternative and choose the option corresponding to it. In case no improvement is needed, click the option corresponding to 'No improvement required'.

Q.39 There's going to be a new headteacher in September, who is good. It's time for a change

A. who are
B. that is
C. which is
D. No improvement required

Q.40 He slapped the team into action and they headed for the town at a **more leisure pace**.

[IBPS PO, 2021]

A. many leisurely
B. many leisured
C. more leisurely pace
D. No improvement required

Q.41 I have great **antipathy towards** the people who are born with a silver spoon.

A. antipathy for
B. antipathy to
C. antipathy against
D. No correction required

Ques (42-43):Direction: A sentence/ a part of the sentence is underlined. Five alternatives are given to the underlined part which will improve the meaning of the sentence. Choose the correct alternative. In case no improvement is needed, click the option corresponding to 'No improvement'.

Q.42 The arrest of five prominent activists by the Pune police on a coordinated operation across four States has resulted in such indignation.

A. by a coordinated operation
B. in a coordinated operation
C. to a coordinated operation
D. a coordinated operation

Q.43 Yoga develops the functioning of deep organs included oxygenation of the brain and skin

A. including oxygenation
B. included by oxgenation
C. includes oxygen
D. No improvement

Ques (44-45):Direction: In the following questions, some part of the sentence is underlined. Which of the options given below the sentence should replace the part underlined to make the sentence grammatically correct? If the sentence is correct as it is given then choose option (D) 'No Correction required' as the answer.

Q.44 He is a very lazy person and hate doing any kind of work.

A. hated doing
B. hate does
C. hates doing
D. No correction required

Q.45 If he were in Australia he would be getting up now.

A. were been getting
B. had been getting
C. has being getting
D. No correction required

// Smart Answer Sheet //

Correct   Indicates percentage of students who answered questions correctly.

Skipped   Indicates percentage of students who skipped questions.

Q.	Ans.	Correct / Skipped
1	B	62.07 % / 32.21 %
2	B	41.23 % / 40.74 %
3	B	53.24 % / 33.66 %
4	A	43.96 % / 49.68 %
5	C	54.17 % / 41.89 %
6	C	82.64 % / 14.99 %
7	B	80.08 % / 10.91 %
8	D	87.4 % / 10.27 %
9	C	76.06 % / 12.03 %

Q.	Ans.	Correct / Skipped
10	A	81.11 % / 10.36 %
11	D	62.52 % / 33.69 %
12	D	84.83 % / 12.64 %
13	C	83.95 % / 11.95 %
14	D	28.61 % / 71.29 %
15	D	57.39 % / 38.2 %
16	C	87.17 % / 12.15 %
17	C	63.1 % / 31.71 %
18	D	48.83 % / 44.32 %

Q.	Ans.	Correct / Skipped
19	D	69.29 % / 30.5 %
20	A	48.51 % / 43.29 %
21	C	76.28 % / 16.23 %
22	B	69.14 % / 30.61 %
23	C	46.84 % / 49.94 %
24	B	25.86 % / 72.02 %
25	A	58.5 % / 32.07 %
26	C	43.34 % / 33.88 %
27	A	55.44 % / 34.05 %

Q.	Ans.	Correct / Skipped
28	A	19.17 % / 80.03 %
29	B	88.21 % / 11.25 %
30	B	52.52 % / 41.67 %
31	C	45.23 % / 36.13 %
32	A	44.69 % / 43.2 %
33	C	45.13 % / 41.25 %
34	A	43.79 % / 51.24 %
35	C	43.92 % / 35.32 %
36	B	86.6 % / 11.69 %

Q.	Ans.	Correct / Skipped
37	D	66.93 % / 31.26 %
38	A	46.32 % / 36.88 %
39	C	58.54 % / 31.25 %
40	C	55.18 % / 43.02 %
41	C	40.81 % / 53.78 %
42	B	66.02 % / 33.12 %
43	A	86.99 % / 11.03 %
44	C	63.2 % / 31.6 %
45	D	62.87 % / 36.57 %

Performance Analysis	
Avg. Score (%)	44.44%
Toppers Score (%)	68.89%
Your Score	

//Hints and Solutions//

1. The meaning of given phrases:

- Look up means to become better.
- Look into means to try to discover the facts about something such as a problem.
- Look for means to search for someone or something..
- Look after means to take care of someone or something.

From the meanings, it is clear that looking for should be used in place of looking up to make a sentence grammatically correct.

I am **looking for** my keys but I am unable to find them.

Hence, the correct option is (B).

2. "Who" is always used to refer to people. "That" is always used when you are talking about an object.

So, people in the world that doesn't are replaced with people in the world who don't to make the sentence grammatically correct.

There are very few **people in the world who don't** like ice cream.

Hence, the correct option is (B).

3. The given sentence is an example of subject-verb inversion with negative adverb fronting.

In other words, when a negative adverb (e.g. no sooner . . . than) heads a sentence, an auxiliary verb (e.g. did) changes places with the subject (e.g. the bell).

We need an auxiliary verb for the inversion to work here, so we should replace "do" with "did" and we also change the verb according to the tense to make the sentence grammatically correct.

So, the correct sentence is: No sooner **did the bells ring** than the students ran out of their classes.

Hence, the correct option is (B).

4. The underlined part is grammatically incorrect.

The modal 'should' is always followed by a base form of the verb.

e.g. You should help him.

But in the underlined part, it is followed by the noun "goals".

Thus, add the verb 'be' after the modal 'should'

Option (B): is incorrect as 'to' is followed by 'been' (a V^3).

Option (C): is incorrect as with the plural noun 'goals', the indefinite article 'a' has been used.

Thus, the correct sentence will be: What should be the goals of a vaccination policy during a global pandemic?

Hence, the correct option is (A).

5. 'Exported' is the correct because the sentence is in past tense saying that tulips are always exported to Holland. 'have exported' is wrong because it is in the present perfect tense. 'Export' is in simple present tense and 'had exported' is in the past perfect tense and so both are wrong.

So, the correct sentence is: Every year billions of Tulips are cultivated, a majority of which are grown and exported from Holland.

Hence, the correct option is (C).

6. 'Since' is the correct word because it means from a particular time in the past until the latest point in time.

So, the correct sentence is: Reporters say that Ajith had been a genius since childhood.

Hence, the correct option is (C).

7. 'say' is the correct solution because the sentence is in simple present tense and also 'had say' is grammatically wrong. 'have been saying' is wrong because it is in present perfect continuous tense. 'saying' is wrong because it is in present continuous tense. 'have say' is grammatically wrong.

So the correct solution is, Experts say that people (adults) need at least 6 hours of sleep every night.

Hence, the correct option is (B).

8. The correct phrase to be used is of the opinion. It means to have a certain belief or opinion about someone or something. So, the phrase is correctly used in the sentence and we need no improvement

Hence, the correct option is (D).

9. The most appropriate preposition that can be used before India is across.

In the given context, 'across' means from one side to the other of something which has limits or sides such as a city, river or road.

It means POSHAN Abhiyan is improving nutrition indicators across the lengths and breadths of entire India.

Correct Sentence: POSHAN Abhiyaan or the National Nutrition Mission is playing a major role in improving nutrition indicators across India.

Hence, the correct option is (C).

10. Anemia is a result of a lack of red blood cells in the body which leads to reduced oxygen flow to the body's organs. This causes fatigue, dizziness and shortness of breath. Anemic describes a person who is suffering from anemia.

Correct sentence : While every fifth child under the age five is vitamin A deficient, one in every third baby has vitamin B12 deficiency and two out of every five children are anemic.

Hence, the correct option is (A).

11. Affect means to influence something or someone. Effect, when used as a noun, means the result of an influence. When used as a verb, effect means to bring about or cause something to occur.

Hence, the correct option is (D).

12. As----as is used to compare two things.

Since we are comparing the price of a house ' as high as ' will be used here.

Note: There are no phrases as 'so high so', 'as high to' and 'so high to', and 'as higher' does not form a meaningful sentence when put in this sentence.

Hence, the correct option is (D).

13. The phrase 'it relied heavily upon' does not match the tense of the sentence. The tense of the sentence is simple present tense. But the phrase is in the past tense and is therefore incorrect.

'It relied heavily on' is the same as 'it relied heavily upon' and is therefore rejected.

'It rely heavily upon' is grammatically incorrect and therefore cannot be used.

'It has been relying heavily upon' is incorrect as it makes the sentence belong to the present progressive tense.

'It relies heavily upon' is also grammatically correct as it makes the sentence belong to the simple present tense.

Hence, the correct option is (B).

14. The phrase 'for defeat of God's will' is grammatically incorrect and needs to be corrected.

'At defeat of God's will' is grammatically incorrect and is therefore rejected.

'To defeat God's will', 'At defeating the will of God' and 'In defeating God's will' are correct answers as they fit the grammatical texture of the sentence without changing the meaning of it.

Hence, the correct option is (D).

15. The sentence provided to us is in the Simple Past tense. The phrase 'contends that the' does not follow the tense of the sentence and is therefore incorrect.

'Contend that the' is in the present tense and therefore cannot be used.

'Contending that the' cannot be used as 'contending' is the present participle of the word 'contend'.

'Contended that the' is correct as it fits the tense of the sentence.

'Avowed that the' is correct as it carries the same meaning as the word 'contended' and is also in the correct tense.

Hence, the correct option is (D).

16. The 'Solitary Reaper' is one of the best poems composed by William Wordsworth.

The sentence is comparing poems by William Wordsworth and thus 'one of the best' poems conveys a superlative degree of comparison between the poems and hence is the right answer.

Hence, the correct option is (C).

17. The word "extirpated" means to eradicate or destroy completely and "eradicated" means destroy completely or put an end to.

Therefore, "extirpated" can be replaced with "eradicated" without changing the meaning of the sentence.

Hence, the correct option is (C).

18. Slander: a false spoken statement about someone that damages their reputation, or the making of such a statement

Disparity: lack of equality or similarity, especially in a way that is not fair

Thus, the word 'Slander' should be replaced with 'Disparity' to form a contextually correct sentence.

Hence, the correct option is (D).

19. Compassion: a strong feeling of sympathy and sadness for the suffering of others

Empathy: to have concern or sympathy for others

Inconceivable: Unbelievable

Plausible: (of an argument or statement) seeming reasonable or probable

Indestructible: not able to be destroyed

Therefore, from the given options, the best alternative for the emboldened word is 'empathy'.

Hence, the correct option is (D).

20. The phrasal verb 'Looked up' means 'searched for or located and visited'.

1. I looked up the important points.

2. You should have looked me up when you were in London.

3. I looked up the story.

Hence, the correct option is (A).

21. Take out means 'to remove something from a pocket, bag etc.' Eg- Take out the things from the cupboard.

1. I will take out all the letters.

2. Take out the trash and come here.

3. He will take out the old furniture.

Hence, the correct option is (C).

22. Wistful means having a feeling of vague or longing so the correct word to replace it would be Nostalgic which means a sentimental longing or wistful affection.

Cynical means to be concerned with one's own interests.

Cutesy means cute to a sentimental extent.

Hence, the correct option is (B).

23. Out of the blue is replaced by the word Serendipitous which means occurring or discovered by chance in a happy or beneficial way.

Zemblanity means unpleasant unsurprise.

Misfortune means an unlucky thing or something bad that has happened.

Hence, the correct option is (C).

24. At the drop of the hat means to do things quickly or without hesitation. So the correct word to replace it would be promptly which means quickly.

Grudgingly means reluctantly, it's wrong because Reena was happy to do work and same goes for unwillingly.

Hence, the correct option is (B).

25. 'Break in' means forced entry into a place. Example: Someone had broken in through the bedroom window. This sentence uses the past participle form of 'break'.

1. The break in had occurred just before midnight.

2. The two robbers had an alibi for the time period of the break in.

3. The would-be thieves had smashed the door lock in an attempt to break in.

Hence, the correct option is (A).

26. The phrase 'Hang in there' means 'to continue doing something in a determined way even though it is difficult'. Eg- Hang in there until I come back.

1. Work can get difficult but you just need to hang in there.

2. The second half of the movie was so horrible but we just had to hang in there.

3. You need to hang in there till the driver returns.

Hence, the correct option is (C).

27. The phrasal verb 'Cut off' means 'to remove something by cutting it or to make a place difficult or impossible to enter, leave, or communicate with'. Eg- His leg was cut off to remove the infection.

1. Cut off this item from the list.

2. He tried to cut off sweets.

3. The floods cut off all communication.

Hence, the correct option is (A).

28. Abound in means: to be filled with (something) : contain a very large amount of (something)

1. The story does, however, abound in felicities; the physical descriptions of the planet, for example, are superb.

2. While other ions abound in cytoplasm in their millimoles, liberal estimates of free Ca concentrations run around 0.1 micromolar, maximum.

3. Examples abound in the professions, for example, the question of auditors and joint-stock companies, or solicitors and conveyancing.

Hence, the correct option is (A).

29. Angle for means to try to make someone give you something without asking for it directly. Example: She didn't want Ron thinking that she was angling for sympathy.

1. People are angling for new jobs at hedge funds, corporate buyout shops, boutique banks and startups.

2. They were angling for several tickets to the automobile exhibition show.

3. He's been angling for an invitation, but I don't want him to come.

Hence, the correct option is (B).

30. The phrasal verb 'Chip in' means 'to give some money to pay for something'. Eg- We should all chip in to tidy the room.

1. We will chip in to pay his bills.

2. I will chip in to collect money for the campaign.

3. He will chip in to serve the meal.

Hence, the correct option is (B).

31. Act on means To take action because of something like information received. Example: A patient will usually listen to the doctor's advice and act on it.

1. The police will act on the tip and catch the gang red-handed.

2. It had previously relied on other banks to act on its behalf on an agency basis.

3. Seventeen years later a British government chose to act on that suggestion and dispatch the fleet.

Hence, the correct option is (C).

32. The phrasal verb 'Get back to' means 'return or to phone, write, or speak to someone at a later time because you were busy or could not answer their question earlier'. Eg- Please get back to me with the reports as soon as possible.

1. She promised to get back to after she finishes her work.

2. I don't know when I am going to get back to reading.

3. Can you get back to me with the figures?

Hence, the correct option is (A).

33. The phrasal verb 'Broke in' means 'interrupted a conversation; entered by force'. Eg- Someone had broken in through the bedroom window.

1. He suddenly broke in saying, 'It's a lie'.

2. 'Hey', she broke in, 'I'm just trying to help.'

3. We broke in but we weren't able to find him.

Hence, the correct option is (C).

34. The phrasal verb 'ask around' means 'to ask several people for information or advice or help.' Eg- I asked around, but nobody had seen him for days

1. He had to ask around for some food.

2. You need to ask around for your car.

3. We will have to ask around for help.

Hence, the correct option is (A).

35. Come apart means become separated into pieces or fragments. Example: I picked up the book and it just came apart in my hands.

1. The top and bottom come apart if you pull hard enough.

2. My whole life had come apart at the seams.

3. After the first act, the play begins to come apart at the seams

Hence, the correct option is (C).

36. The phrasal verb 'bawled out' means 'criticized. Eg- They bawled him out for arriving late.

1. He always bawled people out in the meetings.

2. Her mother bawled her out for forgetting the meeting.

3. When he heard the news, he bawled out.

Hence, the correct option is (B).

37. The underlined phrases do not have to be improved because:

'Eat out' means 'to have a meal in a restaurant instead of at home'.

'Do away with' means 'to get rid of something'.

'Counting on' means 'depending on someone to do what you want or expect them to do for you'.

All these phrases fit the sentences properly and make them grammatically and contextually correct.

Hence, the correct option is (D).

38. Point of time (ago) in the past indicates that the action took place at a point in the past. Thus, the action is mentioned in the simple past. For example: I returned to Mumbai two days ago.

The point of time in the past is expressed by since, ever since, last, yesterday, ago, before, etc.

Therefore, the correct sentence is: John Snow returned to Castle Black one month ago.

Hence, the correct option is (A).

39. In the given sentence, the emboldened part **who is** is grammatically incorrect.

Which is used to refer to something previously mentioned when introducing a clause giving further information.

Here, which is good refers to the whole situation of getting a new headteacher in September and not just the headteacher.

So, the correct sentence is, There's going to be a new headteacher in September, which is good. It's time for a change.

Hence, the correct option is (C).

40. In the sentence, more leisure pace is grammatically incorrect.

In the emboldened part, the word leisure is a noun that is followed by another noun pace.

Here, the adjective of leisure i.e. leisurely which means acting, proceeding, or done without haste must be used to describe the noun pace.

So, the correct sentence is, He slapped the team into action and they headed for the town at a more leisurely pace.

Hence, the correct option is (C).

41. 'Antipathy against' will replace 'antipathy towards'

antipathy means hatred or scorn.

Therefore, the correct sentence is: I have great antipathy against the people who are born with a silver spoon.

Hence, the correct option is (C).

42. The preposition 'on' has been incorrectly used in the underlined part of the sentence.

'On' is generally used to denote the position for surfaces or a position just above or outside an area or to show the state of something.

'A coordinated operation' refers to an activity that is in a position with space limitations i.e., it is not spread out all over the country.

Thus, 'in a coordinated operation' is the correct replacement for the underlined phrase.

Hence, the correct option is (B).

43. The error is in the usage of 'included' in the underlined part. The sentence talks about Yoga and its benefits.

The correct word for the underlined part must be 'including' which means containing as part of the whole being considered. In the sentence, the word 'functioning' is in the continuous form so the verb 'include' must also be in continuous form.

'included oxygenation' must be replaced with 'including oxygenation'.

Hence, the correct option is (A).

44. He is a very lazy person and hates doing any kind of work.

The underlined part must be replaced with 'hates doing' as the verb 'hate' has to be in agreement with the the subject 'He' which is singular in number.

Hence, the correct option is (C).

45. The sentence talks of a hypothetical. The future continuous tense is appropriate here. However, the use of 'were" in the sentence means we need to modify 'will' to its 'past tense form' i.e., 'would'. So the correct phrase would be 'would be getting'. Therefore, no correction is needed.

Hence, the correct option is (D).

Q.1 Direction: A sentence has been given in Active/Passive Voice. Out of the four alternatives suggested, select the one which best expresses the same sentence in Passive/Active Voice.

By whom was this window broken? Five packets of milk were delivered by the milkman.

A. Who broke this window? The milkman delivered five packets of milk.

B. Who had broke this window? The milkman had delivered five packets of milk.

C. Whom was break this window? The milkman will deliver five packets of milk.

D. Who is breaking this window? The milkman is delivering five packets of milk.

Q.2 Direction: Choose the option that is the active form of the sentence.

The politician's speech was loudly cheered.

A. The audience cheer the politician's loud speech.

B. The audience was loudly cheered by the politician's speech.

C. The audience loudly cheered the politician's speech.

D. The audience had been loudly cheered by the politician.

Q.3 Direction: Choose the option that is the active form of the sentence.

The child tore the page of the book.

A. The page of the book was torn by the child.

B. The page of the book tore by the child.

C. The book's page is torn by the child.

D. The page of the book is tearing by the child.

Q.4 Direction: Choose the option that is the active form of the sentence.

Shyam saw Abhishek starting the car.

A. Abhishek has seen Shyam starting the car.

B. Abhishek can be seen starting the car by Shyam.

C. Abhishek was seen starting the car by Shyam.

D. Abhishek was saw by Shyam starting the car.

Q.5 Direction: Choose the option that is the active form of the sentence.

The little puppy chewed my new slippers.

A. My new slippers were chewing the little puppy.

B. My new slippers can be chewed by the little puppy.

C. My new slippers were chewed by the little puppy.

D. My new slippers are being chew by the little puppy.

Q.6 Direction: Choose the option that is the active form of the sentence.

Give the command.

A. Let the command be given.

B. You can give the command.

C. The command can be given.

D. The command should be give by you.

Q.7 Direction: Choose the option that is the active form of the sentence.

The class teacher was taking the children to the zoo.

A. The children will go to the zoo by their class teacher.

B. The children can be taking to the zoo by their class teacher.

C. The children being taken to the zoo by their class teacher.

D. The children were being taken to the zoo by their class teacher.

Ques (8-9):Direction: Choose the option that is the active form of the sentence.

Q.8 The manager permitted women employees to leave the office early on that day.

A. Women employees permitted the manager to leave the office early on that day.

B. Women employees had to leave the office early on that day.

C. Women employees should leave the office early on that day.

D. Women employees were permitted to leave the office early on that day.

Q.9 An award was given to the film 'Andhaa Dhund.'

A. The jury had given the film 'Andhaa Dhund' an award.

B. The jury gave the film 'Andhaa Dhund' an award.

C. The jury was gave the film 'Andhaa Dhund' an award.

D. The jury will give the award to the film 'Andhaa Dhund'.

Ques (10-13):Direction: Choose the option that is the passive form of the sentence.

Q.10 I burnt my hand yesterday while cooking.

A. My hand was burning yesterday while cooking.

B. My hand could be burnt yesterday while cooking.

C. My hand was burnt yesterday while cooking.

D. My hand will be burnt yesterday while cooking.

Q.11 The Municipal Corporation changed the manhole covers before the rainy season.

A. The manhole covers is being changed before the rainy season.

B. The manhole covers are change before the rainy season.

C. The manhole covers were changed before the rainy season.

D. The manhole covers can be changed before the rainy season.

Q.12 Switch off the television.

A. Can you switch off the television?

B. May I switch off the television?

C. Let the television be switched off.

D. Let the television being switch off

Q.13 They considered it an impressive building.
A. It was considered to be an impressive building.
B. It can be consider to be an impressive building.
C. It was considering to being an impressive building.
D. It is considered to be an impressive building.

Q.14 Direction: Choose the option that is the active form of the sentence.
By whom was this poem written?
A. Who wrote this poem?
B. Who is wrote this poem?
C. Who write this poem?
D. This poem is wrote by whom?

Ques (15-17):Direction: Choose the option that is the passive form of the sentence.

Q.15 The tennis ball hit Dhiraj on the head.
A. Dhiraj had been hit on the head by the tennis ball.
B. Dhiraj was hit on the head by the tennis ball.
C. The tennis ball was being hit by Dhiraj.
D. Dhiraj was being hit on the head by the tennis ball.

Q.16 They found her guilty of theft.
A. She found them guilty of theft.
B. She was found guilty of theft.
C. She had been find guilty of theft.
D. She is find guilty of theft by them.

Q.17 The fisherman caught a large fish.
A. A large fish should be caught by the fisherman.
B. A large fish was catching the fisherman.
C. A large fish was caught by the fisherman.
D. A large fish had been catched by the fisherman.

Q.18 Direction: A sentence has been given in Active/ Passive Voice. Out of the four alternatives suggested, select one which best expresses the same sentence in Passive/Active Voice.
The detective found the lost necklace.
A. The lost necklace should find the detective.
B. The lost necklace was found by the detective.
C. The lost necklace founded by the detective.
D. The lost necklace had been find by the detective.

Ques (19-21):Direction: Choose the option that is the passive form of the sentence.

Q.19 They need 104 more runs to win the match.
A. 104 more runs are needed for them to win the match.
B. 104 more runs will need for them to win the match.
C. They are needed 104 more runs to win the match.
D. 104 more runs can be needed by them to win the match.

Q.20 The security guard opened the gate using his pass.
A. The gate is open by the security guard by using his pass.
B. The gate was opened by the security guard using his pass.
C. The gate opened the security guard using his pass.
D. The gate was open by the security guard use his pass.

Q.21 Avoid taking the flyover.
A. The flyover can be avoid take.
B. The flyover should be avoided.
C. The flyover should avoid taking.
D. The flyover should be avoid.

Q.22 Direction: Choose the option that is the active form of the sentence.
Has your message been despatched?
A. Has your message despatched?
B. Have you despatched your message?
C. Had you despatch your message?
D. Is your message despatching?

Ques (23-24):Direction: Choose the option that is the passive form of the sentence.

Q.23 The first settlers displaced the original inhabitants.
A. The original inhabitants are displacing the first settlers.
B. The original inhabitants were displaced by the first settlers.
C. The original inhabitants will displace the first settlers.
D. The original inhabitants are being displace by the first settlers.

Q.24 You have not yet responded to several of my complaints.
A. Several of my complaints you have not been responded to yet.
B. My complaints are not been responding yet by you.
C. Several of my complaints are not being responded yet.
D. Several of my complaints have not been responded to yet.

Q.25 Direction: Choose the option that is the active form of the sentence.
I am sometimes puzzled by her actions.
A. Her actions are sometimes puzzled by me.
B. Her actions sometimes puzzle me.
C. She can sometimes puzzle me.
D. Her actions were sometimes puzzling me.

Ques (26-35):Direction: In the following question, a sentence has been given in Active/Passive Voice. Out of the four alternatives suggested, select the one which best expresses the same sentence in Passive/Active Voice.

Q.26 He was not given the information he needed.
A. Somebody was not given the information he needed.
B. The information he needed wasn't given to him.
C. He needed the information he wasn't given.
D. They didn't give him the information he needed.

Q.27 Bipin was not told about the meeting.
A. Somebody did not tell Bipin about the meeting.
B. There was nobody who could tell Bipin about the meeting.
C. Nobody told Bipin about the meeting.
D. The meeting was not told about Bipin.

Q.28 End the war now.
A. Now must the war be ended.
B. Let the war be ended now.
C. You must end the war now.
D. Must the war be ended now.

Q.29 Mrs. Vaijanthi teaches us literature.
A. We have been taught literature by Mrs. Vaijanthi.
B. Literature was being taught by Mrs. Vaijanthi to us.
C. Literature is taught to us by Mrs. Vaijanthi.
D. Literature is being taught by Mrs. Vaijanthi to us.

Q.30 Cacao is bitter when it is tasted.
A. Cacao is bitter.
B. Cacao tastes bitter.
C. Cacao's taste is bitter.
D. Cacao tasted bitter.

Q.31 God gives us happiness.
A. Happiness is given by God.
B. Happiness is being given to us by God.
C. Happiness has been given by God.
D. Happiness will be given by God.

Q.32 A lot of saplings have been planted by the chief guest.
A. The chief guest is planting a lot of saplings.
B. The chief guest has planted a lot of saplings.
C. The chief guest have planted a lot of sapling.
D. The chief guest has been planting a lot of saplings.

Q.33 The invitation cards will be sent today.
A. They will sent the invitation cards today.
B. They will have sent the invitation cards today.
C. They will send the invitation cards today.
D. They will be sending the invitation cards today.

Q.34 How much a month are you paid?
A. How much a month do you pay?
B. In a month how much do you pay?
C. How much a month do they pay you?
D. How much a month do you pay the?

Q.35 Who taught you to dance?
A. Who did teach you to dance?
B. By who were you taught to dance?
C. You were taught to dance by who?
D. By whom were you taught to dance?

Ques (36-45):Direction: In the following question, a sentence has been given in Active/Passive Voice. Out of the four alternatives suggested, select the one which best expresses the same sentence in Passive/Active Voice.

Q.36 Students asked many questions to their teacher.
A. Many teachers were asked questions by the students.
B. The teacher was asked many questions by their students.
C. Their teacher was asked many questions by the students.
D. Their teachers were asked many questions by the students.

Q.37 Your mother called you many times.
A. You was called many times by your mother.
B. You were being called many times by your mother.
C. You called many times by your mother
D. You were called many times by your mother.

Q.38 They were playing hockey in the garden.
A. Hockey is being played by them in the garden.
B. Hockey was played by them in the garden.
C. Hockey were being played by them in the garden.
D. Hockey was being played by them in the garden.

Q.39 Mohan has not eaten anything.
A. Nothing has not been eaten by Mohan.
B. Mohan does not eat anything.
C. Nothing has been eaten by Mohan.
D. Anything had not been eaten by Mohan.

Q.40 Call the police.
A. Let the police be called.
B. Let us be called by the police.
C. The police be called by you.
D. We are calling the police.

Q.41 I have to complete this task by tomorrow.
A. This task had to be completed by me by the next day.
B. This task have to be completed by me by tomorrow.
C. This task has to be completed by me by tomorrow.
D. I will be completing this task by tomorrow.

Q.42 Who helped you with your homework?
A. By who was you helped with your homework?
B. By whom were you helped with your homework?
C. Your homework was helped by whom?
D. Who had helped you with your homework?

Q.43 Why didn't you help your friend?
A. Why were your friend helped by you?
B. Why did your friend not helped by you?
C. Why was your friend not helped by you?
D. Why were you not helping your friend?

Q.44 You should forget the past.
A. Past must be forgotten by you.
B. You should be forgotten by the past.
C. The past should being forgotten by you.
D. The past should be forgotten by you.

Q.45 Kids love chocolate.
A. Chocolate is loved by kids.
B. Chocolate are loved by kids.
C. Chocolate is being loved by kids.
D. Chocolate was loved by kids.

// Smart Answer Sheet //

Correct Indicates percentage of students who answered questions correctly.

Skipped Indicates percentage of students who skipped questions.

Q.	Ans.	Correct / Skipped
1	A	26.96 % / 67.52 %
2	C	51.64 % / 36.66 %
3	A	32.14 % / 67.36 %
4	C	13.55 % / 68.84 %
5	C	66.74 % / 32.31 %
6	A	79.96 % / 11.03 %
7	D	64.77 % / 30.39 %
8	D	84.61 % / 14.59 %
9	B	24.88 % / 70.65 %

Q.	Ans.	Correct / Skipped
10	C	68.1 % / 30.27 %
11	C	17.77 % / 75.57 %
12	C	68.94 % / 30.7 %
13	A	44.63 % / 37.95 %
14	A	80.6 % / 11.09 %
15	B	15.82 % / 69.15 %
16	B	45.58 % / 38.27 %
17	C	45.26 % / 34.45 %
18	B	69.4 % / 30.05 %

Q.	Ans.	Correct / Skipped
19	A	40.52 % / 50.19 %
20	B	85.56 % / 11.91 %
21	B	13.7 % / 74.88 %
22	B	63.8 % / 31.8 %
23	B	52.8 % / 41.71 %
24	D	21.07 % / 74.99 %
25	B	42.65 % / 40.82 %
26	D	18.2 % / 75.73 %
27	C	29.86 % / 69.87 %

Q.	Ans.	Correct / Skipped
28	B	61.23 % / 32.92 %
29	C	85.21 % / 13.7 %
30	B	15.84 % / 76.89 %
31	A	86.42 % / 10.33 %
32	B	45.42 % / 42.11 %
33	C	68.41 % / 31.01 %
34	C	54.41 % / 42.29 %
35	D	43.59 % / 40.02 %
36	C	49.43 % / 30.08 %

Q.	Ans.	Correct / Skipped
37	D	47.1 % / 50.32 %
38	D	47.57 % / 38.41 %
39	C	50.03 % / 34.23 %
40	A	47.11 % / 51.56 %
41	C	46.07 % / 31.2 %
42	B	51.64 % / 46.45 %
43	C	68.03 % / 31.62 %
44	D	47.86 % / 41.68 %
45	A	80.75 % / 15.72 %

Performance Analysis	
Avg. Score (%)	51.11%
Toppers Score (%)	55.56%
Your Score	

//Hints and Solutions//

1. The sentence becomes: Who broke this window? The milkman delivered five packets of milk.

The sentence is given in passive voice to convert it into active:

- While converting the voice, the subject and the object change their place:
- 'Who' becomes the subject. ('Whom' works as the object in the interrogative statement).
- In an assertive statement: 'The milkman' becomes the subject and 'Five packets of the milk' becomes the object.
- Preposition 'by' before the object is removed.
- 'was/were + V_3' in passive voice is changed into 'V_2' in active voice.

Hence, the correct option is (A).

2. The correct answer is:

'The audience loudly cheered the politician's speech.'

In the active form, the subject and the object will get interchanged. So, 'the politician's speech' will become the object. The passive form contains 'was' which means the active form must be in the past tense.

Option (A) is in the present tense.

Option (B) changes the meaning.

Option (D) is in the past perfect tense.

Rules of Conversion from Passive to Active Voice:

1. Identify the subject, the verb and the object: S+V+O.
2. Change the subject into object.
3. Omit the suitable helping verb or auxiliary verb.
4. Change the past participle to simple past tense form of the verb.
5. Omit the preposition "by".
6. Change the object into subject.

Hence, the correct option is (C).

3. The above-given sentence is in the active voice.

We need to change it in the passive voice.

The following steps are required to change the given sentence into passive voice:-

- The subject 'the child' of the active voice will become the object of the passive voice.
- The object 'the page of the book' of the active voice will become the subject of the passive voice.
- The tense(simple past tense) will change according to the following structure:-
  - Active Voice - Subject + did + V_1 or V_2 (tore) + Object.
  - Passive Voice - Object + was/were + V_3 (torn) + by + Object.

Therefore, the correct passive voice is The page of the book was torn by the child.

Hence, the correct option is (A).

4. The correct answer is:

'Abhishek was seen starting the car by Shyam.'

In the passive form, the subject and the object get interchanged.

'Abhishek' will become the subject in the passive form.

The sentence is in the past continuous tense.

So, the passive form will be- subject+ was + past participle form of verb + continuous form of verb + object.

Hence, the correct option is (C).

5. The correct answer is 'My new slippers were chewed by the little puppy'.

The instructions given below should be followed while changing an assertive sentence to a passive voice.

- Find the subject and object of the sentence and exchange their places; make changes in their cases as well if subject and object are pronouns.
- Use preposition 'by' before the agent.
- Use an appropriate helping verb in passive form according to the tense of the active form.
- Always use the third form of the main verb in passive form.
- At last line up the remaining part.

Now let us look at the question:

The subject will become "my new slippers".

The active form contains the past participle form of verb i.e. chewed so the passive form will be in past tense form.

Option (A) is in past continuous form.

Option (B) contains 'can' which is incorrect.

Option (D) is in present continuous form.

Hence, the correct option is (C).

6. The given sentence is an imperative sentence.

The instructions given below should be followed while changing an imperative sentence to passive voice.

Find the subject and object of the sentence and exchange their places; make changes in their cases as well if subject and object are pronouns.

The passive form will be:

Let + object(the command) + be + past participle form (given). For Example:

Active Voice: Open the door.

Passive Voice: Let the door (object) be opened (be + past participle or V_3).

Active Voice: Please calculate the bill.

Passive Voice: Let the bill (object) be calculated (be + past participle or V_3).

Hence, the correct option is (A).

7. The correct answer is:

The children were being taken to the zoo by their class teacher.

The above-given sentence is in the active voice.

We need to change it into passive voice.

We need to follow the given steps for converting the sentence into passive voice:-

- The subject 'the class teacher' of the active voice becomes the object of the passive voice.
- The object 'the children' of the active voice becomes the subject of the passive voice.
- The tense(past continuous tense) will be changed according to the following structure:-
    - Active Voice - Subject + was/were + V_{ing} + Object.
    - Passive Voice - Object + was/were + being + V_3 + Subject.
- Thus, 'was taking' will be replaced by 'were being taken'.
- The rest of the sentence remains the same.

Hence, the correct option is (D).

8. The correct answer is:

Women employees were permitted to leave the office early on that day.

The above-given sentence is in the active voice.

We need to change it in the passive voice.

The following steps are required to change the given sentence into passive voice:

- The subject 'the manager' of the active voice will become the object of the passive voice.
- The object 'women employees' of the active voice will become the subject of the passive voice.
- The tense(simple past tense) will change according to the following structure:-
    - Active Voice - Subject + did + V_1 or V_2 + Object.
    - Passive Voice - Object + was/were + V_3 + by + Object.
- Thus, 'permitted' will be replaced by 'were permitted'.
- The rest of the sentence remains the same.

Hence, the correct option is (D).

9. The correct answer is:

'The jury gave the film 'Andhaa Dhund' an award.'

In the active form, the subject and the object will get interchanged.

In the active form 'award' will become the object.

The passive form contains 'was' + past participle form of verb so the active form will contain the past participle form of the verb.

Option (A) is in past perfect tense.

Option (C) is grammatically incorrect. 'Was gave' is totally incorrect.

Option (D) is in future tense because the word 'will' is used.

Hence, the correct option is (B).

10. The correct answer is:

My hand was burnt yesterday while cooking.

In the passive form, the subject and the object will be interchanged. So, 'my hand' will become the subject. The sentence uses the past participle form of the verb i.e., burnt. The passive form will be in the past tense.

Option (A) is in past continuous tense.

Option (B) uses could which should be used only when 'can' is there in the active form.

Option (D) is in future tense.

Hence, the correct option is (C).

11. The above-given sentence is in the active voice.

We need to change it in the passive voice.

The following steps are required to change the given sentence into passive voice:

- The subject 'the Municipal Corporation' of the active voice will become the object of the passive voice.
- The object 'the manhole covers' of the active voice will become the subject of the passive voice.
- The tense(simple past tense) will change according to the following structure:-
    - Active Voice - Subject + did + V_1 or V_2 + Object.
    - Passive Voice - Object + was/were + V_3 + by + Object.

Hence, the correct option is (C).

12. The passive voice of the given sentence is:

Let the television be switched off.

The given sentence is an imperative sentence.

The instructions given below should be followed while changing an imperative sentence to passive voice.

Find the subject and object of the sentence and exchange their places; make changes in their cases as well if subject and object are pronouns.

The passive form will be - Let + object (the command) + be + past participle form.

Hence, the correct option is (C).

13. The above-given sentence is in the active voice.

We need to change it in the passive voice.

The following steps are required to change the given sentence into passive voice:

- In the passive form, the subject and the object will be interchanged. 'It' will become the subject.
- The tense(simple past tense) will change according to the following structure:-
    - Active Voice - Subject + did + V_1 or V_2 + Object.
    - Passive Voice - Object + was/were + V_3 + by + Object.

Option (B) and (D) are in the present tense.

Option (C) is in the past continuous tense.

Hence, the correct option is (A).

14. The above-given sentence is in the passive voice.

We need to change it into an active voice.

We need to follow the given steps for converting the given sentence into active voice:

- In sentences containing 'who', the passive starts with 'by whom'.
- The following structure is followed:-
    - Active Voice - Who + V_1 + Object?
    - Passive Voice - By whom + helping verb + Object + V_3?
- Thus, 'written' will be converted to 'wrote'.

Hence, the correct option is (A).

15. Dhiraj was hit on the head by the tennis ball.

The above-given sentence is in the active voice.

We need to change it in the passive voice.

The following steps are required to change the given sentence into passive voice:

- The subject 'the tennis ball' of the active voice will become the object of the passive voice.
- The object 'Dhiraj' of the active voice will become the subject of the passive voice.
- The tense(simple past tense) will change according to the following structure:-
    - Active Voice - Subject + did + V_1 or V_2 + Object.
    - Passive Voice - Object + was/were + V_3 + by + Object.
- Thus, 'hit' will be converted to 'was hit'.

Hence, the correct option is (B).

16. The correct answer is:

She was found guilty of theft.

The voice of a verb tells whether the subject of the sentence performs or receives the action.

In active voice, the subject (agent) acts upon the verb; while in passive, the verb acts upon the subject (agent).

Rules of Conversion from Active to Passive Voice:

1. Identify the subject, the verb and the object: S+V+O.
2. Change the object into subject.
3. Put the suitable helping verb or auxiliary verb.
4. Change the verb into past participle of the verb.
5. Add the preposition "by".
6. Change the subject into object.

Option (B) follows all the proper conversion rules.

Hence, the correct option is (B).

17. The correct answer is:

A large fish was caught by the fisherman.

The voice of a verb tells whether the subject of the sentence performs or receives the action.

In active voice, the subject (agent) acts upon the verb; while in passive, the verb acts upon the subject (agent).

Rules of Conversion from Active to Passive Voice:

- Identify the subject, the verb and the object: S+V+O
- Change the object into subject
- Put the suitable helping verb or auxiliary verb
- Change the verb into past participle of the verb
- Add the preposition "by"
- Change the subject into object

Option (C) follows the rules of transformation clearly.

Hence, the correct option is (C).

18. The correct answer is:

The lost necklace was found by the detective. as it follows all the necessary rules for sentence transformation.

The voice of a verb tells whether the subject of the sentence performs or receives the action.

The sentence in question is in the active voice. The principal verb is the simple past tense form of the verb 'find'.

Rules of Conversion from Active to Passive Voice:

1. Identify the subject, the verb and the object: S+V+O.
2. Change the object into subject.
3. Add suitable helping verb or auxiliary verb according to the tense present in the sentence.
4. Change the verb into past participle of the verb.

5.   Add the preposition "by".

6.   Change the subject into object.

Option (B) follows all the required rules of sentence transformation.

Hence, the correct option is (B).

19. The correct answer is:

"104 more runs are needed for them to win the match."

The sentence in question is in active voice. The principal verb in the sentence is in the simple present tense.

Rules of Conversion from Active to Passive Voice:

- Identify the subject, the verb, and the object: S+V+O
- Change the object into subject
- Add suitable helping verb or auxiliary verb
- Change the main verb into past participle form
- Add the preposition "by" or "for"
- Change the subject into object.

Example:

Active Voice: Sameer wrote a letter. (Subject) + (verb) + (object).

Passive Voice: A letter was written by Sameer. (Object) + (auxiliary verb) + (past participle) + (by subject).

Option (A) follows all the sentence transformation rules correctly.

Hence, the correct option is (A).

20. The gate was opened by the security guard using his pass.

The above-given sentence is in the active voice.

We need to change it in the passive voice.

The following steps are required to change the given sentence into passive voice:

- The subject 'the security guard' of the active voice will become the object of the passive voice.
- The object 'the gate' of the active voice will become the subject of the passive voice.
- The tense (simple past tense) will change according to the following structure:-
    - Active Voice - Subject + did + V_1 or V_2 + Object.
    - Passive Voice - Object + was/were + V_3 + by + Object.
- Thus, 'opened' will be converted to 'was opened'.

Hence, the correct option is (B).

21. The correct sentence would be:

The flyover should be avoided.

The voice of a verb tells whether the subject of the sentence performs or receives the action.

Rules of Conversion from Active to Passive Voice:

1.   Identify the subject, the verb and the object: S+V+O.

2.   Change the object into subject.

3.   Put the suitable helping verb or auxiliary verb.

4.   Change the verb into past participle of the verb.

5.   Add the preposition "by".

6.   Change the subject into object.

Option (B) follows all the parameters.

Hence, the correct option is (B).

22. The correct answer is:

Have you despatched your message?

The voice of a verb tells whether the subject of the sentence performs or receives the action.

Rules of Conversion from Passive to Active Voice:

1.   Identify the subject, the verb and the object: S+V+O

2.   Change the subject into object

3.   Omit the suitable helping verb or auxiliary verb

4.   Change the past participle of the verb into its simple form.

5.   Remove the preposition "by"

6.   Change the object into subject.

Option (B) only fulfils all the conversion criteria.

Hence, the correct option is (B).

23. The above-given sentence is in the active voice.

We need to change it in the passive voice.

The following steps are required to change the given sentence into passive voice:

- The subject 'the first settlers' of the active voice will become the object of the passive voice.
- The object 'the original inhabitants' of the active voice will become the subject of the passive voice.
- The tense(simple past tense) will change according to the following structure:-
    - Active Voice - Subject + did + V_1 or V_2 + Object.
    - Passive Voice - Object + was/were + V_3 + by + Object.
- Thus, 'displaced' will be converted to 'were displaced'.

Hence, the correct option is (B).

24. The correct answer is:

Several of my complaints have not been responded to yet.

The given sentence is in the active voice, hence we need to convert it into the passive voice.

Find the subject (You) and object (several of my complaints) of the sentence and exchange their places during transformation.

'You' will be converted to 'my'.

The given sentence is in the present perfect tense.

The passive verb form for the present perfect is:-

Has/have + been + past participle form of the verb.

So, 'have not yet responded' changes to 'have not been responded to yet'.

At last line up the remaining part.

Hence, the correct option is (D).

25. The above-given sentence is in the passive voice.

We need to change it into active voice:

- The subject 'I' becomes the object 'me' of the active voice.
- The object 'her actions' becomes the subject of the active voice.
- Simple present tense changes in the following manner:-
    - Passive Voice - is/am/are + V_3
    - Active Voice - (do/does + V_1) or (V_1 s/es)
- Thus, 'am sometimes puzzled' will be converted to 'sometimes puzzle'.

Hence, the correct option is (B).

26. The given sentence is in passive form and its structure is:

Passive: Object + was/were (not) + verb (IIIrd form) + (by + subject).

Its active structure would be:

Active: Subject + did not + verb (Ist form) + object.

It is optional to include the part (By + subject) in the passive voice. In sentences where the subject is hidden or not given, we need to create a subject accordingly.

The active form of the given sentence would be:

They didn't give him the information he needed.

Hence, the correct option is (D).

27. The sentence is in passive form and needs to be changed into active voice. The structure for passive/active voice has been shown below:

Passive: Object + was/were + verb (IIIrd form) + (by + subject).

Active: Subject + verb (IInd form) + object.

So, according to the above structure, the active voice of the given sentence would be:

Nobody told Bipin about the meeting.

Hence, the correct option is (C).

28. The given sentence is an imperative sentence. It is given in the form:

Active: Verb + object

So, the passive form of the sentence will be:

Passive: Let + object + be + past participle

So, the passive voice of the given sentence would be:

Let the war be ended now.

Hence, the correct option is (B).

29. The given sentence is in the active voice. It is a simple form of present tense. The structures for active/passive voices are:

Active: Subject + verb ("s" or "es" with singular noun) + object.

Passive: Object + is/are/am + verb (IIIrd form) + by + subject.

So, based on the above structures, we can convert the given sentence into passive voice:

Literature is taught to us by Mrs. Vaijanthi.

Hence, the correct option is (C).

30. The sentence is in the passive voice. Such sentences are called Mid-voice or Quasi-Passive voice. Such sentences seem in active voice but their meaning is in the passive voice. Such sentences have verbs that are intransitive (without a direct object).
In the given sentence, the verb 'taste' is intransitive (without any object) and bitter is the adverb. So, we use "it" to refer to the subject on which the action is being taken. In such sentences, we do not use the connector "by". We use "when".
So, the active form of the sentence will be:

Cacao tastes bitter.

Hence, the correct option is (B).

31. The given sentence is in the active voice. It is a simple form of present tense. The structures for active/passive voices are:

Active: Subject + verb ("s" or "es" with singular noun) + object.

Passive: Object + is/are/am + verb (IIIrd form) + by + subject.

So, based on the above structures, we can convert the given sentence into passive voice:

Happiness is given by God.

Hence, the correct option is (A).

32. The given sentence is in the passive voice and its tense is present perfect. The structures for active/passive voices are:
Active: Subject + has/have + verb (IIIrd form) + object.

Passive: Object + has/have + been + verb (IIIrd form) + by + subject.
So, the active voice of the given sentence would be:

The chief guest has planted a lot of saplings.

Hence, the correct option is (B).

33. The given sentence is in the passive voice of simple future tense. Let us understand the structures for active/passive voices for such sentences.
Active: Subject + will/shall + verb (Ist form) + object.
Passive: Object + will/shall + be + verb (IIIrd form) + by + subject.

So, with the help of the above structures, we can convert the sentence into active voice:

They will send the invitation cards today.

Hence, the correct option is (C).

34. The given sentence is in a passive form of present interrogative tense. The structures for active/passive voices are:

Active: Question word + do/does + subject + verb (Ist form) + object?

Passive: Question word + is/are/am + object + verb (IIIrd from) + by + subject?

So, with the help of the above structures, we can convert the given sentence into active voice:

How much a month do they pay you?

Hence, the correct option is (C).

35. The given sentence is of past interrogative tense that starts with "who". The structures for active/passive for such sentences are:

Active: Who + verb (IInd form) + object?

Passive: By whom + was/were + verb (IIIrd form) + object?

So, the passive sentence would be:

By whom were you taught to dance?

Hence, the correct option is (D).

36. Basic rules to be followed for Active/Passive conversions are:
1. The object of the active verb becomes the subject of the passive verb.
2. The finite form of the verb is changed (to be+ past participle).
3. The subject of the active sentence becomes the object of the passive sentence (or is dropped).
4. Preposition "by" is used before the object.
The given sentence is in the active form of simple past tense. The structures for active/passive voices are:

Active: Subject + verb (IInd form) + object.

Passive: Object + was/were + verb (IIIrd form) + by + subject.

So, with the help of the above structures, we can convert the given sentence into passive voice:

Their teacher was asked many questions by the students.

Hence, the correct option is (C).

37. The given sentence is in the active form of simple past tense. The structures for active/passive voices are:
Active: Subject + verb (IInd form) + object.

Passive: Object + was/were + verb (IIIrd form) + by + subject.

So, with the help of the above structures, we can convert the given sentence into passive voice:

You were called many times by your mother.

Hence, the correct option is (D).

38. The given sentence is in the active voice. Its tense is past continuous. The structures for active/passive voices are:
Active: Subject + was/were + verb (ing) + object.

Passive: Object + was/were + being + verb (IIIrd from) + by + subject.

So, with the help of the above structures, we can convert the given sentence into passive voice:

Hockey was being played by them in the garden.

Hence, the correct option is (D).

39. The given sentence is of present perfect tense and it is in the active form. The structures for active/passive voices are:
Active: Subject + has/have + verb (IIIrd form) + object.

Passive: Object + has/have + been + verb (IIIrd form) + by + subject.

So, the passive voice of the given sentence would be:

Anything has not been eaten by Mohan.

OR

Nothing has been eaten by Mohan.

Hence, the correct option is (C).

40. The passive voice of imperative sentences that suggest order, suggestion, or request can be made in two ways:
Active: Verb + object

Passive: 1. Let + object + be + past participle

2. You are requested/ordered/suggested + to + verb (Ist form) + object

So, the passive voice of the given sentence would be:

Let the police be called.

OR

You are requested to call the police.

Since the first type is given in option A, it is the correct answer.

Hence, the correct option is (A).

41. Sentences, as given in the question, show obligation. The structure for such sentences are:

Active: subject + has/have/had + to + verb1 + object.

Passive: Object + has/have/had + to + verb3 + by + subject.

So, with the help of these structures, we can convert the given sentence in passive voice as:

This task has to be completed by me by tomorrow.

Hence, the correct option is (C).

42. For simple past sentences that start with "who", the following structures are followed for active/passive voice:
Active: Who + verb (IInd form) + object?

Passive: By whom + was/were + object + verb (IIIrd form)?

So, the passive sentence would be:

By whom were you helped with your homework?

Hence, the correct option is (B).

43. The given sentence is in active voice and its tense is past indefinite interrogative tense. The structure for active/passive voice of such sentences are:
Active: Question word + did + subject + verb (Ist form) + object?

Passive: Question word + was/were + object + verb (IIIrd form) + by + subject?

So, the passive voice of the given sentence would be:

Why was your friend not helped by you?

Hence, the correct option is (C).

44. The given sentence is of active voice and it uses a modal verb. The structures for active/passive voices for modal verbs are:
Active: Subject + modal verb + verb (Ist form) + object.

Passive: Object + modal verb + be + verb (IIIrd form) + by + subject.

So, with the help of the above structures, we can convert the given sentence into passive voice:

The past should be forgotten by you.

Hence, the correct option is (D).

45. The given sentence is in the active voice. It is a simple form of present tense. The structures for active/passive voices are:
Active: Subject + verb ("s" or "es" with singular noun) + object.

Passive: Object + Is/are/am + verb (IIIrd form) + by + subject.

So, based on the above structures, we can convert the given sentence into passive voice:
Chocolate is loved by kids.

Hence, the correct option is (A).

Ques (1-12):Direction: Choose the correct alternative which will improve the part of the sentence given in quotes.

Q.1 The gas 'is being seeping' out of the rocks.
[SSC Sub Inspector (CPO), 2018], [SSC Sub Inspector (CPO), 2017]

A. Is seeping
B. Is seep
C. Was being seeping
D. No improvement

Q.2 Captain Ranjith 'safety navigated' his ship without an accident for 100 voyages.
[SSC Sub Inspector (CPO), 2018]

A. Safely navigate
B. Safety navigates
C. Safely navigated
D. No improvement

Q.3 The pedestrians 'should to be' cautious while crossing the road.
[SSC Sub Inspector (CPO), 2018], [SSC Sub Inspector (CPO), 2017]

A. Must not
B. Should be
C. Should not
D. No improvement

Q.4 Some children are much more 'aggressive then' others.
[SSC Sub Inspector (CPO), 2018]

A. Aggressively than
B. Aggressive than
C. Aggressively then
D. No improvement

Q.5 It is raining, "isn't it"?
[SSC Sub Inspector (CPO), 2018], [SSC Sub Inspector (CPO), 2017]

A. Haven't it
B. Hasn't it
C. Weren't it
D. No improvement

Q.6 After a 'period for imprisonment,' she renounced terrorism.
[SSC Sub Inspector (CPO), 2018], [SSC Sub Inspector (CPO), 2017]

A. Period of imprisonment
B. Period out imprisonment
C. Period about imprisonment
D. No improvement

Q.7 Santhosh asked me where 'was my pen'.
[SSC Sub Inspector (CPO), 2018], [SSC Sub Inspector (CPO), 2017]

A. My pen was
B. My pen are
C. Is my pen
D. No improvement

Q.8 Apple's new "operate" system for phones and tablets, iOS 11, is getting some much-sought-after updates.
[SSC Sub Inspector (CPO), 2018], [SSC Sub Inspector (CPO), 2017]

A. Operating
B. Operationals
C. Operated
D. No improvement

Q.9 Our company aims 'on help' students with disabilities to live and study independently.
[SSC Sub Inspector (CPO), 2018], [SSC Sub Inspector (CPO), 2017]

A. In help
B. At help
C. To help
D. No improvement

Q.10 The decision ''will leaving her" in a peculiar predicament.
[SSC Sub Inspector (CPO), 2018], [SSC Sub Inspector (CPO), 2017]

A. Will left her
B. Will leave her
C. Leave
D. No improvement

Q.11 I was born 'in' 16 November in 1986.
[SSC Sub Inspector (CPO), 2018], [SSC Sub Inspector (CPO), 2017]

A. On
B. At
C. For
D. No improvement

Q.12 Sumathi was 'a industrious' and willing worker.
[SSC Sub Inspector (CPO), 2018]

A. An industrious
B. A industrious
C. An industriously
D. No improvement

Ques (13-15):Direction: Improve the bracketed part of the sentence.

Q.13 400 million people speak English as (there first language).
A. There native language
B. Their first language
C. His first language
D. No improvement

Q.14 She could have left then, and might have if curiosity hadn't gotten (best of her).
A. The best of her
B. The most best of her
C. A best of her
D. No improvement

Q.15 You don't recognize me, (don't you)?
A. Didn't you
B. Isn't it
C. Do you
D. No improvement

Ques (16-28):Direction: Select the alternative that will improve the underlined part of the sentence in case there is no improvement select "No improvement".

Q.16 Our cook puts too many salt in the food.
A. No improvement
B. Putting too much
C. Puts too much
D. Puts very much

Q.17 Riya went into the shop because <u>it has sale</u>.
A. No improvement
B. it is having sale
C. it having a sale
D. it had a sale

Q.18 You have to wear this uniform <u>whether you likes it or not</u>.
A. whether you like it or not
B. whether you are liking it or not
C. No improvement
D. Whether if you like it or not

Q.19 You have my mobile number, <u>isn't it</u>?
A. don't you
B. No improvement

C. do you   **D.** has you

Q.20 Many people <u>have become aware of</u> the advantages of preventive health care nowadays.
A. are become aware of
B. will be becoming aware to
C. have becoming aware for
D. No improvement

Q.21 The milk has boiled over and <u>falling onto the stove</u>.
A. falls into the stove
B. fallen onto the stove
C. No improvement
D. fall over in the stove

Q.22 It <u>has been raining very hardly</u> since morning.
A. is been raining very hardly
B. No improvement
C. has been raining very hard
D. have been raining very hardly

Q.23 Dinesh requested the lady at the counter to give him a <u>seat besides the window</u>.
A. No improvement
B. a seat beside the window
C. an seat beside a window
D. one seat besides the window

Q.24 In the major cities <u>cost of life</u> is very high.
A. cost of life are
B. the cost of living are
C. No improvement
D. the cost of living is

Q.25 The floods this year <u>cause a lot of</u> damage to the crops.
A. causing a lot of   **B.** cause lots of
C. have caused a lot of   **D.** No improvement

Q.26 I had to go to Delhi, <u>however, I changed my mind</u> and decided not to go.
A. therefore I change my mind
B. nevertheless I change my mind
C. however I will change my mind
D. No improvement

Q.27 If I had been there <u>I would surely solve</u> the problem for you.
A. I would surely have solved
B. I will surely solves
C. I would surely solving
D. No improvement

Q.28 Ajit <u>has been played bridge since 2017</u>.
A. is been playing bridge from 2017
B. has been play bridge from 2017
C. No improvement
D. has been playing bridge since 2017

Q.29 Diection: Select the alternative that will improve the underlined part of the sentence.

The news reported that the police <u>have catched the guilty</u> person and are interrogating him.
A. had caught the guilty
B. No improvement
C. have caught the guilty
D. are caught a guilty

Ques (30-35):Direction: Select the alternative that will improve the underlined part of the sentence in case there is no improvement select "No improvement".

Q.30 The watchman <u>prevent him from parking</u> his car near the gate.
A. prevents him for parking
B. prevented him to park
C. prevented him from parking
D. No improvement

Q.31 <u>'Did you brought</u> your drawing books?' the teacher asked the students.
A. Did you bring   **B.** Do you bringing
C. Do you brought   **D.** No improvement

Q.32 The children's cricket ball hit their neighbour's window <u>and it broke.</u>
A. and it is broke   **B.** and it broken
C. and it was breaking   **D.** No improvement

Q.33 The only vacant seat in the bus <u>was right in the corner</u>.
A. right on the corner
B. right into the corner
C. right up to the corner
D. No improvement

Q.34 Using seeds <u>for grow more plants</u> is an exceptionally good way of gardening.
A. No improvement
B. to growing more plants
C. to grow more plants
D. for grew more plants

Q.35 <u>Unless Arjun takes a taxi</u> he will not reach the airport in time.
A. However Arjun takes a taxi
B. If Arjun take a taxi
C. No improvement
D. Unless Arjun take taxi

Ques (36-45):Direction: In the following question, a sentence/part of the sentence is printed in bold. Below are given alternatives to the bold sentence/part of the sentence at (A), (B) and (C) which may improve the sentence. Choose the correct alternative. In case no improvement is needed, your answer is an option (D).

Q.36 While crossing the road, **a snake was seen**.
A. A snake was moving
B. He saw a snake
C. A snake was observed
D. No improvement

Q.37 His speech **was broadcasted** over the radio the last Thursday.

A. was broadcast

B. had been broadcast

C. has been broadcast

D. No improvement

Q.38 We had a grand party and we enjoyed very much.

A. We had a grand party and enjoyed very much.

B. We had a grand party to enjoy very much.

C. We had a grand party and we enjoyed ourselves very much.

D. No improvement

Q.39 If I was you, I would not sign the document.

A. If I have been you

B. If I were you

C. If I had been you

D. No improvement

Q.40 If I had gone to Mumbai, **I would surely bring** your books.

A. Would have surely brought

B. Could have surely brought

C. Might have brought

D. No improvement

Q.41 A very horrifying serial **has telecasted** ten days ago.

A. has telecast

B. was telecasted

C. was telecasting

D. No Improvement

Q.42 After the heavy rains last week, the water in the lake **raised another two feet**.

A. rose another two feet

B. rised another two feet

C. would raise another two feet

D. No improvement

Q.43 It is high time, you **go** home.

A. have gone

B. should go

C. went

D. No improvement

Q.44 The constitution of **India guaranteed** each citizen equal rights and privileges.

A. India guarantees

B. Indian guarantees

C. India guarantee

D. No improvement

Q.45 I won't **have you behaving** like that in my office.

A. have you behave

B. have you to behave

C. have you to behaving

D. No improvement

// Smart Answer Sheet //

Correct Indicates percentage of students who answered questions correctly.

Skipped Indicates percentage of students who skipped questions.

Q.	Ans.	Correct / Skipped
1	A	46.42 % / 41.08 %
2	C	79.32 % / 19.37 %
3	B	89.85 % / 10.12 %
4	B	81.31 % / 14.54 %
5	D	48.13 % / 37.91 %
6	A	66.36 % / 32.28 %
7	A	48.89 % / 38.04 %
8	A	57.31 % / 38.12 %
9	C	14.54 % / 74.96 %
10	B	83.96 % / 14.64 %
11	A	23.95 % / 67.7 %
12	A	67.74 % / 30.49 %
13	B	84.06 % / 10.31 %
14	A	76.08 % / 14.25 %
15	C	82.96 % / 13.49 %
16	C	53.28 % / 30.19 %
17	D	76.56 % / 14.94 %
18	A	87.28 % / 11.43 %
19	A	40.22 % / 42.82 %
20	D	53.37 % / 42.89 %
21	B	47.44 % / 32.1 %
22	C	55.26 % / 36.22 %
23	B	46.0 % / 32.83 %
24	D	42.31 % / 40.48 %
25	C	45.11 % / 33.54 %
26	D	25.66 % / 70.21 %
27	A	87.58 % / 11.18 %
28	D	42.32 % / 47.52 %
29	C	89.21 % / 10.35 %
30	C	68.31 % / 31.54 %
31	A	81.52 % / 18.03 %
32	D	53.33 % / 42.91 %
33	D	66.28 % / 31.09 %
34	C	77.4 % / 22.2 %
35	C	66.09 % / 30.85 %
36	B	56.59 % / 31.42 %
37	A	45.14 % / 54.19 %
38	C	51.25 % / 40.57 %
39	B	43.93 % / 34.25 %
40	A	62.1 % / 35.77 %
41	B	61.66 % / 34.46 %
42	A	56.55 % / 31.39 %
43	C	81.93 % / 15.65 %
44	A	54.54 % / 40.07 %
45	A	65.83 % / 31.13 %

Performance Analysis	
Avg. Score (%)	60.0%
Toppers Score (%)	64.44%
Your Score	

//Hints and Solutions//

1. The sentence should be- The gas 'is seeping' out of the rocks.

The sentence is in Present continuous tense.

A present continuous tense verb form is -- (Subject+ is+v1+ing+object)

Hence, the correct option is (A).

2. The correct sentence is- Captain Ranjith 'safely navigated' his ship without an accident for 100 voyages.

'Safety' means the state of being safe from injury or loss.

The correct alternative should be 'safely' an adverb which means not likely to cause harm or injury.

According to the context of the sentence, the correct word should be-- safely [as it explains how he navigated the ship].

Hence, the correct option is (C).

3. The correct sentence is- The pedestrians 'should be' cautious while crossing the road.

The infinitive 'to' is incorrect as the phrase needs to be 'should be', as it is a suggestion.

Should as a modal conveys the idea of 'suggestion or advice'.

After should you use the base form of the infinitive (= verb without 'To', For example: Use 'Be' instead of 'To be')

Hence, the correct option is (B).

4. The correct sentence is- Some children are much more 'aggressive than' others.

A comparison is done in the sentence, in comparative degree adjective the word 'than' follows the adjective.

The comparison in the sentence should be 'more aggressive than'. In the given sentence 'than' should replace 'then'.

Hence, the correct option is (B).

5. "No improvement" is needed for the given sentence.

A question tag uses the auxiliary in the sentence and the subject pronoun to form a tag.

However, if the auxiliary is positive the tag converts it to negative and if it is negative the tag converts it to a positive before using it.

The auxiliary in the given sentence is --'is' and the tag, therefore, should be 'isn't'.

Hence, the correct option is (D).

6. The correct sentence is--After a 'period of imprisonment,' she renounced terrorism.

'Of' is a preposition that is used to mean relates to, while 'for' is a preposition of time.

So, the phrase in quotes should be --'period of imprisonment' as it relates to imprisonment.

Hence, the correct option is (A).

7. The correct sentence is- Santhosh asked me where 'my pen was'.

The question word should be followed by the 'noun /pronoun' related to it.

Here the noun /pronoun is 'my pen', so the correct phrase is 'my pen was'.

Hence, the correct option is (A).

8. The correct sentence is --Apple's new "operating" system for phones and tablets, iOS 11, is getting some much-sought-after updates.

The correct term for the system for phones and tablets is 'operating system'.

Hence, the correct option is (A).

9. The correct sentence is - Our company aims 'to help' students with disabilities to live and study independently.

'Help' by itself is a verb, but when it is used as a complement to another word it needs an infinitive 'to'.

So, the phrase in quotes should be 'to help' as it complements 'company aims'.

Hence, the correct option is (C).

10. The correct sentence should be- The decision "will leave her" in a peculiar predicament.

The Future tense verb form is 'will + verb 1st form' i.e., 'will + leave'.

Hence, the correct option is (B).

11. The correct sentence is- I was born 'on' 16 November in 1986.

Specific prepositions are used for indicating time.

Use 'on' for days or dates--on Monday / on 5 April.

So, the part of the sentence in quotes should be the preposition 'on' not 'in'.

Hence, the correct option is (A).

12. The correct sentence is Sumathi was 'an industrious' and willing worker.

The indefinite article 'an' is used before words beginning with a vowel sound.[A,E,I,O,U]

'Industriously' begins with 'I' thus needs the article 'an' before it.

Hence, the correct option is (A).

13. The correct sentence is 400 million people speak english as 'their first language'.

The word "there" refers to a place, "their" means belonging to, or associated with, a group of people. Here, "their" should be used in place of there.

Hence, the correct option is (B).

14. The correct sentence is She could have left then, and might have if curiosity hadn't gotten 'the best of her'.

Before the superlative degree "best", article 'the' should come. For option B, "most" can't be used before "best".

Hence, the correct option is (A).

15. The correct sentence is She could have left then, and might have if curiosity hadn't gotten 'the best of her'.

A positive statement is followed by a negative question tag. A negative statement is followed by a positive question tag. The sentence is negative so the tag should be positive and only option (C) is positive.

Hence, the correct option is (C).

16. The correct sentence is our cook puts too much salt in the food.

The subject of the sentence 'our cook' is a singular subject.

- So, it will take a singular verb i.e., puts.
- 'Puts' is used with third person singular noun.
- So, it is correctly used.

'Many' is used with countable nouns and 'much' is used with uncountable nouns.

For Examples:

- How much petrol is in the car?
- How many people were at the meeting?
- Here 'salt' is uncountable, so we will use 'much'.

Therefore, the correct sentence is "Our cook puts too much salt in the food".

Hence, the correct option is (C).

17. The correct sentence is: "Riya went into the shop because it had a sale."

The error lies in 'it has sale'.

- The sentence is in the past tense. The action has already happened.
- The word 'went' indicates that the sentence is in past tense and past tense form of 'has' is 'had'.
- Article 'a' is used before indefinite things.

Hence, the correct option is (D).

18. The correct sentence is You have to wear this uniform whether you like it or not.

'Likes' is used with the third person singular noun like he or she.

With the second person pronoun, we use the base form of the verb i.e., like.

Hence, the correct option is (A).

19. The correct sentence is You have my mobile number, don't you?

The underlined phrase is a question tag.

A positive statement is followed by a negative question tag. Example: Jack is from Spain, isn't he?

Mary can speak English, can't she?

A negative statement is followed by a positive question tag. Example: They aren't funny, are they?

He shouldn't say things like that, should he?

Since, the sentence is positive, the question tag should be negative so we can reject options (C) and (D).

'It' is used while referring to a thing. Example: I like your jacket. Is it new? Here, 'it' is referring to 'jacket'.

Here, the speaker is referring to a person i.e., you.

Hence, the correct option is (A).

20. No Improvement is needed in the above sentence.

'Nowadays' is used which means the speaker is talking about the days which are ongoing at the present.

So, we need to use the present perfect tense.

Option (A) is in the simple present tense.

Option (B) is in the future continuous tense.

Option (C) uses 'have' which is incorrect.

Hence, the correct option is (D).

21. The correct sentence is - The milk has boiled over and fallen onto the stove.

The sentence is in the present perfect tense as indicated by the words 'has boiled'. So, we will use the past participle form of verb i.e., fallen.

Onto means moving to a location on the surface.

'Into' means expressing movement or action with the result that someone or something becomes enclosed or surrounded by something else.

Over means extending directly upwards from.

Hence, the correct option is (B).

22. The correct sentence is - It has been raining very hard since morning.

The word 'since' is used which means that the sentence is highlighting an event that has begun from a time in the past. So, the use of 'has' is correct.

'hardly' means scarcely which is incorrectly used. Instead of 'hardly', 'hard' must be used which means that it was raining heavily.

Hence, the correct option is (C).

23. The correct sentence will be: "Dinesh requested the lady at the counter to give him a seat beside the window."

Since, 'seat' starts with a consonant, so the use of 'a' is correct.

'Beside' means 'at the side of'.

'Besides' mean 'in addition to something'.

Here, beside must be used as the sentence talks about the location.

Hence, the correct option is (B).

24. The correct sentence is 'in the major cities the cost of living is very high'.

Since, the subject of the be verb here' is 'cost', we have to use the singular form of the verb. Thus, neither options (A), nor (B) can be the answer to the question.

Hence, the correct option is (D).

25. The correct sentence is -The floods this year have caused a lot of damage to the crops.

We are talking about an event that happened in the current year. Thus, we have to use the present perfect form of the verb 'cause'.

So, the correct sentence is:

The floods this year have caused a lot of damage to the crops.

Hence, the correct option is (C).

26. None of the phrases given in the options can be a substitute for the underlined part of the sentence in question.

Since, two conflicting events are taking place, we can't use 'therefore', as it puts emphasis on and follows the first event.

Nevertheless is an adverb which means 'in spite of' or 'despite'. It is used when one argument is especially strong.

Hence, the correct option is (D).

27. The correct sentence is If I had been there I would surely have solved solve the problem for you.

The first part of the sentence contains the past perfect form of the 'be' verb. The second part must agree with the tense present in the first part. Only option (A) has the required past perfect tense.

Hence, the correct option is (A).

28. The correct sentence is- Ajit has been playing bridge since 2017.

When we refer to something that has been going on for quite some time, we use the present perfect continuous tense of the verb.

Only option (D) contains 'has been playing', the present perfect continuous tense.

Hence, the correct option is (D).

29. The news reported that the police have catched the guilty person and are interrogating him.

The correct form of the verb 'catch', when used with either the present perfect or the past perfect tense, is 'caught' (V3).

So, the correct sentence would be:

The news reported that the police have caught the guilty person and are interrogating him.

Hence, the correct option is (C).

30. The correct sentence would be: The watchman prevented him from parking his car near the gate.

In this case, the sentence talks about a particular event which occurred in the past.

Since, we have no idea about the time frame, we use simple past. The use of present tense is grammatically incorrect.

Hence, the correct option is (C).

31. The correct sentence is: 'Did you bring your drawing books?' the teacher asked.

The sentence is in the simple past tense. When we use the past form of the verb 'do', we have to use the present form of the following verb. Thus, 'did brought' is an incorrect usage.

Hence, the correct option is (A).

32. The given sentence is in simple past tense so we will use the past tense form of the verb i.e., broke.

With the past tense form of the verb, 'is' cannot be used.

Option (A) is making no sense.

Option (B) is grammatically incorrect.

Option (C) is in the past continuous tense.

Hence, the correct option is (D).

33. The sentence is correct.

When 'corner' means an interior angle formed by two meeting walls, we use the preposition in.

Example:

The keys are lying in the corner of the room.

Into means expressing movement or action with the result that someone or something becomes enclosed or surrounded by something else.

Example:

Put the bowl into the fridge.

Up to means as far as.

Example:

I could not reach up to the wall.

Here, 'in' is correct. It means- at a point within an area or space; within the shape of something; surrounded by something; into something; forming the whole or part of something.

Hence, the correct option is (D).

34. The use of the preposition 'for' with the base form of the verb i.e., grow is incorrect.

Instead of 'for', 'to' should be used.

'To' cannot be used with 'growing' as it is grammatically incorrect.

Hence, the correct option is (C).

35. 'Unless' is used to introduce the case in which a statement being made is not true or valid.

Unless means 'used to say what will or will not happen if something else does not happen or is not true; except if'.

No improvement , Here it is used correctly as the speaker states that Arjun will not reach the airport in time except if he takes a taxi.

With a singular noun, the use of 'takes' is correct.

Hence, the correct option is (C).

36. Here we need a subject of reference so only option (B) is needed here.

So, the correct sentence is: While crossing the road, he saw a snake.

Hence, the correct option is (B).

37. The third form of the broadcast is "broadcast".

So, the correct sentence is: His speech was broadcast over the radio the last Thursday.

Hence, the correct option is (A).

38. Option (C) is correct as enjoy is the transitive verb that must have an object with it, so a reflexive pronoun needs to be added as an object as there is no object given for "enjoy".

So, the correct sentence is: We had a grand party and we enjoyed ourselves very much.

Hence, the correct option is (C).

39. In conditional sentence subject takes "were" after it.

So, the correct sentence is- If I were you, I would not sign the document.

Hence, the correct option is (B).

40. Past Perfect Tense (would have surely brought) will be used with this Conditional Sentence (that starts with an if)

The sentence structure will be as follows: If + Past Perfect (had gone) …. would + have + past Participle-brought.

So, the correct sentence is- If I had gone to Mumbai, I would have surely brought your books.

Hence, the correct option is (A).

41. The past tense of the telecast is "telecast" or "telecasted".

The third-person singular simple present indicative form of the telecast is "telecasts".

The present participle of the telecast is "telecasting".

The past participle of the telecast is "telecast" or "telecasted".

So, the correct sentence is: A very horrifying serial was telecasted ten days ago.

Hence, the correct option is (B).

42. Rise does not take an object, as it is an intransitive verb. It is an irregular verb; its forms are:

Base Form (Infinitive):	Rise
Past Simple:	Rose
Past Participle:	Risen
3rd Person Singular:	Rises
Present Participle/Gerund:	Rising

So, the correct sentence is: After the heavy rains last week, the water in the lake rose another two feet.

Hence, the correct option is (A).

43. It is high time:- if you feel that it is already late for something to happen, you can use the expression 'It's high time…' This structure might look unusual because it uses a past tense form to talk about the present or future. In fact, past tenses are used to talk about the present/future in many phrases with time.

Since the presence of 'high time, the word 'go' must be in the past tense.

Therefore, 'go' must be replaced by 'went'.

So, the correct sentence is: It is high time, you **went** home.

Hence, the correct option is (C).

44. Universal truths and facts are expressed in simple present tense thus "India guarantees".

So, the correct sentence is: The constitution of India guarantees each citizen equal rights and privileges.

Hence, the correct option is (A).

45. Have is a causative verb that takes bare infinitive with it, thus "behaving" should be replaced with "behave".

So, the correct sentence is: I won't have you behave like that in my office.

Hence, the correct option is (A).

Q.1 Select the wrongly spelt word.

A. Abhorrent   **B.** Privarticate
C. Circuitous   **D.** Finicky

Q.2 Select the wrongly spelt word.

A. Transgresser   **B.** Accommodate
C. Perspicuous   **D.** Assassin

Q.3 Select the wrongly spelt word.

A. Specialist   **B.** Expecially
C. Specially   **D.** Specialization

Q.4 Select the wrongly spelt word.

A. Particular   **B.** Impateint
C. Fortunate   **D.** Thoroughly

Q.5 Select the wrongly spelt word.

A. Summarize   **B.** Reidiculous
C. Receptionist   **D.** Inhuman

Q.6 Direction: In this section, a word is spelt in four different ways. Identify the one which is correct and mark your answer accordingly.

[Indian Military Academy (IMA), 2020], [Officers Training Academy (OTA), 2020]

A. Mountaneous   **B.** Mountenous
C. Mountaineous   **D.** Mountainous

Q.7 Direction: In this section, a word is spelt in four different ways. Identify the one which is correct and mark your answer accordingly.

[Indian Military Academy (IMA), 2020], [Officers Training Academy (OTA), 2020]

A. Etiquette   **B.** Etiquete   **C.** Etiequtte   **D.** Etequtte

Q.8 Direction: In this section, a word is spelt in four different ways. Identify the one which is correct and mark your answer accordingly.

[Indian Military Academy (IMA), 2020], [Officers Training Academy (OTA), 2020]

A. Curriculam   **B.** Curiculum
C. Curiculeum   **D.** Curriculum

Q.9 Direction: In this section, a word is spelt in four different ways. Identify the one which is correct and mark your answer accordingly.

[Indian Military Academy (IMA), 2020], [Officers Training Academy (OTA), 2020]

A. Magnificent   **B.** Magnificant
C. Magneficent   **D.** Magenficient

Q.10 Direction: In the given question, four words are given out of which one word is correctly spelt. Choose the correctly spelt word.

[Indian Military Academy (IMA), 2020], [Officers Training Academy (OTA), 2020]

A. Twelth   **B.** Twelfth   **C.** Tweluth   **D.** Twelthe

Q.11 Direction: In this section, a word is spelt in four different ways. Identify the one which is correct and mark your answer accordingly.

[Indian Military Academy (IMA), 2020], [Officers Training Academy (OTA), 2020]

A. Snobbery   **B.** Snoberry
C. Snabbery   **D.** Snobbory

Q.12 Direction: In this section, a word is spelt in four different ways. Identify the one which is correct and mark your answer accordingly.

[Indian Military Academy (IMA), 2020], [Officers Training Academy (OTA), 2020]

A. Neurasis   **B.** Nuroesis   **C.** Neurosis   **D.** Neuresis

Q.13 Direction: In this section, a word is spelt in four different ways. Identify the one which is correct and mark your answer accordingly.

[Indian Military Academy (IMA), 2020], [Officers Training Academy (OTA), 2020]

A. Dipthteria   **B.** Diptheria
C. Diphtheria   **D.** Diphthria

Q.14 Direction: In this section, a word is spelt in four different ways. Identify the one which is correct and mark your answer accordingly.

[Indian Military Academy (IMA), 2020], [Officers Training Academy (OTA), 2020]

A. Meagre   **B.** Megare   **C.** Meagr   **D.** Megear

Q.15 Select the wrongly spelt word.

A. Embarrass   **B.** Embrace
C. Embody   **D.** Embelish

Q.16 Select the wrongly spelt word.

A. Booty   **B.** Blosom   **C.** Brood   **D.** Boast

Q.17 Select the wrongly spelt word.

A. Appellation   **B.** Ammunition
C. Anoint   **D.** Demurage

Q.18 Select the wrongly spelt word.

A. Absense   **B.** Acquiesce
C. Acquisition   **D.** Acquit

Q.19 Select the wrongly spelt word.

A. Ambit   **B.** Embarassment
C. Palpable   **D.** Flabbergast

Q.20 Select the wrongly spelt word.

A. Argument   **B.** Ignorant
C. Conscience   **D.** Appearent

Q.21 Select the correctly spelt word.

A. Ilogical **B.** Achieve
C. Appearence **D.** Grammer

Q.22 Direction: A word is spelled in four different ways. You are to identify the one which is correct. Choose the alternative bearing the correct spelling from the given options.
[Officers Training Academy (OTA), 2019], [Indian Military Academy (IMA), 2019]

A. Accommodate **B.** Acomodate
C. Accomdate **D.** Acomodait

Q.23 Direction: A word is spelled in four different ways. You are to identify the one which is correct. Choose the alternative bearing the correct spelling from the given options.
[Officers Training Academy (OTA), 2019], [Indian Military Academy (IMA), 2019]

A. Recommnd **B.** Reccommend
C. Recommend **D.** Reccomand

Q.24 Direction: A word is spelled in four different ways. You are to identify the one which is correct. Choose the alternative bearing the correct spelling from the given options.
[Officers Training Academy (OTA), 2019], [Indian Military Academy (IMA), 2019]

A. Argyument **B.** Argument
C. Arguement **D.** Argyooment

Q.25 Direction: A word is spelled in four different ways. You are to identify the one which is correct. Choose the alternative bearing the correct spelling from the given options.
[Officers Training Academy (OTA), 2019], [Indian Military Academy (IMA), 2019]

A. Decisive **B.** Desisive
C. Descisive **D.** Desicive

Q.26 Direction: A word is spelled in four different ways. You are to identify the one which is correct. Choose the alternative bearing the correct spelling from the given options.
[Officers Training Academy (OTA), 2019], [Indian Military Academy (IMA), 2019]

A. Aggressive **B.** Agresive
C. Agressive **D.** Aggresive

Q.27 Direction: A word is spelled in four different ways. You are to identify the one which is correct. Choose the alternative bearing the correct spelling from the given options.
[Officers Training Academy (OTA), 2019], [Indian Military Academy (IMA), 2019]

A. Assassination **B.** Asassination
C. Asasination **D.** Assasination

Q.28 Direction: A word is spelled in four different ways. You are to identify the one which is correct. Choose the alternative bearing the correct spelling from the given options.
[Officers Training Academy (OTA), 2019], [Indian Military Academy (IMA), 2019]

A. Embarassment **B.** Embbarasment
C. Embrasement **D.** Embarrassment

Ques (29-34):Direction: In the given question, four words are given, three of which are spelt correctly while one is miss-spelt.

Q.29 Choose the miss-spelt word.
[NCHM JEE (Hotel Mgmt & Catering), 2018]

A. fatuous **B.** obituary
C. Mortury **D.** Congress

Q.30 Choose the miss-spelt word.
[NCHM JEE (Hotel Mgmt & Catering), 2018]

A. Solidarity **B.** Digress
C. Solemn **D.** Congeniall

Q.31 Choose the miss-spelt word.
[NCHM JEE (Hotel Mgmt & Catering), 2018]

A. Impassioned **B.** Abbay
C. Correlation **D.** Tumultous

Q.32 Choose the miss-spelt word.
[NCHM JEE (Hotel Mgmt & Catering), 2018]

A. Philately **B.** Philosophy
C. Actuality **D.** Nomancloture

Q.33 Choose the miss-spelt word.
[NCHM JEE (Hotel Mgmt & Catering), 2018]

A. Sovereign **B.** Persanage
C. Lucid **D.** Bovine

Q.34 Choose the miss-spelt word.
[NCHM JEE (Hotel Mgmt & Catering), 2018]

A. Amicable **B.** Sociable
C. Vulnarable **D.** Malleable

Q.35 Select the correctly spelt word.
A. Judgement **B.** Jujment
C. Judgmeant **D.** Judgemant

Q.36 Select the correctly spelt word.
A. Equelibrium **B.** Equilriam
C. Equilibrium **D.** Equillibrium

Q.37 Select the wrongly spelt word.
A. Courtesy **B.** Diffedent
C. Sincerity **D.** Collapse

Q.38 Select the correctly spelt word.
A. Inchantment **B.** Ingagement
C. Installment **D.** Ingradient

Q.39 Select the correctly spelt word.
A. Magnanemous **B.** Magnanomous
C. Magnanimous **D.** Magnonimus

Q.40 Find out that word, the spelling of which is wrong.
A. Immunity **B.** Immaculate
C. Imminent **D.** Immitate

Q.41 Find out that word, the spelling of which is wrong.
A. Sargeant **B.** Shallot **C.** Shackle **D.** Shellac

Q.42 Find out that word, the spelling of which is wrong.

A. Beetle

B. Beautician

C. Bearable

D. Beautifull

Q.43 Find out that word, the spelling of which is wrong.

A. Anxiety

B. Ankel

C. Accommodation

D. Allergy

Q.44 Find out that word, the spelling of which is wrong.

A. Recuperate

B. Pasture

C. Populace

D. Penence

Q.45 Find out that word, the spelling of which is wrong.

A. Shutter

B. Silhoutte

C. Shepherd

D. Shield

// Smart Answer Sheet //

Correct — Indicates percentage of students who answered questions correctly.

Skipped — Indicates percentage of students who skipped questions.

Q.	Ans.	Correct / Skipped
1	B	55.21 % / 34.41 %
2	A	55.47 % / 44.1 %
3	B	52.13 % / 42.7 %
4	B	77.8 % / 13.97 %
5	B	85.96 % / 12.59 %
6	D	53.9 % / 37.83 %
7	A	19.83 % / 70.5 %
8	D	89.58 % / 10.35 %
9	A	69.16 % / 30.47 %
10	B	62.89 % / 36.61 %
11	A	46.13 % / 49.71 %
12	C	86.85 % / 13.06 %
13	C	51.77 % / 47.71 %
14	A	29.0 % / 70.18 %
15	D	83.8 % / 14.58 %
16	B	79.11 % / 12.09 %
17	D	52.36 % / 34.29 %
18	A	83.53 % / 11.25 %
19	B	80.14 % / 16.75 %
20	D	79.08 % / 12.5 %
21	B	84.82 % / 14.53 %
22	A	87.23 % / 10.52 %
23	C	43.83 % / 45.09 %
24	B	79.7 % / 11.77 %
25	A	56.91 % / 36.1 %
26	A	46.38 % / 39.76 %
27	A	79.22 % / 19.32 %
28	D	67.42 % / 30.56 %
29	C	51.96 % / 35.1 %
30	D	61.41 % / 31.16 %
31	B	46.57 % / 52.54 %
32	D	51.41 % / 45.35 %
33	B	48.64 % / 44.02 %
34	C	31.79 % / 67.4 %
35	A	76.49 % / 19.94 %
36	C	80.38 % / 11.9 %
37	B	40.96 % / 32.45 %
38	C	79.93 % / 18.29 %
39	C	52.74 % / 42.73 %
40	D	89.44 % / 10.17 %
41	A	49.5 % / 33.83 %
42	D	85.4 % / 14.16 %
43	B	56.46 % / 37.12 %
44	D	51.08 % / 48.66 %
45	B	55.53 % / 33.18 %

Performance Analysis

Avg. Score (%)	37.78%
Toppers Score (%)	60.0%
Your Score	

//Hints and Solutions//

1. Privarticate is the wrongly spelt word. The correct word is Prevaricate. It means speak or act in an evasive way.

Hence, the correct option is (B).

2. Transgresser is the wrongly spelt word. The correct word is Transgressor. It means 'a person who breaks a law or moral rule'.

Hence, the correct option is (A).

3. Expecially is the wrongly spelt word. The correct word is Especially. It is used to single out one person or thing over all others.

Hence, the correct option is (B).

4. Impateint is the wrongly spelt word. The correct word is Inpatient. It means 'having or showing a tendency to be quickly irritated or provoked'.

Hence, the correct option is (B).

5. Reidiculous is the wrongly spelt word. The correct word is Ridiculous. It means deserving or inviting derision or mockery; absurd.

Hence, the correct option is (B).

6. The correct answer is 'Mountainous.'

Mountainous': The correctly spelled word is 'Mountainous' and it means (of a region) having many mountains.

Example: The Antarctic is a mountainous area.

Hence, the correct option is (D).

7. The correct answer is 'Etiquette.'

'Etiquette': The correctly spelled word is 'Etiquette' and it means the customary code of polite behavior in society or among members of a particular profession or group.

Example: He refused to bow to the Queen, in deliberate breach of etiquette.

Hence, the correct option is (A).

8. The correct answer is 'Curriculum.'

'Curriculum': The correctly spelt word is 'Curriculum' and it means the subjects comprising a course of study in a school or college.

Example: The curriculum is rigidly prescribed from an early age.

Hence, the correct option is (D).

9. The correct answer is 'Magnificent.'

'Magnificent': The correctly spelt word is 'Magnificent' and it means extremely beautiful, elaborate, or impressive.

Example: She looked magnificent in her wedding dress.

Hence, the correct option is (A).

10. The correct answer is 'Twelfth.'

'Twelfth': The correctly spelt word is 'Twelfth' and it means constituting number twelve in a sequence; 12th.

Example: 1 December is the twelfth month of the year.

Hence, the correct option is (B).

11. The correct answer is 'Snobbery.'

'Snobbery': The correctly spelt word is 'Snobbery' and it means the character or quality of being a snob.

Example: We will end the snobbery that has damaged vocational education.

Hence, the correct option is (A).

12. The correct answer is 'Neurosis.'

'Neurosis': The correctly spelt word is 'Neurosis' and it means excessive and irrational anxiety or obsession.

Example: Behavior therapists believe that neurosis is learned and can be unlearned.

Hence, the correct option is (C).

13. The correct answer is 'Diphtheria.'

'Diphtheria': The correctly spelt word is 'Diphtheria' and it is a serious infection caused by strains of bacteria called Corynebacterium diphtheriae that make a toxin (poison).

Example: Europe now accounts for 80 percent of diphtheria cases reported worldwide.

Hence, the correct option is (C).

14. The correct answer is 'Meagre.'

'Meagre': The correctly spelt word is 'Meagre' and it means (of something provided or available) lacking in quantity or quality.

Example: Dietaries differed, here too ample, there meagre to starvation.

Hence, the correct option is (A).

15. The correct spelling is 'Embellish' which means 'to make something more beautiful by adding decoration to it'.

Embarrass: to make somebody feel shy, uncomfortable, or ashamed, especially in a social situation.

Embrace: an act of putting your arms around somebody as a sign of love or friendship.

Embody: to express or represent an idea or a quality.

Hence, the correct option is (D).

16. The correct spelling is blossom which means mature or develop in a promising or healthy way.

Booty: valuable stolen goods, especially those seized in war.

Brood: a family of birds or other young animals produced at one hatching or birth.

Boast: an act of talking with excessive pride and self-satisfaction.

Hence, the correct option is (B).

17. Demurage is the wrongly spelt word. The correct spelling is Demurrage.

Demurrage (noun) - a charge payable to the owner of a chartered ship on failure to load or discharge the ship within the time agreed.

Example: The House of Lords held that the company was not liable as principal to pay demurrage.

Hence, the correct option is (D).

18. Absense is the wrongly spelt word. The correct spelling is 'Absence'.

Absence - the fact of something/somebody not being there; lack.

Example: In the absence of a doctor, try to help the injured person yourself.

Hence, the correct option is (A).

19. Embarassment is the wrongly spelt word. The correct spelling is Embarrassment.

Embarrassment - a feeling of self-consciousness, shame, or awkwardness.

Example: I turned red with embarrassment.

Hence, the correct option is (B).

20. Appearent is the wrongly spelt word. The correct spelling is Apparent.

Apparent - clearly visible or understood; obvious.

Example: She laughed for no apparent reason.

Hence, the correct option is (D).

21. Out of all the options, only 'Achieve' is correctly spelt.

Achieve - to gain something, usually by effort or skill.

Example: You have achieved the success you deserve.

Hence, the correct option is (B).

22. The correct spelling is 'Accommodate'.

Accommodate: to have enough space for somebody/something, especially for a certain number of people; to provide somebody with a place to stay, live or work.

For example: The ceilings were too low to accommodate his terrific height.

The other words are incorrectly spelled.

Hence, the correct option is (A).

23. The correct spelling is 'Recommend'.

Recommend: put forward (someone or something) with approval as being suitable for a particular purpose or role; advocate; endorse

For example: Can you recommend a good dictionary?

The other words are incorrectly spelled.

Hence, the correct option is (C).

24. The correct spelling is 'Argument'.

Argument: a disagreement, or the process of disagreeing, an angry discussion between two or more people who disagree with each other.

For example: He got into an argument with Jeff in the pub last night.

The other words are incorrectly spelled.

Hence, the correct option is (B).

25. The correct spelling is 'Decisive'.

Decisive: the ability to settle an issue, producing a definite result; having or showing the ability to make decisions quickly and effectively.

For example: You must be decisive and persistent to succeed in this competitive field.

The other words are incorrectly spelled.

Hence, the correct option is (A).

26. The correct spelling is 'Aggressive'.

Aggressive: ready or likely to attack or confront, characterized by or resulting from aggression; behaving or done in a determined and forceful way.

For example: You'd better keep the two aggressive people apart.

The other words are incorrectly spelled.

Hence, the correct option is (A).

27. The correct spelling is 'Assassination'.

Assassination: to kill someone famous or important, such as a head of state, head of government, politician, member of a royal family, or CEO.

For example: The CIA discovered the plot of the President's assassination.

The other words are incorrectly spelled.

Hence, the correct option is (A).

28. The correct spelling is 'Embarrassment'.

Embarrassment: an emotional state that is associated with mild to severe levels of discomfort, and which is usually experienced when someone commits a socially unacceptable or frowned-upon act that is witnessed by or revealed to others. the feeling of being embarrassed, or something that makes you feel embarrassed,

For example: Unshed tears of embarrassment were starting to burn her eyes.

The other words are incorrectly spelled.

Hence, the correct option is (D).

29. 'Mortury' is a miss-spelt word.

The correct spelling is 'Morcuary'.

Meaning: a room or building in which dead bodies are kept,for hygienic storage for examination,until burial or cremation.

Sentence:Two mortuary attendants escorted the deceased body from the morgue to the burial site.

Hence, the correct option is (C).

30. Congeniall is the miss-spelt word.

The correct spelling is congenial.

Meaning:pleasant

Sentence:We studied in the congenial atmosphere of the library. He found the work to be congenial. She was congenial and easygoing.

Hence, the correct option is (D).

31. Abbay is the miss-spelt word.

The correct word is **'Abbey'**.

Meaning:a large church together with a group of buildings where religious communities of monks or nuns live or used to live.

Sentence:1. We were going to a concert in Bath Abbey. 2. Then he came to a white abbey.

Hence, the correct option is (B).

32. Nomencloture is the miss-spelt word.

The correct spelling is 'nomenclature'.

Meaning:a system of naming things, especially in science.

Sentence:The committee of the Royal Geographical Society settled the existing nomenclature of the three great oceans.

Hence, the correct optiob is (D).

33. 'Persanage' is the miss-spelt word.

The correct spelling is 'personage'.

Meaning: an important or famous person.

Sentence:Every prince of the blood is a royal personage.

Hence, the correct option is (B).

34. 'Vulnarable' is the miss-spelt word.

The correct spelling is 'vulnerable'.

Meaning: weak and easy to hurt physically or emotionally.

Sentence: Poor organization left the troops vulnerable to enemy attack.

Hence, the correct option is (C).

35. The correct spelling is Judgement.

Judgement - the ability to make considered decisions or come to sensible conclusions.

Hence, the correct option is (A).

36. Among all the given options, equilibrium is correctly spelt.

Equilibrium- a state in which opposing forces or influences are balanced

Hence, the correct option is (C).

37. Diffedent is the wrongly spelt word. The correct spelling is Diffident.

Diffident means modest or shy because of a lack of self-confidence.

Hence, the correct option is (B).

38. Installment is the correctly spelt word.

It means one of several parts into which a story, plan, or amount of money owed has been divided so that each part happens or is paid at different times until the end or total is reached.

Hence, the correct option is (C).

39. The correctly spelt word is 'Magnanimous'.

The meaning of the word 'Magnanimous' is 'charitable or generous'.

Hence, the correct option is (C).

40. Immitate will be Imitate

Hence, the correct option is (D).

41. Sargeant will be Sergeant.

Hence, the correct option is (A).

42. Beautifull is the wrongly spelt word. The correct spelling is Beautiful.

Beautiful: pleasing the senses or mind aesthetically.

Hence, the correct option is (D).

43. Ankel is the wrongly spelt word. The correct spelling is Ankle.

The ankle is a large joint made up of three bones: The shin bone (tibia) The thinner bone running next to the shin bone (fibula) A foot bone that sits above the heel bone (talus).

Hence, the correct option is (B).

44. Penence will be Penance.

Hence, the correct option is (D).

45. Silhoutte is the wrongly spelt word. The correct spelling is Silhouette.

Silhouette: the dark shape and outline of someone or something visible in restricted light against a brighter background.

Hence, the correct option is (B).

Q.1 Direction: Choose the correct meaning of the idiom and mark the answer.

Be in eclipse

[Officers Training Academy (OTA), 2021], [Indian Military Academy (IMA), 2021]

A. Less successful   **B.** Feeling happy

C. Very successful   **D.** Being defeated

Q.2 Direction: Choose the correct meaning of the idiom and mark the answer.

Ways and means

[Officers Training Academy (OTA), 2021], [Indian Military Academy (IMA), 2021]

A. A technique

B. Methods of achieving something

C. Norms and regulations of doing something

D. Improving one's way of doing

Q.3 Direction: Choose the correct meaning of the idiom and mark the answer.

Up in arms

[Officers Training Academy (OTA), 2021], [Indian Military Academy (IMA), 2021]

A. Very happy   **B.** Very satisfied

C. Very angry   **D.** Feeling fine

Q.4 Direction: Choose the correct meaning of the idiom and mark the answer.

Big ticket

[Officers Training Academy (OTA), 2021], [Indian Military Academy (IMA), 2021]

A. Very less   **B.** Very costly

C. Very easy   **D.** Not much

Q.5 Direction: Choose the correct meaning of the idiom and mark the answer.

Bolt from the blue

[Officers Training Academy (OTA), 2021], [Indian Military Academy (IMA), 2021]

A. An event or piece of news which is unexpected

B. Desirable event or news

C. An event which takes place as planned

D. News which has been long expected, but arrives late

Q.6 Direction: Choose the correct meaning of the idiom and mark the answer.

Be a law unto yourself

[Officers Training Academy (OTA), 2021], [Indian Military Academy (IMA), 2021]

A. Behave unconventional and unpredictable

B. Abide by law and order

C. Ask others to follow the law

D. Create law and order for others

Q.7 Direction: Choose the correct meaning of the idiom and mark the answer.

Spiff up

[Officers Training Academy (OTA), 2021], [Indian Military Academy (IMA), 2021]

A. To make oneself look neat

B. To make oneself look untidy

C. To make oneself look arrogant

D. To appear on the stage as a baboon

Q.8 Direction: Direction: Choose the correct meaning of the idiom and mark the answer.

Run wild

[Officers Training Academy (OTA), 2021], [Indian Military Academy (IMA), 2021]

A. To run like a wild animal

B. To treat anyone like a wild creature

C. To feel like a wild animal

D. To behave without any control

Q.9 Direction: Choose the correct meaning of the idiom and mark the answer.

Wind down

[Officers Training Academy (OTA), 2021], [Indian Military Academy (IMA), 2021]

A. To relax after a period of activity

B. To act furiously after a period of silence

C. To speak out the truth to people

D. To act on the ground

Q.10 Direction: Choose the correct meaning of the idiom and mark the answer.

Mellow out

[Officers Training Academy (OTA), 2021], [Indian Military Academy (IMA), 2021]

A. To feel bad about other's enjoyment

B. To like and dislike people concurrently

C. To enjoy oneself without doing much

D. To work hard and doing much work

Q.11 Direction: Given below is an idiom/phrase which is followed by four alternative meanings to each. Choose the correct option which is the most appropriate meaning.

Dirt cheap

[Officers Training Academy (OTA), 2019], [Indian Military Academy (IMA), 2019]

A. Extremely cheap   **B.** Extremely costly

C. Very cheap person   **D.** Very cheap item

Q.12 Direction: Given below is an idiom/phrase which is followed by four alternative meanings to each. Choose the correct option which is the most appropriate meaning.

A shrinking violet

[Officers Training Academy (OTA), 2019], [Indian Military Academy (IMA), 2019]

A. A lean person **B.** A shy person
C. A happy person **D.** A sad person

Q.13 Direction: Given below is an idiom/phrase which is followed by four alternative meanings to each. Choose the correct option which is the most appropriate meaning.

Gordian knot

[Officers Training Academy (OTA), 2019], [Indian Military Academy (IMA), 2019]

A. Undoable job **B.** A difficult problem
C. A different problem **D.** Doable job

Q.14 Direction: Given below is an idiom/phrase which is followed by four alternative meanings to each. Choose the correct option which is the most appropriate meaning.

Fall in a heap

[Officers Training Academy (OTA), 2019], [Indian Military Academy (IMA), 2019]

A. To be at the mercy of someone else
B. To be thinking about someone
C. To lose control of one's own feelings
D. To be in control of one's own feelings

Q.15 Direction: Given below is an idiom/phrase which is followed by four alternative meanings to each. Choose the correct option which is the most appropriate meaning.

Have a conniption fit

[Officers Training Academy (OTA), 2019], [Indian Military Academy (IMA), 2019]

A. To be very angry
B. To be very happy
C. To be very sad
D. To be a jubilant person

Q.16 Direction: Given below is an idiom/phrase which is followed by four alternative meanings to each. Choose the correct option which is the most appropriate meaning.

Be in seventh heaven

[Officers Training Academy (OTA), 2019], [Indian Military Academy (IMA), 2019]

A. To be extremely happy
B. To be extremely upset
C. To be extremely adventurous
D. To be extremely silent

Q.17 Direction: Given below is an idiom/phrase which is followed by four alternative meanings to each. Choose the correct option which is the most appropriate meaning.

Hand in glove

[Officers Training Academy (OTA), 2019], [Indian Military Academy (IMA), 2019]

A. Working separately
B. Working together
C. Working for someone
D. Not willing to work

Q.18 Direction: Given below is an idiom/phrase which is followed by four alternative meanings to each. Choose the correct option which is the most appropriate meaning.

Nip in the bud

[Officers Training Academy (OTA), 2019], [Indian Military Academy (IMA), 2019]

A. Prevent a small problem before it becomes severe
B. Prevent the big problems
C. Make it severe
D. Beating the problem

Q.19 Direction: Given below is an idiom/phrase which is followed by four alternative meanings to each. Choose the correct option which is the most appropriate meaning.

Like a shag on a rock

[Officers Training Academy (OTA), 2019], [Indian Military Academy (IMA), 2019]

A. Completely alone **B.** Completely idle
C. Complete silence **D.** Complete happy

Q.20 Direction: Given below is an idiom/phrase which is followed by four alternative meanings to each. Choose the correct option which is the most appropriate meaning.

A pearl of wisdom

[Officers Training Academy (OTA), 2019], [Indian Military Academy (IMA), 2019]

A. An important piece of news
B. An important person
C. An important thing for life
D. An important piece of advice

Q.21 Direction: Some proverb/idiom is given below together with their meanings. Choose the correct meaning of proverb/idiom.

To cry wolf
A. To listen eagerly
B. To give false alarm
C. To turn pale
D. To keep off starvation

Q.22 Direction: Select the option that means the same as the given idiom.

To pull oneself together
A. To hide important facts and reasons
B. To put necessary matters on the table
C. To keep working constantly with attention
D. To calm oneself and begin to think or act

Q.23 Direction: Select the most appropriate meaning of the underlined idiom in the given sentence.

I will not go to work today as I am feeling <u>under the weather</u>.
A. Bad weather **B.** Too hot to go out
C. Being sick **D.** Rainy weather

Q.24 Direction: Select the most appropriate for the phrase.

Hard-nosed attitude
A. Quality to forgive **B.** Protective

C. Aggressive   **D.** Calm

Q.25 Direction: Read the following information carefully and answer the question given below-

In the given question, a word or phrase is underlined. Beneath each sentence, four alternative meanings are given. Select the best alternative that has the closest meaning to the underlined phrase.

Readers are advised to take this information <u>with a grain of salt</u>.

A. Taking something under consideration.

B. Taking responsibility to maintain privacy.

C. Not taking something too seriously.

D. Not taking something easily.

Q.26 Direction: Select the option that means the same as the given idiom.

Alive and kicking

A. To be dead inside   **B.** To excel

C. Lively and active   **D.** To participate

Q.27 Direction: Choose the option which best expresses the meaning of the idiom/phrase given below.

Be in the same boat

A. To ask someone to travel on the same boat

B. To be in the same difficult situation

C. Willing to do something immediately

D. To force an issue that has already ended

Q.28 Direction: Select the most appropriate meaning of the given idiom.

Dowry is a burning <u>question</u> of the day.

A. A widely debated issue

B. A dying issue

C. A relevant problem

D. An irrelevant issue

Q.29 Direction: You are required to identify the words that are contextually similar to the idiom/phrase given sentence.

All in all

A. Every person

B. Particular thing same in all

C. Call all at once

D. Most important

Q.30 Directions: In the following question given below a/an idiom/phrase is given in bold which is then followed by five options that try to decipher its meaning as used in the sentence. Choose the option which gives the meaning of the phrase most appropriately in the context of the given sentence.

They go to the beach when they should be **hitting the books** and then they wonder why they get low marks.

A. Scrutinizing   **B.** Studying

C. Reflecting   **D.** Exploring

Q.31 Direction: In the following question, out of the four alternatives, choose the alternative which best expresses the meaning of the Idiom/Phrase.

A peeping Tom

A. Tom is peeping from the door.

B. Tom is a cheat.

C. A person working for Police.

D. A person who secretly watches others, especially for sexual gratification.

Q.32 Direction: In the following question, out of the four alternatives, choose the alternative which best expresses the meaning of the Idiom/Phrase.

Achilles heel

A. Runaway

B. Soft feet

C. A small problem or weakness in a person or system that can result in failure

D. Walk slowly

Q.33 Direction : In the following questions, four/five alternatives are given for the meaning of the given Idiom/Phrase. Choose the alternative which best express the meaning of the Idiom/Phrase.

To pick holes

A. To find some reason to quarrel

B. To destroy something

C. To cut some part of an item

D. To criticize someone

Q.34 Direction: You are required to identify the words that are contextually similar to the phrase/idiom given in bold and mark that as your answer.

If I say **"I am going to hit the books now"**.

A. Take a short break from studying

B. Throw my books away

C. To study

D. Worry about study

Q.35 Direction: In the following question, out of the four alternatives, select the alternative which best expresses the meaning of the Idiom/ Phrase.

Face the muisc

A. To listen to something

B. To enjoy something

C. To face the consequences

D. To meet someone

Q.36 Direction: In the given question, four alternatives are given for the meaning of the given Idiom/Phrase. Choose the alternative which best express the meaning of the Idiom/Phrase.

Off the hook

A. Everything prepared and kept ready for you.

B. Accept something without checking its veracity.

C. No longer in difficulty or trouble.

D. Put a person who is helping you into a difficult situation.

Ques (37-45):Direction: Select the most appropriate meaning of the underlined idiom in the given sentence.

Q.37 I told you not to play the prank but you didn't listen, now <u>face the music</u>.

A. accept the consequences

B. put on earphones
C. listen to the songs
D. sing popular songs

Q.38 Pradeep was so tired that <u>he hit the sack</u> as soon as possible.

A. Left work   **B.** Went to bed
C. Accepted defeat   **D.** Kicked the sack

Q.39 Their relationship has <u>run into rough weather</u> ever since they fell in love with the same girl.

[SSC Sub Inspector (CPO), 2019]

A. experienced difficulties
B. brought cool breeze and rains
C. become stronger and firmer
D. become pleasant and cordial

Q.40 You must have a concrete project and <u>not build castles in the air</u> if you want to submit an application for a loan.

[SSC Sub Inspector (CPO), 2019]

A. make unfaithful friends
B. talk irresponsibly
C. have unrealistic ideas
D. make unplanned buildings

Q.41 This problem is <u>a hard nut to crack,</u> it will take longer than they imagined.
A. involves breaking nuts
B. is not interesting enough
C. is difficult to solve
D. needs a lot of work

Q.42 My aunt has <u>the gift of the gab</u> and can socialize in any group.
A. ability to cook well
B. ability to criticize anyone
C. ability to spend time anywhere
D. ability to speak eloquently

Q.43 There was no one in the team who could <u>bell the cat</u> and tell the producer the truth.
A. Tame some animals
B. Warn the owners
C. Do the impossible task
D. Ring the bells regularly

Q.44 The <u>apple of discord</u> among the brothers was their father's mansion in the country.
A. reason for quarrel   **B.** hopeful attention
C. Sincere affection   **D.** Fruitful discussion

Q.45 My neighbour's son is very mischievous and always <u>getting in everyone's hair.</u>
A. Throwing things at them
B. Pulling their hair
C. Entertaining them
D. Annoying them

// Smart Answer Sheet //

Correct Indicates percentage of students who answered questions correctly.

Skipped Indicates percentage of students who skipped questions.

Q.	Ans.	Correct / Skipped	Q.	Ans.	Correct / Skipped	Q.	Ans.	Correct / Skipped	Q.	Ans.	Correct / Skipped	Q.	Ans.	Correct / Skipped
1	A	65.51 % / 33.53 %	10	C	56.27 % / 34.94 %	19	A	57.62 % / 37.99 %	28	A	80.54 % / 11.72 %	37	A	76.23 % / 11.31 %
2	B	46.84 % / 46.22 %	11	A	78.15 % / 10.98 %	20	D	63.75 % / 30.91 %	29	D	50.87 % / 38.45 %	38	B	55.5 % / 35.14 %
3	C	60.09 % / 35.9 %	12	B	47.39 % / 39.45 %	21	B	58.88 % / 30.64 %	30	B	58.71 % / 30.39 %	39	A	52.84 % / 43.44 %
4	B	65.54 % / 30.41 %	13	B	14.32 % / 74.86 %	22	D	11.57 % / 78.45 %	31	D	77.93 % / 20.12 %	40	C	76.71 % / 18.73 %
5	A	53.15 % / 39.21 %	14	C	12.91 % / 84.9 %	23	C	61.12 % / 31.73 %	32	C	47.51 % / 50.91 %	41	C	78.47 % / 18.92 %
6	A	50.13 % / 40.64 %	15	A	50.3 % / 42.88 %	24	C	89.0 % / 10.96 %	33	D	64.98 % / 32.89 %	42	D	56.97 % / 41.12 %
7	A	63.88 % / 32.36 %	16	A	49.81 % / 49.29 %	25	C	52.32 % / 32.03 %	34	C	44.1 % / 53.75 %	43	C	20.9 % / 73.81 %
8	D	58.93 % / 39.13 %	17	B	43.36 % / 40.89 %	26	C	82.74 % / 13.37 %	35	C	26.3 % / 68.87 %	44	A	24.76 % / 73.06 %
9	A	49.4 % / 33.41 %	18	A	51.72 % / 44.55 %	27	B	54.76 % / 44.75 %	36	C	46.28 % / 37.87 %	45	D	12.91 % / 77.29 %

Performance Analysis

Avg. Score (%)	46.67%
Toppers Score (%)	60.0%
Your Score	

//Hints and Solutions//

1. The correct answer is Less successful.

Be in eclipse: much less successful and important than before

For example: Even when her career was temporarily in eclipse she had no financial worries.

Hence, the correct option is (A).

2. The correct answer is 'Methods of achieving something.'

Ways and means: The methods by which something is accomplished or attained, especially in relation to finances

For example: We're here to discuss the goals of the project, not the ways and means.

Hence, the correct option is (B).

3. The correct answer is 'Very angry.'

Up in arms: angry or rebellious

For example: My mom was up in arms about the new salary cuts rumored to be put in place.

Hence, the correct option is (C).

4. The correct answer is 'Very costly'.

Big ticket: Very expensive ,Very costly

For example: We've never had much money, so a brand new furniture set is something of a big-ticket item for us.

Hence, the correct option is (B).

5. The correct answer is, 'An event or piece of news which is unexpected'.

Bolt from the blue: A sudden, unexpected event

For example: The resignation of the chairman came like a bolt from the blue.

Hence, the correct option is (A).

6. The correct answer is, 'Behave unconventional and unpredictable'.

Be a law unto yourself: behave in an independent way, ignoring laws, rules, or conventional ways of doing things

For example: Some of the landowners were a law unto themselves.

Hence, the correct option is (A).

7. The correct answer is, 'To make oneself look neat'.

Spiff up: improve in appearance often by making more neat or stylish

For example: High-school students used to spiff up their college applications with extracurriculars like Model U.N. and student council.

Hence, the correct option is (A).

8. The correct answer is, 'To behave without any control'.

Run wild: to run, go, behave, etc., in a wild and uncontrolled way

For example: The mob was running wild in the streets.

Hence, the correct option is (D).

9. The correct answer is, 'To relax after a period of activity'.

Wind down: (of a person) relax after stress or excitement.

For example: I sank into a hot bath in order to wind down.

Hence, the correct option is (A).

10. The correct answer is, 'To enjoy oneself without doing much'.

Mellow out: to become relaxed and calm

For example: My dad has definitely mellowed out as he's gotten older.

Hence, the correct option is (C).

11. The most appropriate meaning of the given idiom/phrase 'Dirt cheap' is 'Extremely cheap'.

Dirt cheap means something that is extremely cheap. The idea of something being as cheap as dirt.

Extremely cheap means something costing very little, relatively low in price, inexpensive.

For example: In United Kingdom, carrots are dirt cheap.

Hence, the correct option is (A).

12. The most appropriate meaning of the given idiom/phrase 'A shrinking violet' is 'A shy person'.

A shrinking violet means an exaggeratedly shy person.

A shy person is someone who is being nervous or reserved around other people, especially in a social situation.

For example: She was a shrinking violet until she went away to college.

Hence, the correct option is (B).

13. The most appropriate meaning of the given idiom/phrase 'Gordian knot' is 'A difficult problem'.

Gordian knot: A complicated problem that can only be solved with creative or unorthodox thinking.

For example: The coding problem looked like a Gordian knot until we realized we could bypass it altogether with a different approach.

By the given meaning and example we can say that 'A difficult problem' is the appropriate meaning.

Hence, the correct option is (B).

14. The most appropriate meaning of the given idiom/phrase 'Fall in a heap' is 'To lose control of one's own feelings'.

Fall in a heap means to become very emotional, especially sad and perhaps to literally hunch over as a result.

For example: Poor Jane really fell in a heap during the funeral.

By the given meaning and example we can say that 'to lose control of one's own feelings' is the appropriate meaning.

Hence, the correct option is (C).

15. The most appropriate meaning of the given idiom/phrase 'Have a conniption fit' is 'To be very angry'.

To have a conniption fit means to become unreasonably angry or upset, to have an outburst of rage, frustration or ill temper.

For example: My mother is going to have a conniption fit when she sees what has happened to the car!

By the given meaning and example we can say that 'to be very angry' is the appropriate meaning.

Hence, the correct option is (A).

16. The most appropriate meaning of the given idiom/phrase 'Be in seventh heaven' is 'To be extremely happy'.

To be in seventh heaven means to be in a state of bliss or extreme happiness, ecstatic.

For example: I was in my seventh heaven when I received my promotion letter.

By the given meaning and example we can say that 'to be extremely happy' is the appropriate meaning.

Hence, the correct option is (A).

17. The most appropriate meaning of the given idiom/phrase 'Hand in glove' is 'Working together'.

Hand in glove means to work very closely with someone or something, in close collusion or association.

For example: The terrorists are working hand in glove with the drug traffickers.

By the given meaning and example we can say that 'working together' is the appropriate meaning.

Hence, the correct option is (B).

18. The most appropriate meaning of the given idiom/phrase 'Dirt cheap' is 'Extremely cheap'.

Nip in the bud: to stop something before it aggravates or becomes difficult or unmanageable, to put an end to an idea in its initial stage.

For example: Inflation will only get worse if the government doesn't do something right now to nip it in the bud.

By the given meaning and example we can say that 'prevent a small problem before it becomes severe' is the appropriate meaning.

Hence, the correct option is (A).

19. The most appropriate meaning of the given idiom/phrase 'Like a shag on a rock' is 'Completely alone'.

Like a shag on a rock means someone who is lonely or completely isolated.

For example: Even at parties around lots of people, I still tend to feel like a shag on a rock.

By the given meaning and example we can say that 'completely alone' is the appropriate meaning.

Hence, the correct option is (A).

20. The most appropriate meaning of the given idiom/phrase 'A pearl of wisdom' is 'An important piece of advice'.

A pearl of wisdom means a wise saying or a valuable piece of advice.

For example: A parent always shares a pearl of wisdom with their child.

By the given meaning and example we can say that 'an important piece of advice' is the appropriate meaning.

Hence, the correct option is (D).

21. The correct answer is 'To cry wolf' is 'to give false alarm'.

Meaning: call for help when it is not needed, with the effect that one is not believed when one really does need help.

Sentence: If you cry wolf too often, people will stop believing you.

Hence, the correct option is (B).

22. To pull oneself together means To calm oneself and begin to think or act.

Hence, the correct option is (D).

23. The idiom 'under the weather' means 'slightly unwell or in low spirits.'

Therefore, 'being sick' is the correct answer.

Hence, the correct option is (C).

24. Hard nose attitude: being tough, stubborn, or uncompromising

For example, That guy seems so hard-nosed that I'm afraid to say hi to him.

Thus, 'aggressive' is the most suitable meaning.

Hence, the correct option is (C).

25. The meaning of the phrase "take with a grain of salt" means not taking something too seriously.

Example: The Indian players took the issue of racism with a grain of salt.

Hence, the correct option is (C).

26. The idiom, 'Alive and kicking' means continue to live or exist and be full of energy.

For example, She hadn't met her younger sister after her marriage and was delighted to see her alive and kicking at a social event last weekend.

Hence, the correct option is (C).

27. The meaning of the idiom "Be in the same boat" is 'To be in the same difficult situation'.

Example: When he lost his job he did not feel too bad as, after the company downsized, many others were in the same boat.

Hence, the correct option is (B).

28. Burning question: an important question that requires an answer.

Hence, the correct option is (A).

29. All in all is 'Most important'.

As she is only girl in a big family, so she is all in all in her home.

Hence, the correct option is (D)

30. "Hitting the books" means to study especially in time of tests and exams. Here the sentence means implying the meaning of the idiom as "They go to the beach when they should be studying really hard and then they wonder why they don't get good marks."

Hence, the correct option is (B).

31. The idiom A peeping Tom refers to a person who secretly watches others, especially for sexual gratification.

Example: Reynolds contended that the Chinese man was a peeping tom whom he caught spying on his wife one last night March while she was toweling herself after a shower.

Hence, the correct option is (D).

32. The correct answer is 'a small problem or weakness in a person or system that can result in failure'.

Someone's Achilles heel is the weakest point in their character or nature, where it is easiest for other people to attack or criticize them.

Example- His Achilles heel is his quick temper.
Hence, the correct option is (C).

33. To pick holes means To find mistakes and 'criticize someone' has done or said, to show that it is not good or not correct.

Hence, the correct option is (D).

34. Hit the Books means: To study

Example: "Danny was in danger of failing, so before his last math test he left the show early to go home and hit the books."

Hence, the correct option is (C).

35. The correct answer is Face the music is 'To face the consequences'.

'Face the music' means 'to accept the unpleasant results of one's action.

Sentence: After Janine was caught stealing, she had to face the music.

Hence, the correct option is (C).

36. The idiom off the hook is 'no longer in difficulty or trouble'.

Sentence: At first, Sam was suspected of stealing money from the safe, but he was let off the hook after security camera footage showed it was someone else.

Hence, the correct option is (C).

37. To face the music means to 'accept the consequences'.

sentence: He would later have to face the music for his improper decisions.

Hence, the correct option is (A).

38. To Hit the sack means to go to bed.

Example: After the long journey, he hit the sack as soon as he reached home.

He wanted to hit the sack and did not feel like going out to party with his friends.

Hence, the correct option is (B).

39. The correct answer is:

Their relationship has experienced difficulties ever since they fell in love with the same girl.

Run into rough weather means you run into problems and begin to experience them. For eg: The new policy can run into rough weather.

Synonyms: Affliction, be devoured by something, etc.

Hence, the correct option is (A).

40. The correct answer is: You must have a concrete project and not have unrealistic ideas if you want to submit an application for a loan.

Build castles in the air means have unrealistic ideas.

sentence: You need good advice to start your business- don't just build castles in the sir.

Hence, the correct option is (C).

41. Let's look at the meaning of the given idiom:

A Hard nut to crack - a problem that is very difficult to solve or a person who is very difficult to understand. For Example: The test problem was a hard nut to crack.

Hence, the correct option is (C).

42. 'Gift of the gab' is an idiom which means the ability to speak fluently and eloquently. A person with this gift would be a good orator.

Hence, the correct option is (D).

43. To "bell the cat" is an idiom which means to do something which is very daunting/difficult or to do an impossible task.

Hence, the correct option is (C).

44. Apple of discord is an idiom that means a bone of contention (a reason for quarrel).

Example:

- The ancestral property became an apple of discord among the three brothers.
- The water-sharing pact has been the apple of discord between the two states.

Hence, the correct option is (A).

45. Let's look at the meaning of the given idiom:

Getting in everyone's hair - to annoy everyone, usually by being present all the time. For Example: My sister has a habit of getting in everyone's hair whenever there is an important discussion.

Hence, the correct option is (D).

Ques (1-5):Direction: In the question, two statements are given to you followed by four possible conjunctions that can join the sentences to form one sentence. Identify which of the following conjunctions can join both the sentences such that meaning of the two statements would not change.

Q.1 I. Immediately after the summit, Trump did nothing to dispel the suspicions of his Russian connections.

II. He had been following orders from the Kremlin and this made people wonder about his priorities.

A. Because   **B. As if**   **C.** As of   **D.** Though

Q.2 I. Thunderstorms brought the first significant rainfall in weeks to the UK

II. Belfast international airport received 88.2mm in a matter of hours, more than the region's monthly July average.

A. As   **B.** If   **C.** Because   **D.** So

Q.3 I. Unlike other business leaders she has not shunned political leaders but engaged with them

II. She believes that society needs political leaders to bring about change and citizens need to engage with them.

A. In lieu of   **B.** Because   **C.** As in   **D.** As of

Q.4 I. The ultimate target is to test the medicine on human beings so that it can be cured in them as well.

II. All the medicines discovered by doctors have been successfully tested on animals of all kinds to treat carcinogenic cells.

A. Whereas   **B.** As   **C.** And   **D.** But

Q.5 I. The fever not going down even for a moment for almost a week.

II. Prasun decided to give the examination his best shot so that there is no regret in future.

A. As   **B.** Despite   **C.** Unless   **D.** Whereas

Ques (6-10):Direction: In the question, two statements are given to you followed by four possible conjunctions that can join the sentences to form one sentence. Identify which of the following conjunctions can join both the sentences such that meaning of the two statements would not change.

Q.6 I. I saw a stranger in my room.

II. I was roaming in the garden.

A. Once   **B.** Because   **C.** When   **D.** Whereas

Q.7 I. You are a hardworking and intelligent student.

II. Your sister doesn't pay attention in the class.

A. Once   **B.** Because

C. Although   **D.** Whereas

Q.8 I. I shall inform you.

II. I am done with this assignment.

A. Once   **B.** Because

C. Though   **D.** Therefore

Q.9 I. I did not pass the final exam.

II. It was a lucky day for me.

A. Whereas   **B.** Because

C. Still   **D.** Therefore

Q.10 I. The fruit of success is always sweet.

II. It can be enjoyed only after a prolonged period of hard work.

A. Unless   **B.** Because

C. But   **D.** Therefore

Ques (11-14):Direction: In the question, two statements are given to you followed by four possible conjunctions that can join the sentences to form one sentence. Identify which of the following conjunctions can join both the sentences such that meaning of the two statements would not change.

Q.11 A. Harry squelched along the deserted corridor.

B. He came across somebody who looked just as preoccupied as he was.

I. As

II. And

III. But

IV. Nevertheless

A. Only II and III   **B.** Only I

C. Only I and II   **D.** Only IV

Q.12 A. Journalistic freedom is inextricably and inalienably linked to good practices.

B. Some media houses publicize pointless news just to gain more TRP ratings.

I. Even though

II. Yet

III. But

IV. Because

A. Only I and III   **B.** Only IV

C. Only II, III and IV   **D.** Only I, II and III

Q.13 A. Sharan and Ram started their game very well.

B. They lost against Lukasz Kubot and Marcelo Melo in an exhilarating match.

A. But, therefore   **B.** Which, since

C. However, despite   **D.** And, so

Q.14 A. Too much is at stake for not only the nearly 11.3 million undocumented workers.

B. It's at stake for the nearly 1.5 million temporary foreign workers.

A. But also   **B.** And

C. Therefore   **D.** Only (A) and (B)

Ques (15-19):Direction: In the question, two statements are given to you followed by four possible conjunctions that can join the sentences to form one sentence. Identify which of the following conjunctions can join both the sentences such that meaning of the two statements would not change.

Q.15 I. The school has the best research infrastructure in the town.

II. The students are not at all interested in pursuing education.

A. Owing to   **B.** Hence
C. Because of   **D.** However

Q.16 I. I didn't want to get into the depth of the matter at any cost.

II. I took the book from the shelf and started reading with great attention.

A. Instead   **B.** In contrast
C. On the other hand   **D.** However

Q.17 I. I am of the opinion that there is no problem with his technique to play the short ball.

II. I will talk to him about this the first thing after the match today.

A. Nonetheless   **B.** Because
C. Hence   **D.** By comparison

Q.18 I. The monsoon has been very late this year and it has only started raining now.

II. The farmers are demanding compensation from the government for their revenue loss.

A. Nevertheless   **B.** Though
C. Owing to   **D.** Yet

Q.19 I. The team played its heart out in the match.

II. The result had nothing to show for the efforts put into the match by them.

A. Nonetheless   **B.** Since
C. As   **D.** Because

Ques (20-24):Direction: In the question, two statements are given to you followed by four possible conjunctions that can join the sentences to form one sentence. Identify which of the following conjunctions can join both the sentences such that meaning of the two statements would not change.

Q.20 I. The current changes in the tax rate would raise significant revenue.

II. Analysts believe the new tax rate would be very progressive.

A. Finally, such as
B. Also, instead
C. Subsequently, clearly
D. Furthermore, in addition

Q.21 I. Organizations want to cut costs and improve their agility to meet constantly changing consumer demands.

II. Today's employees crave flexibility and control of work in their hands.

A. But, since   **B.** With, thereafter
C. Whereas, while   **D.** From, beside

Q.22 I. A few years ago, more than half of India's banking sector had female chiefs.

II. India lags behind the world in female workforce participation, and is ranked 11th from the bottom among 131 countries.

A. On the whole, in short
B. However, nonetheless
C. Further, even so
D. Anyway, Again

Q.23 I. The Reserve Bank of India started an easing cycle in 2015.

II. It cut policy rates seven times and bond yields fell to levels not seen since the global financial crisis..

A. Eventually, Subsequently
B. Meanwhile, otherwise
C. Thereafter, nearby
D. Currently, illustrated

Q.24 I. China has decided to ban the imports of plastic waste into the country.

II. A lot of countries will have to make new plans for their disposal.

A. Now, hence   **B.** As, since
C. Finally, meanwhile   **D.** Both (A) and (B)

Ques (25-29):Direction: In the question, two statements and four connectors are given. Only one of the connectors from those given can be used to combine the given two statements into one sentence without changing the meaning. Choose that connector as your answer.

Q.25 I. The teacher has asked the students not to copy from others during the examination.

II. The students kept on copying during the final examination resulting in the expulsion of two of them from the university.

A. Yet   **B.** If
C. As   **D.** On account of

Q.26 I. I was not in a situation to step out of the house yesterday because of my severe headache.

II. I attended the sales meeting at my office on the instructions of my senior management.

A. Since   **B.** Nevertheless
C. On the other hand   **D.** By comparison

Q.27 I. I was very tired and exhausted after spending the whole day at the hospital.

II. I went to sleep without having dinner after coming back.

A. So   **B.** In fact
C. Especially   **D.** And

Q.28 I. The minister will definitely come to this locality for election campaigning within the next two days.

II. He may not come here if he is denied the ticket from this constituency by his party.

A. Since   **B.** Unless
C. In addition to   **D.** Of course

Q.29 I. Like every second Indian, I am a big fan of sports and I also like to watch a lot of matches with my friends.

II. I love to watch football matches and enjoy the nail-biting finish most of the matches have.

A. Especially	B. Although
C. Whether	D. Nevertheless

Ques (30-34):Directions: You are required to match statements from columns 1 and 2 and find which of the following pairs of statement make sense meaningfully and grammatically.

Q.30

Column (1)		Column (2)	
A.	The automobile industry employs 37 million	D.	and it was a lovely sight.
B.	A Suddenly the lights went out	E.	people and contributes to seven percent of the country's GDP.
C.	The waves were crashing on the shore	F.	dust finally settled.

A. Only A-E	B. Only B-F
C. Only C-D, B-F	D. Only A-E, C-D

Q.31

Column (1)		Column (2)	
A.	The International Monetary Fund has already	D.	dancer than a singer.
B.	She has started to gain weight suddenly	E.	pared India's growth projections citing lowered domestic demand.
C.	I would rather be a	F.	the wild elephant was no longer sane.

A. Only A-E	B. Only B-F
C. Only B-F, C-D	D. Only A-E, C-D

Q.32

Column (1)		Column (2)	
A.	Entering into parallel pecuniary relationships with stakeholders can be detrimental	D.	was summoned for a hearing.
B.	We thought he loved her but it	E.	to the interests of a company, given that such parties influence decision making.
C.	She always speaks to him	F.	turned out that he loved another girl.

A. Only C-D	B. Only A-E
C. Only A-E, B-F	D. Only B-F

Q.33

Column (1)		Column (2)	
A.	The US had given a conditional waiver	D.	than I had initially thought it would be.
B.	The scores are low because the	E.	task is cognitively demanding.
C.	Writing a list of random sentences is harder	F.	to eight nations to keep buying oil from Iran.

A. Only C-D	B. A-F, B-E, C-D
C. Only B-E	D. Only A-F, C-D

Q.34

Column (1)		Column (2)	
A.	Trade secrets could be anything ranging from	D.	she wanted to buy a jumpsuit.
B.	Despite knowing that it won't suit her	E.	and he went to the theatre instead.
C.	He was supposed to go to school	F.	designs and processes to methods or information.

A. Only A-F	B. Only B-D
C. Only A-F, C-E	D. Only A-F, B-D

Q.35 Direction: You are required to match statements from columns (1) and (2) and find which of the following pairs of statement make sense meaningfully and grammatically.

Column (1)	Column (2)
A. Freelancing is an attractive profession now	D. it is not possible for anything to yield results
B. It is often seen that creative people suffer from	E. though it is costing a lot in marketing
C. The new scheme of the bank is paying dividends	F. with lot of websites offering decent payments

A. A-E, B-F	B. B-D
C. A-F, C-E	D. B-F, A-F, C-D

Ques (36-40):Direction: You are presented with two statements followed by four possible conjunctions that can join the two sentences to form one sentence. Identify which conjunction can join both the sentences in such a way that meaning of the two statements would not change.

Q.36 I. The rupee suffered a drastic loss of about 20% in just a few months.

II. The fall in value of Rupee has raised fears of a repeat of the currency crisis of 2013.

A. Like	B. Unlike
C. Whereas	D. None of these

Q.37 I. It is time that the Environment ministry does away with all kinds of illegal mining activities in the country.

II. The irreparable damage caused by these illegal mining activities is going to contribute a lot to global warming.

A. In lieu of	B. Because of
C. Because	D. Otherwise

Q.38 I. The popularity of cricket eating into the share of revenue of other sports in India for many years now.

II. All other sports are suffering and India is not able to win medals in Olympics in all such sports.

A. Because	B. Therefore
C. Henceforth	D. Due to

Q.39 I. I am of the opinion that my father would have done it the same way had he known this fact.

II. The differences we had when he was alive.

A. Due to	B. Instead of
C. Because of	D. As

Q.40 I. The notification by the Reserve Bank of India to do away with stapling of currency notes by banks has not done much difference.

II. Banks are left with no other option but to issue the old notes to their customers in the absence of fresh notes from the RBI.

A. Due to   **B.** Because of

C. As   **D.** Hence

Ques (41-45):Direction: Select the phrase/connector (it must be at the start) from the given three phrases which can be used to form a single sentence from the two sentences given below, implying the same meaning as expressed in the statement sentences.

Q.41 The Five Year Planning has been done away with in India. The Government of India has decided to go ahead with a 20-year blueprint for development.

I. As the Government of India has decided to go ahead _____.

II. Since the Five Year Planning has been done away with _____.

III. That the Five Year Planning has been done away with _____.

A. Only II   **B.** Only I

C. Both I and III   **D.** Both I and II

Q.42 The Supreme Court has made it clear that only long term motor insurance policies will be there in India. This will make all the insurance companies issue policies for long term.

I. That the Supreme Court has made it clear that _____.

II. As the Supreme Court has made it clear _____.

III. The Supreme Court has made it clear yet _____.

A. Both II and III   **B.** Both I and II

C. Only III   **D.** Only II

Q.43 Many students are now very concerned about the environment. It is a good sign for the country as well as the society.

I. As many students are now very concerned about the environment _____.

II. That many students are now very concerned about the environment _____.

III. Though many students are now very concerned about the environment_____.

A. Both II and III   **B.** Only II

C. Both I and III   **D.** Both I and II

Q.44 The Government is going to launch GPS based technology to track the agriculture land in the country. Google is going to help the Government develop technology for this.

I. Since the Government is going to launch _____.

II. While Google is going to help the Government develop technology _____.

III. Hardly has the Google been helping the government develop technology for this when _____.

A. Only III   **B.** Both II and III

C. Only I   **D.** None of the above

Q.45 The Good Samaritan Law of the Government is not at all effective. This law will not be put into practice by the police.

I. Since the Good Samaritan Law will not be put into practice by the police _____.

II. As the Good Samaritan Law of the government is not at all effective _____.

III. Scarcely the Good Samaritan Law of the Government is not at all effective ___.

A. Both II and III   **B.** Only II

C. Only I   **D.** None of the above

// Smart Answer Sheet //

Correct Indicates percentage of students who answered questions correctly.

Skipped Indicates percentage of students who skipped questions.

Q.	Ans.	Correct / Skipped
1	B	31.04 % / 67.99 %
2	A	45.57 % / 53.42 %
3	B	62.54 % / 30.97 %
4	A	16.51 % / 74.56 %
5	B	61.6 % / 36.61 %
6	C	81.07 % / 10.82 %
7	D	77.75 % / 12.85 %
8	A	42.63 % / 50.15 %
9	C	85.89 % / 13.58 %

Q.	Ans.	Correct / Skipped
10	C	48.93 % / 34.29 %
11	C	87.78 % / 11.93 %
12	D	53.24 % / 44.96 %
13	C	61.15 % / 31.37 %
14	A	45.5 % / 31.72 %
15	D	80.79 % / 13.75 %
16	A	83.49 % / 16.41 %
17	A	87.33 % / 11.34 %
18	C	86.66 % / 11.33 %

Q.	Ans.	Correct / Skipped
19	A	89.94 % / 10.06 %
20	D	43.35 % / 35.37 %
21	C	56.65 % / 39.86 %
22	B	66.13 % / 32.59 %
23	A	54.14 % / 37.0 %
24	D	86.49 % / 12.65 %
25	A	82.99 % / 11.93 %
26	B	67.79 % / 31.11 %
27	A	44.44 % / 47.02 %

Q.	Ans.	Correct / Skipped
28	B	67.69 % / 30.26 %
29	A	46.96 % / 41.46 %
30	D	65.25 % / 33.78 %
31	D	78.12 % / 18.27 %
32	C	52.25 % / 41.48 %
33	B	40.38 % / 42.92 %
34	D	67.66 % / 32.09 %
35	C	42.21 % / 42.53 %
36	D	61.99 % / 33.92 %

Q.	Ans.	Correct / Skipped
37	C	40.61 % / 41.54 %
38	D	67.08 % / 31.9 %
39	B	68.27 % / 30.77 %
40	C	62.37 % / 34.45 %
41	B	46.62 % / 41.34 %
42	B	53.36 % / 45.95 %
43	D	69.61 % / 30.12 %
44	D	48.06 % / 47.98 %
45	D	55.57 % / 31.42 %

Performance Analysis	
Avg. Score (%)	48.89%
Toppers Score (%)	60.0%
Your Score	

//Hints and Solutions//

1. If we read the two sentences, we can observe that the second statement is trying to highlight what the situation seems like. And among the choices available, only 'as if' can be used because it is used to describe how a situation seems to be.

Combing the two sentences the new sentence will be:

Immediately after the summit, Trump did nothing to dispel the suspicions of his Russian connections as if he had been following orders from the Kremlin and this made people wonder about his priorities.

Hence, the correct option is (B).

2. If we read the two sentences, we can observe the second sentence discusses an event which happens while another is in progress. And among the choices available, only 'as' can be used because we use as to introduce two events happening at the same time

Combing the two sentences the new sentence will be:

As thunderstorms brought the first significant rainfall in weeks to the UK, Belfast international airport received 88.2mm in a matter of hours, more than the region's monthly July average.

Hence, the correct option is (A).

3. If we read the two sentences, we can observe that they are related by cause and effect relationship. And among the choices available, only 'because' can be used in this context since it means 'the reasons thereof'

Combing the two sentences the new sentence will be:

Unlike other business leaders she has not shunned political leaders but engaged with them because she believes that society needs political leaders to bring about change and citizens need to engage with them.

Hence, the correct option is (B).

4. If we go through the sentences, it is evident that both the sentences are contrasting in nature. Besides, sentence II should come in the beginning as it introduces the topic and with sentence I in the beginning; it is not possible to understand the disease the author is talking about. Among the given options, only 'whereas' can be used in the given context as it can connect two contrasting sentences.

Hence, the complete sentence after combining the two will be:

All the medicines discovered by doctors have been successfully tested on animals of all kinds to treat carcinogenic cells whereas the ultimate target is to test the medicine on human beings so that it can be cured in them as well.

Hence, the correct option is (A).

5. If we go through the sentences, it implies that both are contrasting sentences. Out of the given options, only 'despite' refers to 'without being affected by' and it fits the context with perfection.

The complete sentence after combining the two will be:

Despite the fever not going down even for a moment for almost a week, Prasun decided to give the examination his best shot so that there is no regret in future.

Hence, the correct option is (B).

6. Here, both the events simultaneously took place, event in statement II was already happening when event in statement I started occuring.

Thus "When" suits best the purpose.

New sentence: I was roaming in the garden when I saw a stranger in my room.

Hence, the correct option is (C).

7. Here both the statements show some kind of contradiction with each other, where one person possess A quality and second person (connected to first person) lacks it.

Whereas conveys such thought appropriately. Here one of the siblings possess qualities like hard work and intelligence whereas the other one lacks it.

New sentence: You are a hardworking and intelligent student whereas your sister doesn't pay attention in the class.

Hence, the correct option is (D).

8. Here both the statements are connected with each other. Thus to combine these two , such conjunction is required which can join the two interrelated facts.

Here it is clear that the event in statement I will occur provided the event in statement II has occured. Statement II will have to occur definitely in order to make statement I happen.

Once defines the relationship in an absolutely correct manner.

New sentence: I shall inform you once I am done with this assignment.

Hence, the correct option is (A).

9. Here both the statements are contradictory to each other. Thus to combine these two, such conjunction is required which can join the two contradicting facts.

Here it is clear that the event in statement I has occured before the event in statement II.

Whereas is not contextually correct in the given statement.

Still is one such conjunction which can join the two contradictory facts mentioned over here.

New sentence: I did not pass the exam, still it was a lucky day for me.

Hence, the correct option is (C).

10. Here both the statements are connected with each other. Thus to combine these two , such conjunction is required which can join the two interrelated facts.

Here it is clear that the event in statement I expresses contradiction to the event in statement II. We know that fruit of success is always sweet but to achieve a real success is not an easy task.

Clearly, But will be used here as it is used to connect ideas that contrast.

Unless is used to express a condition and usage of it would be absurd here in the context.

Because shows a cause and effect kind of relationship and would be irrelevant here.

Therefore is used to define a conclusion. Thus is wrong in this case.

New sentence: The fruit of success is always sweet but it can be enjoyed only after a prolonged period of hard work.

Hence, the correct option is (C).

11. The sentence given here shows a sequence or coherence. As Harry passed by the corridor he saw somebody. There is no contradiction between the statements. Thus use of 'But' is inappropriate here. Thus choice III gets eliminated and option A as well.

Choice IV 'Nevertheless' is contextually not making any sense. This makes option D incorrect.

Now left with 'as' and 'and'. 'As' is very much appropriate here to denote the coherence of the events of passing by and looking someone.

As Harry squelched along the deserted corridor he came across somebody who looked just as preoccupied as he was.

Similarly 'and' can also be used to connect the sentences, as it carry forwards the flow of the event.

Harry squelched along the deserted corridor and came across somebody who looked just as preoccupied as he was.

As both connectors given as choices I and II are fitting well.

Hence, the correct option is (C).

12. Both the statements show contradiction. On one hand, first statement signifies journalism as indistinguishably attached to good practices. On the other hand, second statement talks about the malpractices in one of the branches of journalism i.e. Electronic media.

'Because' is used to define a reason, thus in contextual here.

All other choices connect the sentences very well.

Even though Journalistic freedom is inextricably and inalienably linked to good practices, some media houses publicize pointless news just to gain more TRP ratings.

Journalistic freedom is inextricably and inalienably linked to good practices yet some media houses publicize pointless news just to gain more TRP ratings.

Journalistic freedom is inextricably and inalienably linked to good practices but some media houses publicize pointless news just to gain more TRP ratings.

Hence, the correct option is (D).

13. Here the two statements show contradiction. The first statements talks about the good play and second statements tells about losing the play.

Evidently option D which consist 'and' and 'so' gets eliminated.

Option B- 'since' is absurd to be used here.

Option A- 'therefore' signifies the concluding effect in an sentence. Here we cannot see any such reasoning. If one started off very well then one has to win. So use of 'therefore' is incorrect here.

Option C- Both the connectors 'however' and 'despite' connect the sentence without changing the context and grammar.

Sharan and Ram started their game very well however they lost against Lukasz Kubot and Marcelo Melo in an exhilarating match.

Despite starting the game very well Sharan and Ram lost against Lukasz Kubot and Marcelo Melo in an exhilarating match.

Hence, the correct option is (C).

14. Here both the statements are co-related. As they show the same concern for undocumented as well as foreign workers.

Also, use of 'not only' implies the use of conjunction 'but also' here, as they are the correlative conjunctions.

Too much is at stake for not only the nearly 11.3 million undocumented workers but also for the nearly 1.5 million temporary foreign workers.

Hence, the correct option is (A).

15. Here the two statements have been used in the sense that the school has the best infrastructure for conducting research but the students are not at all interested in taking advantage of that. Only however can be used to connect these two sentences since the first one is about some facility whereas the next is about how that is going in vain. All the other connectors are used to connect sentences that have cause and effect relationship between them. So, all of them can be eliminated.

The connected sentence would be: The school has the best research infrastructure in the town however the students are not at all interested in pursuing education.

Hence, the correct option is (D).

16. If we take into account the context of the two given statements, it is regarding the fact that I did not want to listen to the matter and started reading the book. In contrast is not correct because it is used to indicate something that is opposite to the other and it is certainly not fit in the given context. On the other hand and however can also be eliminated since they cannot connect these two given statements. Only instead can be used in order to connect the two sentences without changing the meaning.

The connected statement would be: I didn't want to get into the depth of the matter at any cost instead I took the book from the shelf and started reading with great attention.

Hence, the correct option is (A).

17. The two statements are regarding the context that the person does not think that there is no problem with his technique to play the short ball but he will definitely talk about it with him after the match. Among the given connectors, both because and hence are mainly used for statements that have cause and effect relationship whereas by comparison is used in order to indicate any kind of comparison. Only nonetheless can connect these two statements since it implies in spite of that and that is why it can be used to connect these two statements without changing the meaning.

The connected sentence would be: I am of the opinion that there is no problem with his technique to play the short ball nonetheless I will talk to him about this the first thing after the match today.

Hence, the correct option is (A).

18. Here the given two statements carry a cause and effect relationship. The reason the farmers are asking for compensation is because of the late onset of monsoon in the country. That is the main reason the farmers have lost their revenue. Among the given connectors, we can see that nevertheless can be used to indicate that in spite of something we have done something else whereas though and yet are also not correct here. There is only one connector that can be used here i.e. owing to.

The connected sentence would be: Owing to the late monsoon and rains this year, the farmers are demanding compensation from the government for their revenue loss.

Hence, the correct option is (C).

19. According to the given context we can see that the players in the team played very well but at the end of the day they lost of the match. Therefore nothing could be shown against the efforts put forward by the players in the match. Nonetheless is used to imply in spite of whereas the rest of the three connectors are mainly used for the purpose of connecting the cause and effect related sentences.

The connected sentence would be:

The team played its heart out in the match nonetheless the result had nothing to show for the efforts put into the match by them.

Hence, the correct option is (A).

20. Both statements supplement each other i.e. they add to each other and carry forward the idea. Out of the given options only 'Furthermore' and 'in addition' fits the context with perfection.

I. In addition to the current changes in the tax rate raising significant revenues, analysts believe the new tax rate would be very progressive.

II. Analysts believe the new tax rate would be very progressive and furthermore, the current changes in the tax rate would raise significant revenue.

Hence, the correct option is (D).

21. Both the statements have the same tone while stating different sides of the same coin (organization and employees). Since they state perspectives which have the same direction, but cannot be used and option A is eliminated.

Option B is also incorrect since thereafter indicates something happening after another event. This is incorrect as there is no indication of a timeline here.

Option D is incorrect as from is used to indicate the point in time at which a particular process starts and is incorrect here. Beside means next to and is incorrect.

Option C is correct:

I. Whereas organizations want to cut costs and improve their agility to meet constantly changing consumer demands, today's employees crave flexibility and control of work in their hands.

II. Organizations want to cut costs and improve their agility to meet constantly changing consumer demands while today's employees crave flexibility and control of work in their hands.

Hence, the correct option is (C).

22. Out of the given options only 'However' and 'nonetheless' fits the context with perfection.

The complete statement would be:

A few years ago, more than half of India's banking sector had female chiefs however, India lags behind the world in female workforce participation, and is ranked 11th from the bottom among 131 countries.

A few years ago, more than half of India's banking sector had female chiefs nonetheless, India lags behind the world in female workforce participation, and is ranked 11th from the bottom among 131 countries.

Hence, the correct option is (B).

23. Out of the given options only 'Eventually' and 'Subsequently' fits the context with perfection.

I. The Reserve Bank of India started an easing cycle in 2015, eventually cutting policy rates seven times and leading to bond yields falling to levels not seen since the global financial crisis.

II. The Reserve Bank of India started an easing cycle in 2015 and subsequently cut policy rates seven times, leading to bond yields falling to levels not seen since the global financial crisis.

Hence, the correct option is (A).

24. Out of the given options 'Now' and 'hence' fits the context with perfection.

I. China has decided to ban the imports of plastic waste into the country and now a lot of countries will have to make new plans for their disposal.

II. China has decided to ban the imports of plastic waste into the country and hence a lot of countries will have to make new plans for their disposal.

Out of the given options 'As' and 'since' also fits the context with perfection.

I. A lot of countries will have to make new plans for their disposal as China has decided to ban the imports of plastic waste into the country.

II. A lot of countries will have to make new plans for their disposal since China has decided to ban the imports of plastic waste into the country.

Hence, the correct option is (D).

25. The first statement is regarding something that has already been said but still somebody did it, as is explained in the second statement.

Among the given options, yet is the correct choice since it is used to imply that despite something whereas if is mainly used in a conditional clause. All the other three connectors given are used to indicate some cause and effect relationship. Hence they can be eliminated as the given statements do not share the cause and effect relationship.

The connected statement would be:

The teacher has asked the students not to copy from others during the examination, yet the students kept on copying during the final examination resulting in the expulsion of two of the them from the university.

Hence, the correct option is (A).

26. The first statement is regarding the issue faced by the person whereas the second statement is regarding the activity on the part of the person despite the problems faced by him or her. Among the given connectors, only B can connect these two statements since it implies 'in spite of something'. Other connectors are out of context in case of these two statements.

Since is mainly used to indicate the cause-effect relationship whereas on the other hand is used in order to imply something contrasting to what has been said already. By comparison is also not correct for the given context.

The complete statement would be:

I was not in a situation to step out of the house yesterday because of my severe headache nevertheless I attended the sales meeting at my office on the instructions of my senior management.

Hence, the correct option is (B).

27. These two statements share a relationship of cause and effect since we are talking about the reason of going to sleep without having dinner also. The reason is that I was very tired for spending the whole day at the hospital.

Among the given options, so can only be used in the given context to imply the cause and effect relationship. Other connectors will not connect these two statements since they do not imply the cause and effect relationship.

The complete sentence would be:

I was very tired and exhausted after spending the whole day at the hospital so I went to sleep without having dinner after coming back.

Hence, the correct option is (A).

28. Here, the first statement is regarding the certainty of the minister coming to this locality in order to do election campaigning but the second statement gives a condition in which there is a possibility that the minister may not come here for the purpose of election campaigning.

Among the given options, unless may be used to connect the two statements since it can give the condition imposed on something taking place. Since is used to imply the cause-effect relationship whereas in addition to is used to imply that something more may have to be said. Other two connectors are also not correct according to the given context.

The complete sentence would be: The minister will definitely come to this locality for election campaigning within the next two days unless he is denied the ticket from this constituency by his party.

Hence, the correct option is (B).

29. The two statements can be connected in the way that the second statement is elaborating on the information already provided in the first statement. The person loves watching matches with his friends and then we get to know that he loves watching football as compared to other sports.

Among the gien options, we may use especially in order to connect the two statements because it also elaborates on the information already available with us.

The connected statement would be:

Like every second Indian, I am a big fan of sports and I like to watch a lot matches especially of football with nail-biting finish with my friends.

Other connectors will not fit in the given context.

Hence, the correct option is (A).

30. Checking B-F:

Suddenly the lights went out dust finally settled.

The sentence doesn't make any sense. The pair B-F is hence invalid.

Checking A-E:

The automobile industry employs 37 million people and contributes to seven percent of the country's GDP.

The above sentence is correct both grammatically and contextually.

Checking C-D:

The waves were crashing on the shore and it was a lovely sight.

The above sentence too is correct both grammatically and contextually.

Hence, the correct option is (D).

31. Checking B-F:

She has started to gain weight suddenly the wild elephant was no longer sane.

The sentence doesn't make any sense. The pair B-F is hence invalid.

Checking A-E:

The International Monetary Fund has already pared India's growth projections citing lowered domestic demand.

The above sentence is correct both grammatically and contextually.

Checking C-D:

I would rather be a dancer than a singer.

The above sentence too is correct both grammatically and contextually.

Hence, the correct option is (D).

32. Checking C-D:

She always speaks to him was summoned for a hearing.

The sentence doesn't make any sense contextually. So the pair C-D is invalid.

Checking A-E:

Entering into parallel pecuniary relationships with stakeholders can be detrimental to the interests of a company, given that such parties influence decision making.

The above sentence is correct both grammatically and contextually.

Checking B-F:

We thought he loved her but it turned out that he loved another girl.

The above sentence is also correct both grammatically and contextually.

Hence, the correct option is (C).

33. Checking A-F:

The US had given a conditional waiver to eight nations to keep buying oil from Iran.

The above sentence is correct both grammatically and contextually.

Checking B-E:

The scores are low because the task is cognitively demanding.

The above sentence is correct both grammatically and contextually as well.

Checking C-D:

Writing a list of random sentences is harder than I had initially thought it would be.

The above sentence too is correct both grammatically and contextually.

Hence, the correct option is (B).

34. Checking A-F:

Trade secrets could be anything ranging from designs and processes to methods or information.

The above sentence is correct both grammatically and contextually.

Checking B-D:

Despite knowing that it won't suit her she wanted to buy a jumpsuit.

The above sentence is also correct both grammatically and contextually.

Checking C-E:

He was supposed to go to school and he went to the theatre instead.

Here, as the sentence implies contrast in ideas, usage of the conjunction 'and' is absurd. Instead of 'and' 'but' should have been used. Hence, the sentence doesn't make any sense. The pair C-E is hence invalid.

Hence, the correct option is (D).

35. Connectors: A and F

A: Freelancing is an attractive profession now

F: with lot of websites offering decent payments

Connectors: C and E

C: The new scheme of the bank is paying dividends

E: though it is costing a lot in marketing

Other pairs do not have any such relationship and therefore cannot be combined to make a meaningful sentence.

Hence, the correct option is (C).

36. If we read both the sentences carefully we can observe that the sentence II refers to an event of past which is related to time (year 2013) whereas sentence I talks about an event that happened recently.

Clearly, none of the given connectors seems to fit in.

However, we can connect these two statements using 'when' as connector.

The fall in value of Rupee has raised fears of a repeat of the currency crisis of 2013 when the rupee suffered a drastic loss of about 20% in just a few months.

Hence, the correct option is (D).

37. If we read the two sentences, we can observe that they are related by cause and effect relationship. And among the choices available, only 'because' can be used in this context since it means 'the reasons thereof'.

Combing the two sentences the complete sentence will be:

It is time that the Environment ministry does away with all kinds of illegal mining activities in the country because the irreparable damage caused by these activities is going to contribute a lot to the global warming.

Hence, the correct option is (C).

38. If we read the two sentences, we shall observe that they are connected by the cause and effect relationship. Hence, 'due to' will be the perfect fit in the given context as it means that 'for this reason'.

Combing the two sentences the new sentence will be:

Due to the popularity of cricket eating into the share of revenue of other sports in India for many years now, all other sports are suffering and India is not able to win medals in Olympics in all such sports.

Hence, the correct option is (D).

39. If we read the sentences it is clear that it talks about two contrasting things. Among the given choices, 'instead of' is the right fit as it means that 'despite the fact that'.

Combing the two sentences the new statement will be:

Instead of the differences we had when he was alive, I am of the opinion that my father would have done it the same way had he known this fact.

Hence, the correct option is (B).

40. If we read the two sentences they are connected by the cause and effect relationship where one is the reason and the other is the result of something. Among the given options, 'as' is the correct choice since it connects the sentences as cause and effect.

Combining the two sentences the new sentence will be:

As banks are left with no other option but to issue the old notes to their customers in the absence of fresh notes from the RBI, the notification by the Reserve Bank of India to do away with stapling off currency notes by banks has not done much difference.

Hence, the correct option is (C).

41. Statement I As the Government of India has decided to go ahead with a 20-year blueprint for development, the Five Year Planning has been done away with in India.

It is correct since it connects both the statements meaningfully.

Statement II is not correct since the reason of cancellation of the Five Year Planning is the new plan of the government of going ahead with a 20-year blueprint and not the other way around as has been implied in the given statement.

Statement III is not correct since it does not connect the two sentences meaningfully.

Hence, the correct option is (B).

42. Statement I That the Supreme Court has made it clear that only long term motor insurance policies will be there in India will make all the insurance companies issue such policies.

This is correct since both the sentences are connected meaningfully.

Statement II As the Supreme Court has made it clear that only long term motor insurance policies will be there in India, it will make all the insurance companies issue policies for long term.

This is correct since the combined sentence makes a meaningful and contextually correct statement.

Statement III is not correct because the sentence connector used is 'yet' which implies in spite of something. It is not fit for the given context as here the insurance companies are going to abide by the Supreme Court ruling and there is no space for neglecting the same on the part of the insurance companies.

Hence, the correct option is (B).

43. Statement I As many students are now very concerned about the environment, it is a good sign for the country as well as the society.

This is correct since both the statements are connected meaningfully.

Statement II That many students are now very concerned about the environment is a good sign for the country as well as the society.

This is also correct since both the statements are connected meaningfully.

Statement III is not correct since the connector is used is not correct. 'Though' is used to denote that despite of something it is taking place. In this context, it will not be applicable.

Hence, the correct option is (D)

44. Statement I is not correct since the connector used here is 'since' which is used in case of cause and effect relationship between two statements. In the given statement, there is no such relationship between the two sentences as one is about an initiative of the government and the other is about the same subject with more details only.

Statement II is not correct because 'while' is used to denote that something is taking place while something else is also happening. In the given statement, 'while' will not fit in the context as the sentences are mere descriptions regarding the same subject and there is no reference to any activity being carried out simultaneously with another.

Statement III is also incorrect since with the given beginning, it is not possible to connect the two sentences. 'Hardly _________when' is used to denote barely or unlikely. It does not fit in the given context and will not make meaningful statement when combined.

Hence, the correct option is (D).

45. Statement I is incorrect since the reason that the Police are not going to adopt a law will not make it ineffective. The Police have to take cognizance of the law and it is not their prerogative to judge any law passed by the Parliament. These two statements given cannot share the cause and effect relationship required for connecting them with the given connector 'since'.

Statement II is not correct since there should be cause and effect relationship between the given statements in order to connect them with the given connector 'as'. In these sentences, no such relationship is there because a law cannot be ineffective if the Police are not practicing it but they have to abide by it. Had it been the case that the law cannot be implemented, it would have been ineffective as stated in the sentences but so is not the case in this context.

Statement III is also incorrect because it is completely out of context to even think about connecting the given two statements with the connector 'scarcely' which actually implies barely. It has no bearing on the given two statements as far as connecting them is concerned.

Hence, the correct option is (D).

Ques (1-5):Direction: Each question consists of a sentence with an underlined word/words followed by four words. Select the option that is opposite in meaning to the underlined word/words.

Q.1 His ideas are <u>obscure</u>.
[Officers Training Academy (OTA), 2018], [Indian Military Academy (IMA), 2018]

A. new
B. clear
C. infamous
D. obscene

Q.2 Ravi is jovial and he makes the environment <u>sanguine</u>.
[Officers Training Academy (OTA), 2018], [Indian Military Academy (IMA), 2018]

A. pessimistic
B. optimistic
C. humorous
D. rebellious

Q.3 There prevailed a <u>woebegone</u> feeling in the room.
[Officers Training Academy (OTA), 2018], [Indian Military Academy (IMA), 2018]

A. sad
B. cheerful
C. sleepy
D. thoughtful

Q.4 It appears that the whole group is <u>mutinous</u>.
[Officers Training Academy (OTA), 2018], [Indian Military Academy (IMA), 2018]

A. arrogant
B. lucky
C. obedient
D. sincere

Q.5 They consider themselves as <u>foes</u> from birth.
[Officers Training Academy (OTA), 2018], [Indian Military Academy (IMA), 2018]

A. protagonists
B. opponents
C. friends
D. soul mates

Q.6 Direction: The following sentence consists an underlined word(s) followed by four options. Select the option that is nearest in meaning to the underlined word and mark your response accordingly.
Having got excited she opened up the Pandora's Box which led to lot of <u>commotion</u>.
[Officers Training Academy (OTA), 2021], [Indian Military Academy (IMA), 2021]

A. uproar
B. peace
C. sound
D. furious

Q.7 Direction: The following sentence consists an underlined word(s) followed by four options. Select the option that is nearest in meaning to the underlined word and mark your response accordingly.
The <u>inherent</u> danger in the problem is that it would lead to many more problems.
[Officers Training Academy (OTA), 2021], [Indian Military Academy (IMA), 2021]

A. outward
B. difficult
C. hallow
D. inbuilt

Q.8 Direction: The following sentence consists an underlined word(s) followed by four options. Select the option that is nearest in meaning to the underlined word and mark your response accordingly.
The officer was <u>reprimanded</u> by the court for delaying the case.
[Officers Training Academy (OTA), 2021], [Indian Military Academy (IMA), 2021]

A. admonished
B. appreciated
C. praised
D. disliked

Q.9 Direction: The following sentence consists an underlined word(s) followed by four options. Select the option that is nearest in meaning to the underlined word and mark your response accordingly.
Some people think that their strength is <u>perpetual.</u>
[Officers Training Academy (OTA), 2021], [Indian Military Academy (IMA), 2021]

A. temporary
B. powerful
C. everlasting
D. all persuasive

Q.10 Direction: The following sentence consists an underlined word(s) followed by four options. Select the option that is nearest in meaning to the underlined word and mark your response accordingly.
One's actions <u>exemplify</u> one's attitude and values.
[Officers Training Academy (OTA), 2021], [Indian Military Academy (IMA), 2021]

A. Devise
B. Sympathize
C. Asks for
D. Demonstrate

Q.11 Direction: The following sentence consists an underlined word(s) followed by four options. Select the option that is nearest in meaning to the underlined word and mark your response accordingly.
The <u>crux</u> of the issue was that there was no evidence to prove the accused guilty of the act.
[Officers Training Academy (OTA), 2021], [Indian Military Academy (IMA), 2021]

A. core
B. part
C. idea
D. tip

Q.12 Direction: The following sentence consists an underlined word(s) followed by four options. Select the option that is nearest in meaning to the underlined word and mark your response accordingly.
Each child develops his/her <u>competency</u> based on the contexts and the inputs for learning.
[Officers Training Academy (OTA), 2021], [Indian Military Academy (IMA), 2021]

A. capability
B. thinking
C. knowledge
D. ideal

Q.13 Direction: The following sentence consists an underlined word(s) followed by four options. Select the option that is nearest in meaning to the underlined word and mark your response accordingly.

He appears to be very <u>haughty</u>, but he is a humble person.

[Officers Training Academy (OTA), 2021], [Indian Military Academy (IMA), 2021]

A. tough   **B.** modest
C. arrogant   **D.** knowledgeable

Q.14 Direction: The following sentence consists an underlined word(s) followed by four options. Select the option that is nearest in meaning to the underlined word and mark your response accordingly.

The newly appointed secretary is <u>industrious.</u>

[Officers Training Academy (OTA), 2021], [Indian Military Academy (IMA), 2021]

A. diligent   **B.** knowledgeable
C. indolent   **D.** insincere

Q.15 Direction: The following sentence consists an underlined word(s) followed by four options. Select the option that is nearest in meaning to the underlined word and mark your response accordingly.

The <u>indignant</u> attitude of the speaker made the groups unhappy.

[Officers Training Academy (OTA), 2021], [Indian Military Academy (IMA), 2021]

A. resentful   **B.** congenial
C. unruly   **D.** supportive

Q.16 Direction: The following sentence consists an underlined word followed by four options. Select the option that is opposite in meaning to the underlined word and mark your response accordingly.

His arguments are not valid. People consider it <u>bombastic.</u>

[Officers Training Academy (OTA), 2021], [Indian Military Academy (IMA), 2021]

A. outdated   **B.** straightforward
C. verbose   **D.** untrue

Q.17 Direction: The following sentence consists an underlined word followed by four options. Select the option that is opposite in meaning to the underlined word and mark your response accordingly.

The decision was <u>absurd</u> for many of the members of the team.

[Officers Training Academy (OTA), 2021], [Indian Military Academy (IMA), 2021]

A. bizarre   **B.** meaningless
C. reasonable   **D.** thoughtful

Q.18 Direction: The following sentence consists an underlined word followed by four options. Select the option that is opposite in meaning to the underlined word and mark your response accordingly.

Relatives of the <u>deceased</u> have been informed about the accident.

[Officers Training Academy (OTA), 2021], [Indian Military Academy (IMA), 2021]

A. injured   **B.** alive   **C.** dead   **D.** survived

Q.19 Direction: The following sentence consists an underlined word followed by four options. Select the option that is opposite in meaning to the underlined word and mark your response accordingly.

At last, she was able to get some <u>solace</u> as the matter had been resolved amicably.

[Officers Training Academy (OTA), 2021], [Indian Military Academy (IMA), 2021]

A. comfort   **B.** relief
C. punishment   **D.** aggravation

Q.20 Direction: The following sentence consists an underlined word followed by four options. Select the option that is opposite in meaning to the underlined word and mark your response accordingly.

Twenty first century has turned out to be a century of problems <u>contrary</u> to the thinking that it would be a better time.

[Officers Training Academy (OTA), 2021], [Indian Military Academy (IMA), 2021]

A. similar   **B.** different
C. divergent   **D.** faith

Q.21 Direction: The following sentence consists an underlined word followed by four options. Select the option that is opposite in meaning to the underlined word and mark your response accordingly.

The poet said that poetry is a <u>spontaneous</u> overflow of powerful feelings.

[Officers Training Academy (OTA), 2021], [Indian Military Academy (IMA), 2021]

A. prepared   **B.** alerted
C. automatic   **D.** well executed

Q.22 Direction: The following sentence consists an underlined word followed by four options. Select the option that is opposite in meaning to the underlined word and mark your response accordingly.

Language is an instrument for <u>asserting</u> one's identity, attitude and perspective.

[Officers Training Academy (OTA), 2021], [Indian Military Academy (IMA), 2021]

A. declaring   **B.** supporting
C. denying   **D.** propagating

Q.23 Direction: The following sentence consists an underlined word followed by four options. Select the option that is opposite in meaning to the underlined word and mark your response accordingly.

He has been <u>exonerated</u> as he tendered an apology.

[Officers Training Academy (OTA), 2021], [Indian Military Academy (IMA), 2021]

A. honoured   **B.** pardoned
C. convicted   **D.** felicitated

Q.24 Direction: The following sentence consists an underlined word followed by four options. Select the option that is opposite in meaning to the underlined word and mark your response accordingly.

Persuasion is essential for people to work as a team.

[Officers Training Academy (OTA), 2021], [Indian Military Academy (IMA), 2021]

A. Dislike
B. Discouraging
C. Convincing
D. Induce

Q.25 Direction: The following sentence consists an underlined word followed by four options. Select the option that is opposite in meaning to the underlined word and mark your response accordingly.

Every habitat has some distinctive vegetation which defines the ecosystem.

[Officers Training Academy (OTA), 2021], [Indian Military Academy (IMA), 2021]

A. Unique
B. Common
C. Special
D. Unfamiliar

Q.26 Direction: In the sentence, a word is underlined followed by four words/groups of words. Select the option that is nearest in meaning to the underlined word and Choose the correct option.

The properties of the family have been impounded by the order of the court.

[Officers Training Academy (OTA), 2019], [Indian Military Academy (IMA), 2019]

A. Confiscated
B. Permitted
C. Sold
D. Put on hold

Q.27 Direction: In the sentence, a word is underlined followed by four words/groups of words. Select the option that is nearest in meaning to the underlined word and Choose the correct option.

The officer in charge of the operations has been impugned for the excesses.

[Officers Training Academy (OTA), 2019], [Indian Military Academy (IMA), 2019]

A. Expelled
B. Rewarded
C. Challenged
D. Given allowance

Q.28 Direction: In the sentence, a word is underlined followed by four words/groups of words. Select the option that is nearest in meaning to the underlined word and Choose the correct option.

Cognitivist and linguists believe that every child is born with innate qualities.

[Officers Training Academy (OTA), 2019], [Indian Military Academy (IMA), 2019]

A. Biological
B. Intrinsic
C. Extrinsic
D. Unnatural

Q.29 Direction: In the sentence, a word is underlined followed by four words/groups of words. Select the option that is nearest in meaning to the underlined word and Choose the correct option.

It was obligatory for the board to implement the rule.

[Officers Training Academy (OTA), 2019], [Indian Military Academy (IMA), 2019]

A. Compulsory
B. Unnecessary

C. By chance
D. Problematic

Q.30 Direction: In the sentence, a word is underlined followed by four words/groups of words. Select the option that is nearest in meaning to the underlined word and Choose the correct option.

They describe the act as a blatant betrayal of faith.

[Officers Training Academy (OTA), 2019], [Indian Military Academy (IMA), 2019]

A. Loyal
B. Faithfulness
C. Treachery
D. Honesty

Q.31 Direction: In the sentence, a word is underlined followed by four words/groups of words. Select the option that is nearest in meaning to the underlined word and Choose the correct option.

However, if it must decide, then it should do so on the narrowest ground possible.

[Officers Training Academy (OTA), 2019], [Indian Military Academy (IMA), 2019]

A. Widest
B. Slightly
C. Smallest
D. Thick

Q.32 Direction: In the sentence, a word is underlined followed by four words/groups of words. Select the option that is nearest in meaning to the underlined word and Choose the correct option.

This is akin to a contractual relationship that places obligations on the entities entrusted with data.

[Officers Training Academy (OTA), 2019], [Indian Military Academy (IMA), 2019]

A. Removed
B. Narrow
C. Similar
D. Unparallel

Q.33 Direction: In the sentence, a word is underlined followed by four words/groups of words. Select the option that is nearest in meaning to the underlined word and Choose the correct option.

Many communication problems can be attributed directly to misunderstandings and inaccuracies.

[Officers Training Academy (OTA), 2019], [Indian Military Academy (IMA), 2019]

A. Disapproved
B. Unofficial
C. Ascribed
D. Tribute

Q.34 Direction: In the sentence, a word is underlined followed by four words/groups of words. Select the option that is nearest in meaning to the underlined word and Choose the correct option.

The exemptions granted to State institutions for acquiring informed consent from processing personal data in many cases appear to be too blanket.

[Officers Training Academy (OTA), 2019], [Indian Military Academy (IMA), 2019]

A. Obtain
B. Lose
C. Giving
D. Thinking

Q.35 Direction: In the sentence, a word is underlined followed by four words/groups of words. Select the option that is nearest in meaning to the underlined word and Choose the correct option.

The manner in which this exercise has been undertaken leaves much to be <u>desired</u>.
[*Officers Training Academy (OTA), 2019*], [*Indian Military Academy (IMA), 2019*]

A. Dislike

B. Unlikely

C. Wish for

D. Asked for

Q.36 Select the most appropriate antonym of the given word.

Empathy

A. Sympathy

B. Appreciation

C. Warmth

D. Empathy

Q.37 Select the most appropriate synonym of the given word.

Chaste

A. Liberated

B. Divine

C. Defiled

D. Pure

Q.38 Choose the word which best expresses the opposite meaning of the word.

Sapient

A. Wise

B. Foolish

C. Wasteful

D. Culvert

Q.39 Pick out the synonym of 'ERUDITE' from the following–

A. Execute

B. Expanse

C. Academic

D. Settle

Q.40 Select the most appropriate synonym of the given word.

Assertion

A. Discussion

B. Rejection

C. Declaration

D. Continuation

Q.41 Select the most appropriate ANTONYM of the given word.

Exonerate

A. vindicate

B. sentence

C. acquit

D. absolve

Q.42 Select the most appropriate ANTONYM of the given word.

Instant

A. Similar

B. Gradual

C. Prompt

D. Diverse

Q.43 Select the most appropriate synonym of the given word.

Benign

A. severe

B. malignant

C. favourable

D. harsh

Q.44 Choose the word which best expresses the opposite meaning of the word.

Cajole

A. pester

B. persuade

C. bitter

D. lament

Q.45 Choose the word which best expresses nearly the same meaning of the given word

Injuction

A. order

B. coincidence

C. shot of medicine

D. meeting point of railway tracks

// Smart Answer Sheet //

| Correct | Indicates percentage of students who answered questions correctly. |

| Skipped | Indicates percentage of students who skipped questions. |

Q.	Ans.	Correct / Skipped		Q.	Ans.	Correct / Skipped		Q.	Ans.	Correct / Skipped		Q.	Ans.	Correct / Skipped		Q.	Ans.	Correct / Skipped
1	B	86.3 % / 10.55 %		10	D	59.14 % / 34.18 %		19	D	53.7 % / 45.2 %		28	A	64.38 % / 35.62 %		37	D	83.73 % / 11.79 %
2	A	44.16 % / 48.2 %		11	A	67.74 % / 31.42 %		20	A	62.65 % / 33.02 %		29	A	69.74 % / 30.08 %		38	B	86.76 % / 11.79 %
3	B	13.1 % / 83.48 %		12	A	16.53 % / 76.17 %		21	A	50.24 % / 40.23 %		30	C	77.49 % / 21.03 %		39	C	89.21 % / 10.64 %
4	C	86.85 % / 10.3 %		13	C	89.28 % / 10.63 %		22	C	54.25 % / 35.38 %		31	C	40.85 % / 35.67 %		40	C	83.87 % / 14.94 %
5	C	89.7 % / 10.12 %		14	A	82.4 % / 12.23 %		23	C	23.07 % / 69.6 %		32	C	87.78 % / 12.21 %		41	B	79.42 % / 13.1 %
6	A	89.22 % / 10.34 %		15	A	41.37 % / 49.56 %		24	B	60.43 % / 33.76 %		33	C	59.57 % / 33.64 %		42	B	79.49 % / 13.45 %
7	D	21.96 % / 72.76 %		16	A	81.33 % / 13.81 %		25	B	60.44 % / 38.89 %		34	A	79.25 % / 12.42 %		43	C	81.51 % / 17.93 %
8	A	49.11 % / 32.29 %		17	C	78.68 % / 13.65 %		26	A	64.79 % / 30.43 %		35	C	55.32 % / 44.49 %		44	A	89.31 % / 10.14 %
9	C	30.74 % / 69.11 %		18	B	88.28 % / 11.04 %		27	C	25.62 % / 71.1 %		36	D	76.68 % / 19.07 %		45	A	85.33 % / 13.97 %

Performance Analysis

Avg. Score (%)	62.22%
Toppers Score (%)	66.67%
Your Score	

//Hints and Solutions//

1. The meaning of the given words:

- Obscure refers to something that is unclear or vague
- Clear refers to something that is obvious and is easy to understand
- New refers to something that is unused
- Infamous refers to someone who is well known for a bad deed
- Obscene refers to something that is offensive or disgusting

From the meanings, it is clear that Clear is the opposite of Obscure.

Hence, the correct option is (B).

2. The meaning of the given words:

- Sanguine refers to someone who is optimistic and positive.
- Pessimistic refers to someone who always looks at the negative side of things.
- Optimistic refers to someone who always looks at the positive side of things.
- Humorous refers to someone who is funny and jovial.
- Rebellious refers to someone who goes against authority and what is expected of them.

From the meanings, it is clear that Pessimistic is the opposite of Sanguine.

Hence, the correct option is (A).

3. The meaning of the given words:

- Woebegone refers to someone who is miserable or sad.
- Cheerful refers to someone who is happy or excited.
- Sad refers to someone who is unhappy.
- Sleepy refers to someone who is ready to go to sleep.
- Thoughtful refers to someone who is considerate.

From the meanings, it is clear that Cheerful is the opposite of Woebegone.

Hence, the correct option is (B).

4. The meaning of the given words:

- Mutinous refers to someone who is unwilling to obey the orders of authority.
- Obedient refers to someone who listens to orders.
- Arrogant refers to someone who has an exaggerated sense of their own importance.
- Lucky refers to someone who is fortunate.
- Sincere refers to someone who is free from pretense.

From the meanings, it is clear that Obedient is the opposite of Mutinous.

Hence, the correct option is (C).

5. The meaning of the given words:

- Foes refer to people who are enemies.
- Friends refer to people that have mutual affection.
- Protagonists refer to the positive characters or the hero/heroine of a story.
- Opponents refer to people that are against each other, rivals.
- Soulmates refer to people that are connected by their souls.

From the meanings, it is clear that Friends is the opposite of Foes.

Hence, the correct option is (C).

6. The correct answer is uproar.

commotion: a state of confused and noisy disturbance

uproar: a loud and impassioned noise or disturbance

Let's look at the meanings of the other given options:

- peace- freedom from disturbance; tranquility
- sound- vibrations that travel through the air or another medium and can be heard when they reach a person's or animal's ear
- furious- extremely angry

Thus, from the given meanings, we find that commotion and uproar are synonyms.

Hence, the correct option is (A).

7. The correct answer is inbuilt.

inherent: existing in something as a permanent, essential, or characteristic attribute

inbuilt: existing as an original or essential part of something or someone

Let's look at the meanings of the other given options:

- outward- of, on, or from the outside
- difficult- needing much effort or skill to accomplish, deal with, or understand
- hallow- honor as holy

Thus, from the given meanings, we find that inherent and inbuilt are synonyms.

Hence, the correct option is (D).

8. The correct answer is admonished.

reprimanded: rebuke (someone), especially officially

admonished: warn or reprimand someone firmly

Let's look at the meanings of the other given options:

- appreciated- recognize the full worth of
- praised- express warm approval or admiration of
- disliked- feel distaste for or hostility toward

Thus, from the given meanings, we find that reprimanded and admonished are synonyms.

Hence, the correct option is (A).

9. The correct answer is everlasting.

perpetual: never-ending or changing

everlasting: lasting forever or a very long time

Let's look at the meanings of the other given options:

- temporary- lasting for only a limited period of time; not permanent
- powerful- having great power or strength
- persuasive- good at persuading someone to do or believe something through reasoning or the use of temptation

Thus, from the given meanings, we find that perpetual and everlasting are synonyms.

Hence, the correct option is (C).

10. The correct answer is demonstrate.

exemplify: be a typical example of

demonstrate: give a practical exhibition and explanation of (how a machine, skill, or craftworks or is performed)

Let's look at the meanings of the other given options:

- devise- plan or invent (a complex procedure, system, or mechanism) by careful thought
- sympathize- feel or express sympathy
- ask for- put a question or seek an answer from someone

Thus, from the given meanings, we find that exemplify and demonstrate are synonyms.

Hence, the correct option is (D).

11. The correct answer is core.

crux: the decisive or most important point at issue

core: the central or most important part of something

Let's look at the meanings of the other given options:

- part- an element or constituent that belongs to something and is essential to its nature
- idea- a thought or suggestion as to a possible course of action
- tip- the pointed or rounded end or extremity of something slender or tapering

Thus, from the given meanings, we find that crux and core are synonyms.

Hence, the correct option is (A).

12. The correct answer is **capability**.

competency: the ability to do something successfully or efficiently

capability: the ability or power to do, experience, or understand something

Let's look at the meanings of the other given options: thinking- the process of using one's mind to consider or reason about something

- knowledge- what is known in a particular field or in total; facts and information
- ideal- satisfying one's conception of what is perfect; most suitable

Thus, from the given meanings, we find that competency and capability are synonyms.

Hence, the correct option is (A).

13. The correct answer is arrogant.

haughty: arrogantly superior and disdainful

arrogant: having or revealing an exaggerated sense of one's own importance or abilities

Let's look at the meanings of the other given options:

- tough- (of a substance or object) strong enough to withstand adverse conditions or rough or careless handling
- modest- unassuming or moderate in the estimation of one's abilities or achievements
- knowledgeable- intelligent and well informed

Thus, from the given meanings, we find that haughty and arrogant are synonyms.

Hence, the correct option is (C).

14. The correct answer is diligent.

industrious: diligent and hard-working

diligent: having or showing care and conscientiousness in one's work or duties

Let's look at the meanings of the other given options:

- knowledgeable- intelligent and well informed
- indolent- wanting to avoid activity or exertion; lazy
- insincere- not expressing genuine feelings

Thus, from the given meanings, we find that industrious and diligent are synonyms.

Hence, the correct option is (A).

15. The correct answer is resentful.

resentful: feeling or expressing bitterness or indignation at having been treated unfairly

indignant: feeling or showing anger or annoyance at what is perceived as unfair treatment

Let's look at the meanings of the other given options:

- congenial- (of a person) pleasant because of a personality, qualities, or interests that are similar to one's own

- unruly- disorderly and disruptive and not amenable to discipline or control
- supportive- providing encouragement or emotional help

Thus, from the given meanings, we find that resentful and indignant are synonyms.

Hence, the correct option is (A).

16. The correct answer is straightforward.

bombastic: high-sounding but with little meaning; inflated

straightforward: uncomplicated and easy to do or understand

Let's look at the meanings of the other given options:

- outdated- out of date; obsolete
- verbose- using or expressed in more words than are needed
- untrue- not in accordance with fact or reality; false or incorrect

Thus, from the given meanings, we find that bombastic and straightforward are antonyms.

Hence, the correct option is (A).

17. The correct answer is reasonable.

absurd: wildly unreasonable, illogical, or inappropriate

reasonable: (of a person) having sound judgment; fair and sensible

Let's look at the meanings of the other given options:

- bizarre- very strange or unusual, especially so as to cause interest or amusement
- meaningless- having no meaning or significance
- thoughtful- absorbed in or involving thought

Thus, from the given meanings, we find that absurd and reasonable are antonyms.

Hence, the correct option is (C).

18. The correct answer is alive.

deceased: a person who has died

alive: (of a person, animal, or plant) living, not dead

Let's look at the meanings of the other given options:

- injured- harmed, damaged, or impaired
- dead- no longer alive
- survived- continue to live or exist, especially in spite of danger or hardship

Thus, from the given meanings, we find that deceased and alive are antonyms.

Hence, the correct option is (B).

19. The correct answer is aggravation.

solace: comfort or consolation in a time of distress or sadness

aggravation: an intensification of a negative quality or aspect

Let's look at the meanings of the other given options:

- comfort- a state of physical ease and freedom from pain or constraint
- relief- a feeling of reassurance and relaxation following release from anxiety or distress.
- punishment- the infliction or imposition of a penalty as retribution for an offense

Thus, from the given meanings, we find that solace and aggravation are antonyms.

Hence, the correct option is (D).

20. The correct answer is similar.

contrary: opposite in nature, direction, or meaning

similar: resembling without being identical

Let's look at the meanings of the other given options:

- different- not the same as another or each other; unlike in nature, form, or quality
- divergent- tending to be different or develop in different directions
- faith- complete trust or confidence in someone or something

Thus, from the given meanings, we find that contrary and similar are antonyms.

Hence, the correct option is (A).

21. The correct answer is prepared.

prepared: make (something) ready for use or consideration

spontaneous: performed or occurring as a result of a sudden inner impulse or inclination and without premeditation or external stimulus

Let's look at the meanings of the other given options:

- alerted- warn (someone) of danger, threat, or problem, typically with the intention of having it avoided or dealt with
- automatic- working by itself with little or no direct human control
- well-executed- skillfully carried out

Thus, from the given meanings, we find that spontaneous and prepared are antonyms.

Hence, the correct option is (A).

22. The correct answer is denying.

asserting: state a fact or belief confidently and forcefully

denying: state that one refuses to admit the truth or existence of

Let's look at the meanings of the other given options:

- declaring- say something in a solemn and emphatic manner

- supporting- bear all or part of the weight of; hold up
- propagating- breed specimens of (a plant or animal) by natural processes from the parent stock

Thus, from the given meanings, we find that asserting and denying are antonyms.

Hence, the correct option is (C).

23. The correct answer is convicted.

exonerated: (especially of an official body) absolve (someone) from blame for a fault or wrongdoing, especially after due consideration of the case

convicted: having been declared guilty of a criminal offense by the verdict of a jury or the decision of a judge

Let's look at the meanings of the other given options:

- honoured- regard with great respect
- pardoned- forgive or excuse (a person, error, or offense)
- felicitated- congratulate

Thus, from the given meanings, we find that exonerated and convicted are antonyms.

Hence, the correct option is (C).

24. The correct answer is Discouraging.

Persuasion: the action or fact of persuading someone or of being persuaded to do or believe something

Discouraging: causing someone to lose confidence or enthusiasm; depressing

Let's look at the meanings of the other given options:

- Dislike- feel distaste for or hostility toward
- Convincing- capable of causing someone to believe that something is true or real
- Induce- to cause something to happen

Thus, from the given meanings, we find that Persuasion and Discouraging are antonyms.

Hence, the correct option is (B).

25. The correct answer is common.

distinctive: characteristic of one person or thing, and so serving to distinguish it from others

common: occurring, found, or done often; prevalent

Let's look at the meanings of the other given options:

- unique- being the only one of its kind; unlike anything else
- special- better, greater, or otherwise different from what is usual
- unfamiliar- not known or recognized

Thus, from the given meanings, we find that distinctive and common are antonyms.

Hence, the correct option is (B).

26. The correct answer is 'Confiscated'.

Impounded: to not let somebody use something by taking it away from them, especially because they have broken the law, seized and taken legal custody of something, especially a vehicle, goods or documents because of infringement of a law.

For example: He recovered all the immense grants of crown lands and rents, impounded by the nobles during his minority.

Confiscated: to take something away from somebody as a punishment.

For example: All Biren's vast property was confiscated , including his diamonds, worth millions.

Hence, the correct option is (A).

27. The correct answer is 'Challenged'.

Impugned: disputed the truth, validity, or honesty of a statement.

For example: His motives have been scrutinized and impugned.

Challenged: used to indicate that someone or something is lacking or deficient in a specified respect.

For example: He challenged the orthodox views on education.

Hence, the correct option is (C).

28. The correct answer is 'Biological'.

Innate: inborn, natural, existing in one from birth, inherent.

For example: He had an innate modesty and simplicity of character.

Biological: (of a member of a person's family) genetically related; related by blood; relating to biology or living organism.

For example: She decided to search for her biological mother after her adoptive parents died.

Hence, the correct option is (A).

29. The correct answer is 'Compulsory'.

Obligatory: required by a legal, moral or other rules; having binding force.

For example: It is obligatory to get insurance before you drive a car.

Compulsory: required by a law or a rule.

For example: Maths and English are compulsory subjects for this course.

Hence, the correct option is (A).

30. The correct answer is 'Treachery'.

Betrayal: the action of betraying someone or something; breaking or violation of trust, or confidence that produces moral and psychological conflict within a relationship amongst individuals or organizations, disloyalty.

For example: She felt that what she had done was a betrayal of Patrick.

Treachery: betrayal of trust; the quality of being deceptive, behaviour that deceives or is not loyal to someone who trusts you.

For example: I was shocked by the treachery of my best friend.

Hence, the correct option is (C).

31. The correct answer is 'Smallest'.

Narrowest: of small width in relation to length; limited in extent, having only a short distance from side to side.

For example: He had escaped death by the narrowest of margins.

Smallest: a superlative degree of the adjective small; of a size that.

For example: He was one of the youngest, and certainly the smallest.

Hence, the correct option is (C).

32. The correct answer is 'Similar'.

Akin: of similar character; related by blood; related, close.

For example: This game is closely akin to rugby.

Similar: having a resemblance in appearance, character or quantity; without being identical.

For example: I would have reacted in a similar way if it had happened to me.

Hence, the correct option is (C).

33. The correct answer is 'Ascribed'.

Attributed: regard something as caused by, to believe that something was caused or done by somebody/something.

For example: Many ancient peoples attributed natural phenomenon such as lightning and volcanoes to the emotions of gods.

Ascribed: regard something as being due to, to say that something was written by or belonged to somebody; to say what caused something.

For example: These differences cannot be ascribed to the action of environment upon each generation.

Hence, the correct option is (C).

34. The correct answer is 'Obtain'.

Acquiring: buying or obtaining (an asset or object) for oneself; learning or developing (a skill, habit, or quality).

For example: The key to acquiring proficiency in any task is repetition.

Obtain: get, acquire, or secure (something); be prevalent, customary, or established.

For example: I should like much to see it, and to obtain a few copies if possible.

Hence, the correct option is (A).

35. The correct answer is 'Wish for'.

Desired: strongly wished for or intended, to find somebody or something really attractive.

For example: Their strategy produced the desired outcome.

Wish for: feel or express a strong desire or hope for something, desire, want

For example: We know what she'll be wishing for on her birthday.

Hence, the correct option is (C).

36. Empathy means the ability to understand another person's feelings, experience, etc.

Apathy means the feeling of not being interested or lack of emotion.

Hence, from the above meanings, we find that both words are opposite in meaning.

Hence, the correct option is (D).

37. The word 'Chaste' means free from any trace of the coarse or indecent.

The word 'pure' means free from any trace of the coarse or indecent.

The synonyms of the word 'Chaste' are "pure, modest, clean".

From the synonym of the given word, we can say that the word 'pure' is the same in meaning.

Hence, the correct option is (D).

38. Let's look at the meanings of the given word and marked option:

Sapient- having or showing deep understanding and intelligent application of knowledge

foolish- showing or marked by a lack of good sense or judgment

Hence, the correct option is (B).

39. Erudite means scholar or academic

hence, the correct option is (C).

40. The word 'Assertion' means a solemn and often public declaration of the truth or existence of something.

The synonyms of the word 'Assertion' are "declaration, affirmation, claim".

From the synonym of the given word, we can say that the word 'Declaration' is the same in meaning.

The word 'Declaration' means a formal or explicit statement or announcement

Hence, the correct option is (C).

41. The word 'Exonerate' means to free from a charge of wrongdoing.

The antonyms of the word 'Exonerate' are "sentence, accuse, convict".

From the antonym of the given word, we can say that the word 'sentence' is the opposite in meaning.

The word 'sentence' means the punishment assigned to a defendant found guilty by a court or fixed by law for a particular offence.

Hence, the correct option is (B).

42. Let's see the meanings of the given words-

Instant→ Happening immediately.

Gradual→ Taking place over an extended period.

Similar→ Of the same kind in appearance.

Prompt→ cause or bring about.

Hence, the correct option is (B).

43. The word 'Benign' means not harsh or stern, especially in nature or effect.

The synonyms of the word 'Benign' are "favourable, gentle, peaceful".

From the synonym of the given word, we can say that the word 'favourable' is the same in meaning.

The word 'favourable' means promoting or contributing to personal or social well-being.

Let's see the meaning of other given options-

severe-strict or harsh

malignant-evil in nature or effect

harsh-cruel or severe

Hence, the correct option is (C).

44. Let's look at the meaning of the given word and the marked option:

Cajole- to get (someone) to do something by gentle urging, special attention, or flattery

pester- to thrust oneself upon (another) without invitation

Let's look at the meanings of the other given options:

persuade- to cause (someone) to agree with a belief or course of action by using arguments or earnest request

bitter- having or showing deep-seated resentment

lament- to feel or express sorrow for

Hence, the correct option is (A).

45. The meaning of the given 'Injunction' is 'A judicial order'.

The meaning of the other options are

Coincidence→ A remarkable concurrence of events.

Hence, the correct option is (A).

Ques (1-10):Direction: Correct the bracket part of the sentence.

Q.1 The man (who had jumped into the lake) managed to swim ashore.

A. who jumping into the lake
B. jumping into the lake
C. who jumped into the lake
D. No correction required

Q.2 He avoids (to speak) to me.

A. to talk
B. speaking
C. speech
D. No correction required

Q.3 The light went out while (I read).

A. was reading
B. am reading
C. had read
D. No correction required

Q.4 My car (broke off) on my way to the office.

A. broke out
B. broke in
C. broke down
D. No correction required

Q.5 These troubles are a direct consequence of the country's prolonged domestic recession and (faltering economics recovery).

A. faltering economic's recovery
B. faltering economic recovery
C. faltering economical recovery
D. No correction required

Q.6 She was (the oldest of the two sisters).

A. Elder of the two sisters
B. Oldest between the two sisters
C. Older than her sister
D. No correction required

Q.7 His brother (never has) and never will be dependable.

A. Never had
B. Never has been
C. Was never being
D. No correction required

Q.8 It is easy to see why cities grew (on the river banks).

A. Along the river banks
B. In the river banks
C. Upon the river banks
D. No correction required

Q.9 After a long lunch-break, business (resurfaces) as usual.

A. Resumes
B. Continues
C. Delays
D. No correction required

Q.10 The whole country is disappointed (over) the defeat of the cricket team.

A. On
B. Above
C. By
D. No correction required

Ques (11-20):Direction: Correct the bracket part of the sentence.

Q.11 Kamal (is and will do) his work sincerely forever.

A. Is done and will do
B. is doing and will do
C. Is and will doing
D. No correction required

Q.12 Children have been expecting a lot more gifts. (Doesn't he)?

A. Hasn't they
B. Don't they
C. Haven't they
D. No correction required

Q.13 The statement logically (infers) a certain conclusion.

A. Infers to
B. Implies
C. Implies to
D. No correction required

Q.14 Some parents (are not agree) to the what principal announced last month.

A. Are not agreeing
B. Does not agree
C. Do not agree
D. No correction required

Q.15 The man (saw a horrible dream) the previous night.

A. Saw a nightmare
B. Had a horrible dream
C. Had a horrible nightmare
D. No correction required

Q.16 We don't think that this news channel (deserves to watch.)

A. Deserve to watch
B. Deserves to be watched
C. Deserves to be watching
D. No correction required

Q.17 You must remember (meeting) the manager tomorrow.

A. Meet

B. To meet

C. To have met

D. No correction required

Q.18 They are (migratory) citizens from another country.

A. Immigrant

B. Migratory

C. Emigrant

D. No correction required

Q.19 (He had his lunch,) when she went to his home.

A. He would have taken his lunch

B. He had his lunch

C. He had have his lunch

D. No correction required

Q.20 (Many a candidate) will come for the next week recruitment process.

A. Many a candidates

B. many candidate

C. A many candidate

D. No correction required

Ques (21-45):Direction: In the following questions, some part of the sentence is underlined. Which of the options given below the sentence should replace the part underlined to make the sentence grammatically correct. If the sentence is correct as it is given then choose option (D) 'No Correction required' as the answer.

Q.21 A student was arrested for displaying an <u>indecently</u> art work in public.

A. indecent

B. unindecently

C. the indecently

D. No correction required

Q.22 He did not like <u>me to smoking</u> in the presence of our teacher yesterday.

A. that I smoke

B. my smoking

C. me smoking

D. No correction required

Q.23 The government has <u>granted permission to prosecute</u> the public servant.

A. granted permission to prosecution

B. sanction to prosecuting

C. sanctioned permission to prosecute

D. No correction required

Q.24 The scenery around the hill station of Himachal Pradesh is <u>quite picturesque and enjoyed</u>.

A. quite picturesque and enjoyable

B. quite picturesque and enjoyed

C. quietly picturesque and enjoyed

D. No correction required

Q.25 Within three years, he demonstrated <u>a dramatic improved</u> business performan

A. the dramatic improved

B. the dramatically improved

C. a dramatically improved

D. No correction required

Q.26 <u>If in case</u> you want to resign within one month, you will have to pay Rs 10,000.

A. if the case

B. if the case of

C. in case

D. No correction required

Q.27 He was visibly upset when he heard the sad news <u>of his debacle</u> in the election.

A. of his debacle of

B. of his being debacled in

C. with his debacle in

D. No correction required

Q.28 <u>Had he been presented</u> there, he would have put an end to the happenings.

A. if he has been presented

B. if he had been present

C. had he presented

D. No correction required

Q.29 Your defence that you found the purse lying on the floor <u>cannot be trust</u>.

A. cannot be trusted

B. can hardly be trust

C. can never be trust

D. No correction required

Q.30 <u>Expeditiously completion</u> of the process will be appreciated by everyone involved.

A. expeditiously complete

B. expeditious complete

C. expeditious completion

D. No correction required

Q.31 Researchers have developed a process <u>to using magnetic</u> with brain-like networks to program and teach devices.

A. to using magnetical

B. to use magnetics

C. for using magnetic

D. No correction required

Q.32 Nala pakam is a term <u>which originated from</u> King Nala's proficiency in cooking.

A. that originated of

B. which has been originated off

C. which has originated from

D. No correction required

Q.33 Poverty is too much with us and its presence across vast stretches of our country <u>disturbed our conscious.</u>

A. disturbed our consciousness

B. disturb its conscience

C. disturbs our conscience

D. No correction required

Q.34 For <u>decade company which</u> make soap, lotions and perfumes have relied on a chemical called Bourgeonal.
A. decades company that
B. decade companies which
C. decades companies that
D. No correction required

Q.35 As far as I know them, they all are atheist <u>and</u> they observe fast during the Navratre.
A. because
B. but
C. yet
D. No correction required

Q.36 Whenever you enter someone else's living room, good manners suggest that you should <u>take out</u> your shoes.
A. put off
B. take off
C. take back
D. No correction required

Q.37 There is nothing <u>quite depressing</u> than low level of unemployment in India.
A. as depressing
B. this depressing
C. more depressing
D. No correction required

Q.38 All the matches of Cricket World Cup <u>will be broadcasted</u> on Start Cricket.
A. will broadcast
B. are going to broadcast
C. going to be broadcasted
D. No correction required

Q.39 After a few hours the kids who fell from the second floor of the building began to <u>come out</u>.
A. come round
B. come on
C. come with
D. No correction required

Q.40 He did not mention how old he was or <u>what is his gender</u>.
A. what was his gender
B. what gender of his was
C. what his gender was
D. No correction required

Q.41 Cash transfers to the poor do not <u>ensue accessibility</u>, affordability or even sustained economic security given falling real wages.
A. Ensure accessibility
B. Ensure excesses
C. Ensures accessibility
D. No correction required

Q.42 With the election <u>round a corner</u> and data revealing that the unemployment rate has hit a 45-year high, there is a spike in concern for the economic security of the people.
A. In the corner
B. Over the corner
C. Around the corner
D. No correction required

Q.43 Afghanistan has <u>historically be an difficult place</u> for external invaders, thanks to its complex tribal equations and its rugged mountainous terrain.
A. historic has a difficult place
B. historically been a difficult place
C. historically being a difficult place
D. No correction required

Q.44 While all rights are available to citizens, persons including foreign citizens <u>are entitle to the rights</u> to equality and the right to life, among others.
A. is entitled to the right
B. are entitled for the right
C. are entitled to a rights
D. No correction required

Q.45 The prospects for Britain's orderly withdrawal from the European Union on March 29 <u>have receded further,</u> even as MPs rallied to stop a no-deal scenario.
A. had recede further
B. have recedes further
C. has receded further
D. No correction required

// Smart Answer Sheet //

Correct Indicates percentage of students who answered questions correctly.

Skipped Indicates percentage of students who skipped questions.

Q.	Ans.	Correct / Skipped
1	C	52.07 % / 33.37 %
2	B	55.87 % / 32.56 %
3	A	61.45 % / 35.1 %
4	C	54.74 % / 35.62 %
5	B	57.51 % / 30.66 %
6	A	63.57 % / 32.05 %
7	B	48.52 % / 50.62 %
8	A	63.94 % / 32.99 %
9	A	40.22 % / 38.28 %
10	C	61.17 % / 32.88 %
11	B	79.13 % / 16.2 %
12	C	29.46 % / 69.61 %
13	B	85.97 % / 12.13 %
14	C	63.49 % / 33.62 %
15	A	85.98 % / 13.74 %
16	B	80.07 % / 10.05 %
17	B	48.08 % / 47.28 %
18	A	53.45 % / 38.79 %
19	B	88.95 % / 10.02 %
20	D	77.75 % / 19.74 %
21	A	49.89 % / 44.79 %
22	B	52.8 % / 44.8 %
23	D	23.7 % / 73.9 %
24	A	29.67 % / 68.94 %
25	C	58.84 % / 35.22 %
26	C	61.32 % / 31.03 %
27	D	61.72 % / 36.04 %
28	A	46.03 % / 40.7 %
29	A	64.04 % / 30.14 %
30	C	48.85 % / 35.96 %
31	B	54.75 % / 38.91 %
32	D	50.5 % / 36.73 %
33	C	44.61 % / 35.82 %
34	C	41.13 % / 50.24 %
35	C	79.03 % / 20.31 %
36	B	59.45 % / 32.15 %
37	C	81.15 % / 13.68 %
38	C	63.89 % / 33.63 %
39	A	32.61 % / 67.06 %
40	C	47.2 % / 51.68 %
41	A	79.28 % / 11.55 %
42	C	51.21 % / 45.44 %
43	B	80.61 % / 14.11 %
44	D	58.93 % / 30.13 %
45	D	32.2 % / 67.74 %

Performance Analysis

Avg. Score (%)	51.11%
Toppers Score (%)	73.33%
Your Score	

//Hints and Solutions//

1. The correct sentence is- The man who jumped into the lake managed to swim ashore.

We use past perfect tense with simple past tense when the one activity finished much time before the second act. Here, jumping into the river and then swimming ashore happened simultaneously. Therefore, there is no need to use past perfect tense in the sentence and it must be kept in simple past.

Hence, the correct option is (C).

2. The correct sentence is- He avoids speaking to me.

There are some verbs that usually take the continuous form of the main verb after them. A few of such verbs are avoid, detest, dislike, hate, enjoy, like, love, etc. Therefore, the verb "avoid" in the given sentence should be followed by the continuous verb "speaking".

Hence, the correct option is (B).

3. The correct sentence is- The light went out while I was reading.

As, when and while are conjunctions. We use them to introduce subordinate clauses. We can use as, when and while to mean 'during the time that', to connect two events happening at the same time. We often use them with the past continuous to refer to background events.

When the men were out working in the field, I helped with milking the cows, feeding the calves and the pigs.

While he was working, he often listened to music.

This implies that the bracketed part is incorrect.

Hence, the correct option is (A).

4. The correct sentence is- My car broke down on my way to the office.

Let's understand the meanings of each phrasal verb given in the options:

Broke off = became separated/detached

Broke out = started/began suddenly

Broke in = force entry to a building

Broke down = suddenly ceased or stopped to function (of a machine or motor vehicle)

As per the context of the sentence, the correct phrasal verb is "broke down".

Hence, the correct option is (C).

5. The correct sentence is- These troubles are a direct consequence of the country's prolonged domestic recession and faltering economic recovery.

To qualify the noun 'recovery', we need the adjective 'economic' not the noun 'economics' to place before it.

Also, we have been provided with two adjectives 'economic' & 'economical' in options B & C respectively.

But 'economical' means not using a lot of money, energy, etc. It doesn't fit in the context.

Hence, the correct option is (B).

6. The correct sentence is- She was the elder of the two sisters.

When the comparison is between two entities, the comparative degree is used. So, using superlative degree is incorrect in the bracketed part. Apart from this, using "oldest" is also incorrect as when there is a comparison of age, we use the adjective "elder". Option A is correct as it follows the correct structure as discussed here.

Hence, the correct option is (A).

7. The correct sentence is- His brother never has been and never will be dependable.

The given sentence uses two forms of auxiliary verb. One is "has" and the other is "will". We know that these auxiliary verbs are followed by different forms of main verbs. "Will" is a future verb and it is followed by the simple form of the main verb. "Has" is a present perfect verb and it is followed by the third form of the main verb. The main verb in the sentence is "be". Thus, "has" will be followed by the third form of "be" which is "been".

Hence, the correct option is (B).

8. The correct sentence is- It is easy to see why cities grew <u>along the river banks</u>.

The use of the preposition "on" is incorrect in the given sentence as is used to show the physical contact to a surface. The correct preposition to be used here is "along" as it means extending in a more or less horizontal line. The cities were established not on the banks but along with the banks.

Hence, the correct option is (A).

9. The correct sentence is- After a long lunch-break, business resumes as usual.

Let's understand the meanings of each word so we can know which fits best in the sentence:

Resurface = 1. to put a new surface on a road, 2. to rise to the surface of the water again, 3. to remember something again which you've forgotten.

Resume = to resume activity after a break.

Continue = to keep happening, existing, or doing something.

Delay = to make something happen at a later time than originally planned or expected.

The correct verb that fits in the sentence is "resume".

Hence, the correct option is (A).

10. The correct sentence is- The whole country is disappointed <u>by</u> the defeat of the cricket team.

The preposition given in the bracketed part is incorrect as the adjective "disappointed" is never used with the preposition "over". The common prepositions which are used with "disappointed" are "in, with", by". Let's understand in what context we use these prepositions with "disappointed".

Disappointment is an emotion. The preposition that follows disappointment hints at the intensity of the emotion involved. "Disappointed in" suggests that a betrayal has taken place.

Example: I am disappointed in you.

"Disappointed by" lacks the sense of betrayal conveyed by "disappointed in".

She was disappointed by the behavior of his uncle.

"Disappointed with" seems to have the broadest application. We're disappointed with products or with how things are done.

I was disappointed with my performance.

The correct preposition to be used in the sentence is "by".

Hence, the correct option is (C).

11. "is" and "will" are the two different helping verbs and they both will take the main verb accordingly, thus the given sentence can be split into two parts as:

Kamal (is doing) his work sincerely forever "and" Kamal (will do) his work sincerely forever.

When combined these two parts into one, the sentence would read as:

Kamal is doing and will do his work sincerely forever.

Hence, the correct option is (B).

12. When we make the question tag, we use the same helping verb as used in the given sentence. And if the sentence is positive we make the question negative and vice versa.

After that, we use a pronoun as per the subject of the sentence.

Since the subject is "children", thus plural pronoun "they" should be used.

The helping verb used in the sentence is "has" thus "has or its form" should be used in the question tag.

Since the given sentence is positive thus the question tag should be negative.

The tense should be the same for both the sentence and question tag.

As per the subject-verb agreement, the verb should be as per the subject, and since the subject of the question tag is "they" thus "have" need to be used.

Hence, the correct option is (C).

13. The statement logically (Implies) a certain conclusion.

"Infer" means to deduce or conclude something and to deduce something there should be some doer but "the statement" cannot be the doer. It cannot deduce anything. A statement can only "imply" something. Imply is a transitive verb, thus "to" should not be written after it as it can take the object directly.

Hence, the correct option is (B).

14. Some parents (Do not agree) to the what principal announced last month.

"Are" when used as a helping verb takes the continuous form of the main verb, however, "agree" is a stative verb that should not be written in the continuous tense. i.e.

Either I agree or I don't but there is no intermediate phase i.e. I am agreeing on this. This is incorrect.

Thus, to negate a sentence keeping the main verb in the base form "do" is used as a helping verb which is changed as per the subject, since the subject is plural thus option (C) should be chosen.

Hence, the correct option is (C).

15. The man (Saw a nightmare) the previous night.

In the English language, we try to keep the sentence short and use alternative words to replace the long phrases. In the sentence, we can use "nightmare" in place of "horrible dream" as they both mean the same thing. So, the bracketed part can be replaced by option (A).

The rest of the options are incorrect as "nightmare" itself is a horrible dream; thus saying horrible nightmare is superfluous.

Hence, the correct option is (A).

16. We don't think that this news channel (Deserves to be watched.)

"This news channel" is a non-living thing that cannot perform any action, but an action can be done on it. thus, the sentence should be passive, so the infinitive part should be written in passive. Thus, the passive of an infinitive "to watch" is "to be watched". A continuous infinitive should not be used as the channel cannot be the doer. E.g. I'd really like to be swimming in a nice cool pool right now.

Hence, the correct option is (B).

17. You must remember (To meet) the manager tomorrow.

Since "time" of future is given thus an infinitive should be used which will show the intention or purpose of action. Thus "to meet" should be chosen.

Hence, the correct option is (B).

18. They are (Immigrant) citizens from another country.

Immigrant means a person who comes to live permanently in a foreign country.

Itinerant means, traveling from place to place.

Emigrant means a person who leaves their own country in order to settle permanently in another.

Hence, the correct option is (A).

19. (He had his lunch,) when she went to his home.

"When "she" visited him" this shows she visited him in past and when she visited him he had already eaten, so he must have eaten before she came, thus past perfect should be used as the action of eating has been done before visiting.

Hence, the correct option is (B).

20. (Many a candidate) will come for the next week recruitment process.

Many a candidate is equivalent to Many candidates. However, since an indefinite article is used thus noun will be in singular form even though it gives the meaning of plural form.

Many a man = many men

Hence, the correct option is (D).

21. A student was arrested for displaying an indecent art work in public.

'Art work' is a noun phrase, before which an appropriate adjective should be used.

The underlined part 'indecently', which is an adverb, hence must be replaced with the adjective 'indecent' to make it a grammatically correct sentence.

Hence, the correct option is (A).

22. He did not like my smoking in the presence of our teacher yesterday.

The underlined part 'me to smoking' must be replaced with 'my smoking' to make it a grammatically correct sentence.

As per the basic usage rules, 'like' is one of the verbs which are followed by a gerund e.g. swmming, dancing or travelling etc.

Since the gerund is a noun, it is logical to find it preceded by a possessive pronoun (his, her, your, my, our, etc) or a noun in the possessive form (Rohan's, Mr. Sharma's, etc).

Hence, the correct option is (B).

23. The government has granted permission to prosecute the public servant.

The sentence is absolutely correct.

Hence, the correct option is (D).

24. The scenery around the hill station of Himachal Pradesh is quite picturesque and enjoyable.

The word 'enjoyed' must be replaced with the adjective 'enjoyable' to make it a grammatically correct sentence.

Hence, the correct option is (A).

25. Within three years, he demonstrated a dramatically improved business performan

In the sentence the word before the phrase 'improved business performance' must be an adverb as it has to add information to the adjective 'improved'.

The underlined part 'a dramatic improved' so must be replaced with 'a dramatically improved' to make it a grammatically correct sentence.

Hence, the correct option is (C).

26. if in case of you want to resign within one month, you will have to pay Rs 10,000.

The idiom 'in case' means 'if it happens' and putting another 'if' before the idiom doesn't make sense.

The underlined part 'If in case' so must be replaced with 'In case' to make it a grammatically correct sentence.

Hence, the correct option is (C).

27. The sentence is absolutely correct and so no correction is required.

Hence, the correct option is (D).

28. If he has been presented there, he would have put an end to the happenings.

In this sentence, which is a type 3 conditional sentence, adding 'ed' to the adjective 'present' is erroneous.

This sentence can be written in two ways:

"Had he been present there, he would have put an end to the happenings." or "If he had been present there, he would have put an end the happenings."

Hence, the correct option is (A).

29. Your defence that you found the purse lying on the floor cannot be trusted.

The sentence is in passive voice and hence past particple (third form) of the verb 'trust' that is 'trusted' will be used to make it a grammatically correct sentence.

Hence, the correct option is (A).

30. Expeditious completion of the process will be appreciated by everyone involved.

As completion is a noun, the word before it has to be an adjective adding information to it. The advrb 'Expeditiously' so must be replaced with the adjective 'Expeditious' to make it a grammatically correct sentence.

Hence, the correct option is (C).

31. The original sentence is incorrect.

Reason: There are two errors in the bold phrase.

1st. Instead of 'to using', the infinitive 'to use' should be used here.

2nd. In the sentence, the writer refers to the subject 'magnetics' and not the adjective 'magnetic'. Therefore, 'magnetic' should be replaced by 'magnetics' to make it a meaningful sentence.

Therefore, among the given choices option (B) replaces the bold part most appropriately.

The sentence after replacement becomes:

Researchers have developed a process to use magnetics with brain-like networks to program and teach devices.

Hence, the correct option is (B).

32. Nala pakam is a term which originated from King Nala's proficiency in cooking.

The original sentence is absolutely correct and needs no correction.

Hence, the correct option is (D).

33. The original sentence is incorrect.

Reason:

1st. As we can observe that the sentence is made in present tense, usage of past form 'disturbed' is erroneous here. Instead of 'disturbed', 'disturbs' (because the subject is singular) should be used here.

2nd. 'Conscious' means 'aware of and responding to one's surroundings' and the word doesn't make any sense in the context of the sentence. Instead of it, the noun 'conscience' that means 'a person's moral sense of right and wrong, viewed as acting as a guide to one's behaviour' should be used here.

Ex. He had a guilty conscience about his desires.

Therefore, among the given choices option (C) replaces the underline part most appropriately.

The sentence after replacement becomes:

Poverty is too much with us and its presence across vast stretches of our country disturbs our conscience.

Hence, the correct option is (C).

34. The original sentence is incorrect.

Reason:

1st. The phrase 'For decades' and not 'for decade' is used to denote a very long time. Therefore, 'decade' must be replaced by 'decades' here.

2nd. As the verb 'make' is used in its plural form, it's clear that the subject has to be plural too. Therefore, the noun 'company' must be replaced by 'companies' here.

3rd. As we need a restrictive relative pronoun in the given case, 'that' should be used in place of 'which' here.

Therefore, among the given choices option (C) replaces the underline part most appropriately.

The sentence after replacement becomes:

For decades companies that make soap, lotions and perfumes have relied on a chemical called Bourgeonal.

Hence, the correct option is (C).

35. The original sentence is erroneous.

Reason: The sentence implies a contradiction of thoughts and therefore usage of 'and as a conjunction is absurd here. Instead, a conjuction that implies the same context should be used.

Among the given choices, only option (C) replaces the given underline part most appropriately.

The sentence after replacement becomes:

As far as I know them, they all are atheist yet they observe fast during the Navratre.

Hence, the correct option is (C).

36. The original sentence is erroneous.

Reason: In the context of the sentence the phrasal verb 'take out' that implies 'to remove something from a pocket, bag etc' seems absurd. Instead of 'take out', 'take off' which means ' to remove something, especially a piece of clothing' should have been used.

Among the given choices, only option (B) replaces the given underline part most appropriately.

The sentence after replacement becomes:

Whenever you enter someone else's living room, good manners suggest that you should take off your shoes.

Hence, the correct option is (B).

37. The original sentence is erroneous.

Reason: As we can observe the usage of 'than' in the sentence, we can infer that the sentence is made in comperative degree. Therefore, instead of 'quite' 'more' should be used.

Among the given choices, only option (C) replaces the given underline part most appropriately.

The sentence after replacement becomes:

There is nothing more depressing than low level of unemployment in India.

Hence, the correct option is (C).

38. The original sentence is erroneous.

Reason: The verb 'broadcast' stays similar in its 'past' as well pas 'past participle' forms. Therefore, usage of 'broadcasted' is erroneous here.

Among the given choices, only option (D) replaces the given underline part most appropriately.

The sentence after replacement becomes:

All the matches of Cricket World Cup will be broadcast on Start Cricket.

Hence, the correct option is (C).

39. The original sentence is erroneous.

Reason: In the context of the sentence the phrasal verb 'come out' which means 'to become known' is not appropriate. Instead of it, 'cme round' which means 'to recover consciousness' should have been used.

Ex. I'd just come round from a drunken stupor.

Among the given choices, only option (A) replaces the given underline part most appropriately.

The sentence after replacement becomes:

After a few hours the kids who fell from the second floor of the building began to come round.

Hence, the correct option is (A).

40. The original sentence is erroneous.

Reason: As the principal clause is made in Past Indefinite Tense, usage of 'is' as be verb in the bold part become ungrammatical.

Besides, in indirect speech a W/H word which is used to start a question becomes relative pronoun and an interrogative sentence changes into an affirmative sentence.

Ex. I know what is your name. (Incorrect)

Ex. I know what your name is. (Correct)

Among the given choices, only option (C) replaces the given underline part most appropriately.

The sentence after replacement becomes:

He did not mention how old he was or what his gender was.

Hence, the correct option is (C).

41. Ensue means result/proceed and does not fit in. This does not make sense in the statement.

Excess means surplus which is opposite of what is needed.

Ensures is incorrect as it leads to subject verb disagreement.

Accessibility is correct and means ease of access.

The phrase 'ensure accessibility' is correct and fits in well meaningfully and grammatically.

Hence, the correct option is (A).

42. The correct phrase is around/round the corner.

Around the corner: Nearby, close by, not far away.

Hence, the correct option is (C).

43. We need the adverb form of 'history'. Thus, 'historically' is correct while 'historic' is incorrect. This eliminates option (A).

Being is incorrect as it is used to refer to an individual/person. Been is correct here. This eliminates option (C).

Due to article 'a', the correct form is 'place' in singular.

Hence, the correct option is (B).

44. The statement talks about multiple people and thus 'are' is correct.

One is entitled 'to' something and not 'for'. This eliminates option (B).

Option (C) is incorrect as 'a rights' is incorrect grammatically.

Option (D) is correct grammatically and contextually.

Hence, the correct option is (D).

45. The statement is correct in its original form and does not need to be changed.

Hence, the correct option is (D).

// Notes //

// Notes //